THE ROAD TO
HASTINGS

THE POLITICS OF POWER IN
ANGLO-SAXON ENGLAND

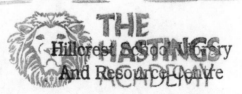

THE ROAD TO
HASTINGS

THE POLITICS OF POWER IN
ANGLO-SAXON ENGLAND

PAUL HILL

TEMPUS

First published 2005

Tempus Publishing Limited
The Mill, Brimscombe Port,
Stroud, Gloucestershire, GL5 2QG
www.tempus-publishing.com

British Library Cataloguing in Publication Data.
A catalogue record for this book is available from the British Library.

ISBN 0 7524 3308 3

Typesetting and origination by Tempus Publishing Limited.
Printed in Great Britain.

CONTENTS

MAP I Map of England showing places mentioned in the book

ACKNOWLEDGEMENTS

The Road to Hastings marks the centrepiece of a trilogy of books on the history of Anglo-Saxon England. I must first thank those who have helped me all the way through my work to date, principal amongst whom is my wife Lucy, whose patience is something more than just a virtue.

To my parents, Richard and Elizabeth Hill, more than ever before my profound gratitude is extended once again for a remarkable network of help which has included the most important aspects of technical back-up, let alone moral support.

To Julie Wileman, I must offer the following sentiment. Had it not been for a remarkable tour of Normandy upon which we both embarked at the great expense of my colleague, I might not have felt able to tackle some important aspects of the Norman argument in this most complex of historical debates. There is nothing quite like a friend who understands a passion. The hospitality with which I was met by Brigitte and Pierre Chantriaux during my all too brief stay in Normandy will never be forgotten. Neither will the gentle comfort with which we were carried by Xavier, a most valuable companion.

Back at home, I am always mindful of the role played in my life by the town of Battle in East Sussex. For me, it is still the very centre of the universe. Michael Lear, a well-known man in this most historic of English towns, must accept my thanks once again for an intriguing journey to hunt for the site of the Malfosse, which I believe we both found very near to his beautiful home.

Thanks are also extended to Chris Gravett who kindly took on the task of providing constructive criticism and advice on the first draft manuscript of *The Road to Hastings*.

Martin Pegler, whose trip to Normandy and Brittany has provided me with one of the most dramatic pictures of Mont-St-Michel that I have ever seen, has become used to my tributes, but must accept them all the same.

John Eagle has stood for a long time beside me during these works. He has provided much inspiration and a good few photographs besides, and to him I extend my thanks.

Just as for *The Age of Athelstan*, the staff at Kingston Museum and Heritage Service in the town where Æthelred II was crowned, deserve more than mere praise. They have not simply helped this author in his work, but have held the torch for a famous royal borough's history and culture which at times has looked as if it was in danger of being overwhelmed by ignorance.

And so to Simon Davies, whose appearance in these acknowledgements goes, I hope, unquestioned. Much as we had approached the complexities of the battle of Brunanburh for *The Age of Athelstan*, so we did for Hastings. The results of our countless table-top encounters were always the same, but it was a great deal of fun.

Paul Hill
Motspur Park, 2004

PREFACE

About 20 years before writing this book I was walking around the abbey remains in Battle on a Sunday afternoon. A man walked alongside me with his son. Soon, they both stopped and the child turned to his father and asked him a question. 'Dad?' he said, with one of those extended syllables which every parent knows precedes a question of great gravity, 'Why did we lose?' The father looked crestfallen. Of course, his fellow countrymen, the English, had indeed lost the battle of Hastings, defeated on home soil by a foreign invader. But there was an expression on his face that aroused my interest. He was embarrassed. He did not seem to know the answer. 'It's a long story', he eventually replied.

Quite by accident, he was right. I did not intervene in their discussion, but began to wonder just how long the story in question really was, so I set about looking into it. Perhaps with this book that little boy, now grown up, will have his answer. Had his father really known, he might have responded along the following lines.

The battle of Hastings was, in fact, a long and unusual battle fought between William, the duke of Normandy and King Harold II of England for the control of the English kingdom. It took place on Senlac Ridge a few miles north of the settlement at Hastings and it lasted from the morning until the early evening of 14 October 1066.

The length of the battle marks it out as extraordinary for battles of its era. The time taken for William to defeat Harold on that famous day had more to do with geography and strategy than it did with tactics. But there is something which makes the Hastings campaign similar in many respects to the other truly great military clashes of Anglo-Saxon England in the Viking Age, and that is that it was a long time in the making.

Alfred the Great's (871-899) triumph over Guthrum at Edington in 878 came only after years of campaigning against the Danish Great Army which had arrived in England in 865. This had been a victory achieved against a section of that army which had split into constituent parts some time before this decisive engagement, its leaders having successfully rearranged the political landscape of central and northern England.

Similarly, King Athelstan's (924-939) celebrated victory over a northern confederacy at Brunanburh in 937 was only made possible by two generations of patient negotiations, fortress building, land purchasing and military campaigning by Edward the Elder (900-924) and Æthelflead, the Lady of the Mercians. And so it was with the great struggles between Danish and English candidates for the throne of England in 1016 which are explored in this book. The death of Edmund Ironside on 30 November 1016 marked the end of a sequence of events which had their root in the political instability created by the collapse of a strong regional power structure in the early years of the reign of Æthelred II (979-1016).

It is against this background of political development, succession crises, negotiations, royal promises and military campaigns that this book is set. Nobody woke up one morning in 1066 and decided to take a kingdom: not even the extraordinary Harald Sigurdsson of Norway, who is often assigned this compulsive characteristic. Punctuation marks in the prose of history – for that is what great battles are – necessarily come at the end of passages in a story. That story, which is told here, begins with a warning to those of us who insist on reading it through modern eyes with contemporary notions of nationality and race. Certainly, there seems to have been a keen grasp of the concept of Englishness, but the secret to understanding the actions of the characters in the story is to recognise exactly what real power meant to the leaders of the age. The road to Hastings was long and dangerous. Along the way, there were signposts instructing the protagonists to follow quite different courses. In the end, it was William and Harold who met on St Calixtus's Day in 1066 in a remote corner of south-east England, but there are many reasons why it could all have been so different.

INTRODUCTION

Early in the morning of 14 October 1066 an English scout ran through the mists which clung to the ridge at Senlac where Battle Abbey now stands. Along the rising ground to the north he scampered towards Caldbec Hill, where the army of his king had camped the night before, awaiting reinforcements. The news he brought to King Harold II of England was most unwelcome; he had seen something unusual across the small valley. William, duke of Normandy had left his own camp at Hastings with his whole army in full order. He had arrived at Telham Hill, 7 miles from his base camp, his force blocking the road to Hastings, thereby preventing Harold from trapping the Norman army in an area of land bounded by rivers and estuaries of greater size and consequence in the eleventh century than they are today.

By the end of that long day, the English king had fallen and with him had gone a whole era of English history. But the extraordinary battle at Hastings notwithstanding, the demise of Anglo-Saxon England had been a slow and tangled affair. In fact, for the final 50 years of Anglo-Saxon England, a very different set of political aspirations at the highest levels were operating than those which had prevailed in the previous age. For that length of time England had been a country with a strong Scandinavian element of soldiery, senior statesmen and for half of that time, kings.

Although it can be argued that England was already a nation in development under the expansionist West Saxon kings of the tenth century in the era after the famous conquests over the Vikings in the north, we should be missing the point if we view the events which led up to the battle of Hastings as being anything to do with notions of nationhood as we currently understand them. Certainly, in fact indisputably, the English people by the eleventh century were thinking of themselves as something much more than a mere loose confederacy of Germanic peoples, but to suppose that the power struggles of the eleventh century were fought over such issues is to misunderstand the essential dynamics of medieval politics. However, as we shall see, because England was indeed a nation in development, the arrival of foreign appointments into key ecclesiastical and political posts during the reign of Edward the Confessor (1042-1066) caused what was then and is now a nationalistic outcry of foul play. Anglo-Saxon cultural identity would become important once again, long after 1066 and it would be used in an overtly political and rather different way than it ever had before, no longer a triumphant clarion call for conquering monarchs, but the brave voice of the oppressed, speaking for the common man. And yet there is a great danger in taking this view.

Let us acknowledge that there was indeed a real power behind the chroniclers' recollections of ancient wise books which told of great battles, each one bigger than ever before, since the English people first came to the shores of Britain and won themselves a country. Stirring as they were, these exhortations were included in poetry and prose for propaganda reasons and were inextricably tied in with the fortunes of dynasties. Before we go on to tell the story of the complex history of marriage alliances, hostage exchanges and battles fought over the period stretching from the reign of Æthelred II (979-1016) to that of Harold II (1066), events which act like beacons along the road to Hastings, let us first take a lesson in the dynamics of Anglo-Saxon politics. It is in the early years of the life of Æthelred II that we can see political fault lines developing and in the attitudes of the leading figures of England at that time we can learn why such things became a recurring feature of later Anglo-Saxon political life.

Succession crises were not unusual in English history. In fact, most kings who came to the throne of the kingdom of the English found that they had to press their claim harder than one or more other candidates to realise their ambitions. Edward the Elder (900-924) had faced a revolt from his cousin Æthelwold who claimed legitimacy via his descent from Edward's uncle, Æthelred I (865-871) who had himself been king of Wessex. The revolt Edward faced was very serious and involved the soliciting of Danish aid against the king. King Athelstan (924-939), the eldest son of Edward, was brought up as a Mercian prince and his rise to power in Wessex had to be a delicately managed affair, given that he was nearly blinded at Winchester by those West Saxon nobles opposed to his succession on the grounds of his mother's status as a concubine. Athelstan, it seems, spent his time as king bringing up his two half-brothers Edmund and Edred as if they were his own sons and both these æthelings, or princes, succeeded to the throne in turn. So, being the eldest son of the king was not necessarily a guarantee of succession, although it clearly meant a great deal. What mattered more to the succession was the nomination by the existing monarch of his heir and the military and political strength of those brave enough to challenge him. The support of the Witan, or High Council of the country, was also a considerable bonus for any prospective candidate. The motor which drove the machinery of succession was the marital history of the monarch in terms of the children which he sired and the political disposition of the mother's family. Sometimes the son of a second, or even third, union could be nominated as heir to the throne to the great irritation of an elder son who might have expected to succeed. By 1066, although there were many other mitigating factors surrounding the long history of the succession crisis which we shall explore, the motor had stopped running.

When in 959 another candidate, Edgar (959-975), more or less wrested the English throne from his incompetent brother Edwy, England entered what has been called its Anglo-Saxon Golden Age. The peaceful reign of Edgar owed much to the martial capabilities of the grandsons of Alfred the Great and consequently Edgar enjoyed the luxury of a huge fleet and imperial-style army. His kingdom also experienced a revival in monasticism which had dramatic effects on the interests of secular leaders who stood to lose from it.

However, the dynamic which governs succession crises came again to the forefront of Anglo-Saxon political life at the end of Edgar's reign in a way that it had not done before. Edgar himself had been brought up in the house of a great nobleman, Athelstan 'Half-King' of East Anglia. Athelstan was one of many regional noblemen in England who had risen during the mid-tenth century as beneficiaries of the royal policy of promoting loyal men in regional posts controlling areas of the former kingdoms such as Mercia, East Anglia and Northumbria. Their power was huge and they were inclined to get involved in national politics at the highest level. They shared with the king the same personal motivations: accrual of wealth, power and land, but above all the promotion of their own line often at the expense of any other. Such motivations became blatantly apparent at the time of a disputed succession to the throne itself, with competing houses favouring different candidates for different reasons, and as we shall see in the run-up to Hastings, sometimes these characters changed sides when it suited them.

And so with Edgar the seeds of a great problem were sewn both in the countryside and at home. From Edgar's early union with Æthelflead Eneda 'the White Duck', daughter of Ordmaer, a boy was born named Edward. Edgar's subsequent marriage to Wulfthryth, the daughter of a

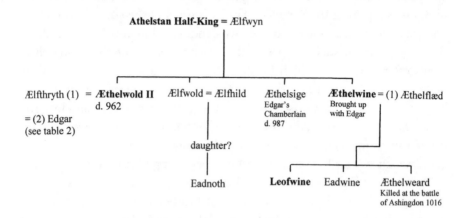

TABLE 1 Descendants of Athelstan 'Half-King' of East Anglia.

(Names in bold indicate ealdormen of East Anglia)

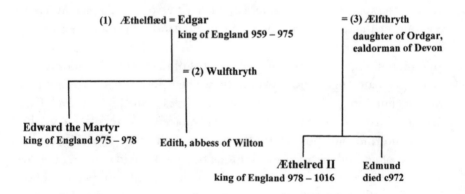

TABLE 2 Descendants of Edgar, king of England

West Saxon nobleman, brought a daughter Edith into the world who went on to become the abbess of Wilton. But from a third marriage to Ælfthryth, the daughter of Ordgar, a Devonshire thegn (which evidently took place while Wulfthryth was still alive) came two children, Edmund and Æthelred. Ælfthryth was the widow of Æthelwold of East Anglia, so she had been the daughter-in-law of Athelstan 'Half-King' and this connection was probably very significant.

It is likely that Edgar's intention was that the inheritance of the throne should go to the sons of the most recent and final relationship, a phenomenon which was not unusual. In fact, Æthelred would repeat the policy himself. It would certainly seem to be the case that Edmund and Ælfthryth's names appear highest in order of preference over that of Edward on a royal grant drawn up by Bishop Æthelwold which conferred privileges to New Minster at Winchester. But to Ælfthryth's dismay, Edmund died in the early 970s and from that moment forward she appears to have devoted some considerable energy to the promotion of her remaining son as heir to the throne. But Edward was still very much in the frame and had powerful supporters himself.

Here, in the succession crisis of 975, we have a situation which shows just how factional Anglo-Saxon England could be, and yet it remains a fact of some interest that, when Edward finally emerged from it as king, he did so as a member of one of the oldest royal lines in the whole of Europe, a line which traced itself back to the sixth century, to the struggles of a sub-Roman polity against the rise of the Saxon invader. The longevity of this line, the line of Cerdic, would become an issue of great potency in the years before Hastings. Among Edward's supporters were Archbishop Dunstan of Canterbury, Ealdorman Æthelwine of East Anglia, Byrhtnoth of Essex and Bishop Oswald of Worcester, who just happened to be the archbishop of York as well. The support of the two archbishops was clearly important, although it might have been given with a little reservation over the legitimacy of Edgar's first union in the eyes of canonical law. Æthelred and his mother had the support of Bishop Æthelwold of Winchester and the very powerful and energetic Ealdorman Ælfhere of Mercia. It seems that it was always going to be the case that whoever Ælfhere supported, Oswald and Æthelwine would go the other way. Ælfhere had good reason to stop the Edward lobby in its tracks. The reasons for the animosity between Oswald and Ælfhere were centred on the great semi-autonomous liberty run by Oswald which became known as Oswaldslow. From here he drew considerable wealth and manpower at the expense of the interests of Ælfhere. Oswaldslow was based on land centred on Worcester, the tenants of which owed service to Oswald and not to the Mercian ealdorman. All this was happening in Ælfhere's backyard. There were also the reforming aspects of Oswald's work, which greatly reduced Ælfhere's sphere of influence at the monastic communities of Pershore, Winchcombe and Westbury. And so it is little wonder that, having set himself up as a key member of the anti-monastic reform movement, Ælfhere became known by some as 'the enemy of the monks'.

There can be little doubt that Ælfhere was angry at the accession of Edward and the victory of the monastic lobby in 975. He set about the monastic community at Evesham by ruthlessly sacking the place and seems also to have destroyed Pershore and Deerhurst, too. Edward had therefore to start his reign with the notion that he must pay close attention to regional politics if he was to tilt the balance of power in his favour.

Oslac, who had been ealdorman of Northumbria since 963, seems to have been ousted by the local Anglo-Scandinavian community in 976. Perhaps they were taking their opportunity to rid themselves of an appointment thrust upon them by King Edgar, or they may have been registering their disapproval of Edward given that Oslac had supported Archbishop Oswald's reforms. Despite this setback for Edward there were some important appointments. One of them shows how closely involved some noblemen

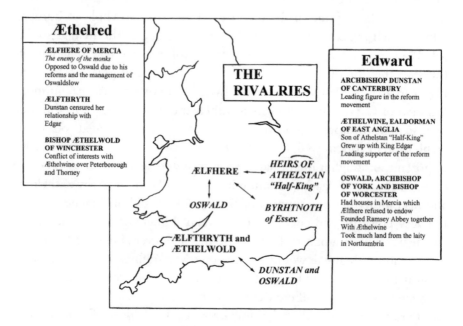

TABLE 3 The rivalries in the accession crisis of 975 – 9

The diagram contains the following labels:

Æthelred

ÆLFHERE OF MERCIA
The enemy of the monks
Opposed to Oswald due to his reforms and the management of Oswaldslow

ÆLFTHRYTH
Dunstan censured her relationship with Edgar

BISHOP ÆTHELWOLD OF WINCHESTER
Conflict of interests with Æthelwold over Peterborough and Thorney

THE RIVALRIES

Edward

ARCHBISHOP DUNSTAN OF CANTERBURY
Leading figure in the reform movement

ÆTHELWINE, EALDORMAN OF EAST ANGLIA
Son of Athelstan "Half-King" Grew up with King Edgar Leading supporter of the reform movement

OSWALD, ARCHBISHOP OF YORK AND BISHOP OF WORCESTER
Had houses in Mercia which Ælfhere refused to endow Founded Ramsey Abbey together With Æthelwine Took much land from the laity in Northumbria

ÆLFHERE ← → HEIRS OF ATHELSTAN "Half-King"

OSWALD

BYRHTNOTH of Essex

ÆLFTHRYTH and ÆTHELWOLD

DUNSTAN and OSWALD

were, not just in the politics of the time, but in the recording of it, too. The five south-western shires of Wessex were given to a man called Æthelweard, who was descended from King Æthelred I of Wessex (865-871) and whose family had a long and noble history, supplying queens to a number of kings. The extraordinary Æthelweard was a well-educated man and it is to his surviving chronicle that we owe some insights into the way in which the English viewed the successes and failures of their time.[1] Æthelweard would also play a part in Æthelred's political negotiations with the Viking armies when they came again, but it seems that his appointment to western Wessex acted in some way as a check to the ambitions of Ælfhere. To a man named Æthelmaer, who also had lands in Rutland, went central Wessex and to an obscure man called Edwin went the control of part of south-east England. This was an area which would soon give rise to some of the most famous characters of later Anglo-Saxon England as well as providing us with the theatre for the final performance in a very long-running show.

Æthelweard's wide-ranging connections with the aristocracy spanned both sides of the succession crisis. It would seem, despite the fact that Edward and Æthelweard shared common ancestry, that the latter was also associated with Ælfthryth and Bishop Æthelwold of Winchester; in a way the appointment to the West Saxon shires might also have been something of a conciliatory gesture to the Æthelred lobby.

And so the patchwork of loyalties and the mixture of motivations which led England on a path towards regicide in 978 are quite clear. But one other thing happened, quite by chance, which seems to have compounded the problem. At a great council held at Calne in Wiltshire in 978, a calamitous accident occurred where many leading figures of the country fell through an upper-storey floor to land on the ground floor below. The *Anglo-Saxon Chronicle* tells us that not everyone was as lucky as St Dunstan:

> Here in this year all the foremost councillors of the English race fell down from an upper floor at Calne, but the holy archbishop Dunstan alone was left standing upon a beam and some were very injured there, and some did not escape it with their life.

These curious deaths notwithstanding, worse was to come if the words of the chronicler are anything to go by. Either Ælfthryth or Ælfhere seem to have seen their chance:

> Here King Edward was killed in the evening-time on 18 March at Corfe 'passage'; and they buried him at Wareham without any royal honours. No

worse deed for the English race was done than this was, since they first sought-out the land of Britain. Men murdered him, but God exalted him. In life he was an earthly king; after death he is now a heavenly saint. His earthly relatives would not avenge him, but his Heavenly Father has much avenged him. Those Earthly slayers wanted to destroy his memory upon earth, but the sublime avenger has spread abroad his memory in the heavens and on the earth. Those who earlier would not bow to his living body, those now humbly bow the knees to his dead bones. Now we can perceive that the wisdom and deliberations of men, and their counsels, are worthless against God's purpose…

Anglo-Saxon Chronicle.
Peterborough Manuscript (E) entry for 979 [978][2]

Edward had been greeted with great warmth and in a moment when he was least expecting it, both his arms were grabbed and an assailant stabbed him. There was a struggle as Edward stayed on his horse and wheeled it around to flee, but he got his foot caught in the stirrup and a little distance later he fell and was dragged along the ground. When his murderers reached him, they simply tossed him down a well. Locals retrieved his body and took it to a church. The body rested for some time at Wareham, perhaps even for a year, lying apparently in a bog where sometimes columns of fire could be seen to mark its position.

Later versions of the event implicate Ælfthryth as the co-ordinator of the assassination, implying that she had intrigued on behalf of her son. The earliest account suggests that the motive lay with the personal retainers of the young Æthelred,[2] but the fact that Ælfhere in 980 arranged for Edward's body to be brought to Shaftesbury might even seem to implicate him in the conspiracy, this being perhaps a form of penance for the deed.

Whoever did it, it had been a lesson for all in the dangers of factional politics. England would not quite be the same after this. It was a horrific murder, whatever the character of the young victim.[3] Kings had been murdered before, but this time it was the result of a long-running internal rift in the power houses of the Anglo-Saxon aristocracy. Although nobody was brought to justice over the murder, the event soon became legend and the legend very quickly turned into a matter of passion and devotion which continues even today. Edward, king and martyr, would be recognised as such, his bones properly translated and his cult established in the reign of his natural and obvious successor, Æthelred. This suspicious incident, and many other things besides would haunt the English monarchy on the eve of the second Viking Age.

I

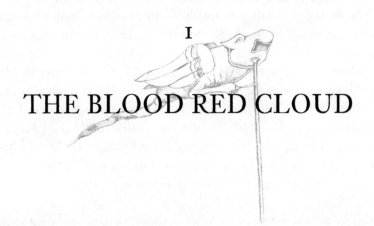

THE BLOOD RED CLOUD

In this year, Æthelred was consecrated as king on the Sunday, fourteen days after Easter, at Kingston; and there were at his consecration two archbishops and ten diocesan bishops. The same year a bloody cloud was seen, many times in the likeness of fire; and it appeared most of all at midnight; and it was formed thus of various beams; then when it became day it glided away.

Anglo-Saxon Chronicle.
Abingdon Manuscript (C) entry for 979

Dire portents indeed. Most accounts of the crowning of Anglo-Saxon kings at Kingston upon Thames in Surrey during the tenth century tell of resplendent halls, of great ceremonies and of monarchs' promises to the people of the kingdom. But here, our scribe with a certain degree of licence, has captured a public mood so different from what had gone before. After the glorious Anglo-Saxon empire of King Athelstan (924-939), upheld by his brothers and nephew, the English had fallen prey to division and weakness, but worst of all, to the second descent upon England of the Viking raiders.

The very young man who came to the English throne amid a climate of suspicion and foreboding would in fact, be one of the longest reigning monarchs in English history. But events during his long reign would conspire to demonstrate the limitations of royal power in the face of powerful and duplicitous magnates and well co-ordinated external threats to the English kingdom. Æthelred II proved to be no Athelstan or Edgar, but he did at least know his lineage and understood the strength of its background. His sons were named after the line of kings of his own ancestry who had done so much to expand ancient Wessex into the kingdom of the English just fifty years earlier, but the memories of the crushing of the barbarians at Brunanburh in 937, of the submission of the northern kings to Edgar and of the serene peace of the Anglo-Saxon Golden Age, must have seemed all the more painful in this time of renewed uncertainty. Nevertheless, the children of Æthelred's first marriage to Ælfgifu, daughter of Thored, earl of Northumbria, bore the names Athelstan, Egbert, Edmund, Edred, Edwy, Edith, Ælfgifu and Wulfhild – an unmistakable signal that Æthelred regarded himself as the rightful heir to the throne of the kingdom of the English. The king would often remind his subjects of his lineage, too. As late as 1014, at the start of his second period in power after his return from exile, in his extensive law code known as Ethelred VIII, he says:

> But let us do as is necessary for us; let us take as our example what former rulers wisely decreed, Athelstan and Edmund, and Edgar who came last – how they honoured God and kept God's law and paid God's tribute, as long as they lived.

But nobody in England could ever forget the way in which Æthelred had come to the throne. Ealdorman Ælfhere and Æthelwold, bishop of Winchester died in 983 and 984 respectively and Ælfthryth thereafter became a quieter figure politically than she had been before. All this came just as the young king was coming of age. The subsequent rise to sainthood of Edward, king and martyr, cast a shadow over the reign of Æthelred and went a long way towards damaging the whole prestige of the crown, notwithstanding the fact that Æthelred himself ordered the observation of Edward's festival. As had been the case with the mighty Athelstan half a century earlier, the circumstances surrounding a royal accession would govern the king's approach to his government. In plain English, this lonely boy had got off to a bad start.

Æthelred's notable misfortunes have led historians to speculate that he never at any time seemed to be entirely in charge of things. It is a view shared by ancient and modern alike. The twelfth-century historian William of Malmesbury is scathing of the man he says more or less let things happen around him, and even the noted historian Sir Frank Stenton suggested that the king was always unsure of himself. Against these notions we must set a few facts. England in the reign of Æthelred was a cosmopolitan place. Despite the impressive conquests of the Anglo-Saxon kings of the last generation, things were still done very differently in the midlands and in the north beyond Watling Street. The unity and sense of purpose which typified the reigns of Athelstan (924-939) and Edgar (959-975) and their empire had proved to be difficult to sustain. Factional family politics played a great part in the problems faced by Æthelred's government and there were also the ever-present cultural and legal differences between communities either side of the well-known Roman road which still divided the country.

Æthelred, rather than showing a lack of sure purpose in his government, seems to have been unable to recognise where careful diplomacy was needed and certainly was capable of making what might seem to be the most extraordinarily rash decisions. But even here, when we closely examine his motives, we find reason behind his actions. The very fact that his reign was such a long one is evidence of a residual strength in the Old English monarchy.

After Ælfhere's death, the office of the Mercian ealdorman was passed to his brother-in-law Ælfric, whose lands in the south-east of the midlands and involvement in the patronage of Peterborough brought him into conflict with the house of Athelstan 'Half-King'. In 985, in one of the king's earliest political manoeuvres, Ælfric was exiled. It is no coincidence that this act occurred at roughly the same time as Ealdorman Æthelwine of East Anglia rose to significance. The office of the Mercian ealdorman would not be revived until 1007. But much would have happened by then.

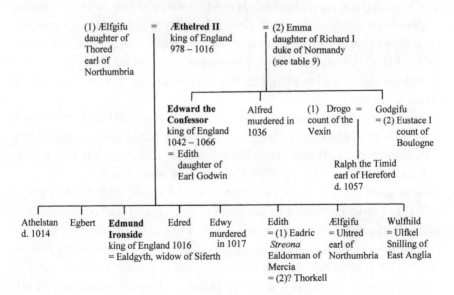

TABLE 4 Descendants of Æthelred II, king of England

(Names in bold indicate kings of England)

It is not entirely true to say that the peaceable years of Edgar's reign had seen no foreign arrivals on the shores of England. In fact, Edgar was frequently chastised for his acceptance of foreigners into the country, particularly the Danes. But the men who arrived in the 960s giving their names to the settlements at Scarborough and Flamborough among others[1] did not do so at the head of great armies of conquest. They came into a country which was strongly controlled and well defended. They were allowed in. No enemy fleet had dared run the gauntlet of the famous patrolling fleets of Edgar's England. But with political weakness in England and disaffection amongst the nobility of the Danish homelands, history was set to repeat itself. The second Viking Age would dawn upon an England which had only just risen from the ashes of the first.

The political situation in Denmark once again was to have a bearing on English fortune. Coincidental with the accession of Æthelred was the rise to comprehensive power in Denmark of Harold Gormsson, who by the twelfth century had acquired the name by which he is popularly referred – 'Bluetooth'. Among his many claims was that he had made the Danes into Christians and had conquered much of Norway. Historians point out that Harold Bluetooth's main areas of interest were in the Baltic world: at the mouth of the Oder he had established a military community which subsequently passed into legend, the Jómsborg Vikings. But such overbearing power in the northern world brought with it many problems. The very ingredients with which Harold intended to rule were unpalatable to those who sought a degree of power themselves and chief amongst these ingredients was the imposition upon a proud pagan culture of Christianity. In 986 Harold's own son Swein, who was opposed to his father, succeeded in driving him from his kingdom. The second Viking Age in England was about to begin.

And so, just eighteen months into Æthelred's reign, the raiders fell upon the shores of England, attacking this time not an island of small competing kingdoms, but a rich and unusually susceptible kingdom ruled, in theory at least, by one king. Hampshire, Thanet and Cheshire were the first areas to feel again the effects of the sword and the torch, with Southampton suffering particular misery in the form of the murder and enslavement of many of its inhabitants at the hands of seven shiploads of Vikings. Then, the following year, Devon and Cornwall suffered, to be followed by Dorset. A six-year gap in the contemporary accounts probably masks the fact that there were other raids in other places, and sure enough, in 988 the old royal estate at Watchet on the Somerset coast, which had been in the hands of Abingdon Abbey for a number of years, was attacked. Then, a

Viking force encountered the men of Devon who are famously recorded as driving away the invader, despite heavy cost to themselves and the loss of an important thegn named Goda.

But the darkest aspect of all for the English was not so much in the nature of the raids themselves. After all, England, Ireland, Scotland and Wales had been through this sort of thing before and each had to reconstitute their military machines to meet the threat, some with more success than others. It had become chillingly apparent that the raiders, although Scandinavian, were not embarking from their homeland before launching their raids, but from somewhere quite different.

There are some hints that in an earlier age, during the reign of King Athelstan (924-939), the Viking attackers had been given some help by the new Scandinavian colonisers of Normandy in northern France. We do not yet know precisely how Athelstan dealt with the threat from the first generation of Normans, or indeed the nature of his relationship with William Longsword, one of their famous leaders. But we do know that the threat to the shores of southern England was clearly there in the early tenth century and now, in Æthelred's time, it was painfully apparent. Here was a maritime power base with harbours just a short sail away from the coast of the heartlands of ancient Wessex, the engine-room of the kingdom of the English. Normandy's Duke Richard I was the thorn in the side. He openly accommodated Scandinavian seafarers in the ports and harbours of his duchy. Æthelred was not unaware of the problem, but it took the direct intervention of Pope John XV to try to thaw the frostiness in the relationship between the two polities who would eventually stand against each other on a ridge outside Hastings.

On Christmas Day 990, a papal envoy came to see King Æthelred. A document was drawn up, the details of which resound with significance. It was to be presented to the duke of the Normans as a list of terms. Early in the spring of the following year, the bishop of Sherborne and two king's thegns escorted the papal envoy to Rouen where the Norman duke agreed to the terms. In a letter concerning the reconciliation in which great sadness is expressed at the rift between two of his faithful sons, the pope explains the nature of the agreement as follows:

> [Richard]…confirmed the same peace with a willing heart, along with his sons and daughters, present and future, and with all his faithful people, on the following terms: that if any of their people, or they themselves, were to commit any wrong against the other, it should be atoned for with a fitting compensation; and the peace should remain forever unshaken,

and confirmed by the mark of both parties, namely on the part of King Æthelred, Æthelsige, bishop of the holy church of Sherborne, and Leofstan, son of Ælfwold, and Æthelnoth, son of Wigstan; on the part of Richard, Bishop Roger [of Lisieux], Rodulf, son of Hugh, Tursten, son of Turgeis.

And Richard is to receive none of the king's men, or of his enemies, nor the king any of his, without their seal.

Without this document, which survives as an early eleventh-century manuscript and which is also included in the work of William of Malmesbury, we should know very little of the enmity between the two power groups either side of the English Channel. This would not be the last time that a pope would have something to say about the Normans and the English, either. But much would happen between England and Normandy before a duke looked over the sea with thoughts of conquest.

The Scandinavian descent on Æthelred's kingdom was about to change its nature entirely. In August, a whole fleet of 93 ships arrived to see what it could get. Just as the early raids of the ninth century had led to larger forces trying their luck, so again the local English leaders were left facing fleets of an alarming size with only their local military resources at their immediate disposal.

After plundering Folkstone and Sandwich, the fleet moved to Ipswich and sacked the settlement. Then it landed in the Blackwater estuary and occupied Northey Island in Essex. The extraordinary battle which took place there has passed into legend. It has become known as the battle of Maldon, named after the nearby burh and it is commemorated in a glorious contemporary poem. The Vikings almost certainly had at their head Olaf Tryggvason, a descendant of the great Harold Fairhair (who had placed his own son Hakon to be fostered at the court of the English King Athelstan). Olaf's fleet had chosen for its moorings the coastal waters of the patrimony of the legendary local Ealdorman Byrhtnoth, whose death at their hands caused a celebrated and vengeful rearguard action.

As battles of the era go, the battle of Maldon was at once unusual and typical. The Danes were initially at a disadvantage, with only pockets of men being able to cross a narrow causeway over the Blackwater estuary. Byrhtnoth's men, who had been denying the Danes access to the mainland, were ordered by their lord to withdraw from their position and form-up with the main army so that battle lines could be drawn between the two opposing forces. In other words, the enemy was to be allowed onto the mainland so that a pitched battle could take place.

Then the Ealdorman permitted in his great pride
to allow land many of these hateful people;
and so then shouted on the shore of the cold water
Byrhthelm's child – and the warriors listened:
'Now the way is open to you: come quickly to us
you men to battle. God alone knows
who on this field of honour may be allowed to be the master of '.

The Battle of Maldon, lines 89-96

The subsequent battle was fought hard in the traditional manner and the Danes eventually held the place of slaughter. The decision to fight had cost the ealdorman his life, but it is worth considering the nature of the gamble he had taken. If he had won the battle, or killed the Danish leader, things might have been so much different for him and the whole eastern seaboard of England. But it was not to be. The Danes were victorious and Byrhtnoth and many of his loyal retainers were dead.

Then he was slain by the heathen warriors;
and both of those warriors which by him stood,
Ælfnoth and Wulmaer were each slain,
close by their lord did they give up their lives.
Then turned away from battle those that would not stay:
there went Odda's child first to flight,
Godric fled from the battle, and the noble abandoned
the one which had often given him many a horse.

So now was laid low the Chief of this army,
Æthelred's Ealdorman. All saw those
sharers of the hearth that their lord lay slain.
But then there advanced onward those splendid retainers,
undaunted men hastening eagerly:
they desired all one of two things,
to leave life or else to avenge their dear lord.

The Battle of Maldon, lines 181-208

The king's response to the new crisis mixed the old with the new. On the advice of the archbishop of Canterbury and of the bishop of Winchester, terms were sought with Olaf with the understanding that he would be baptised. This had been the approach that Alfred had taken with Guthrum

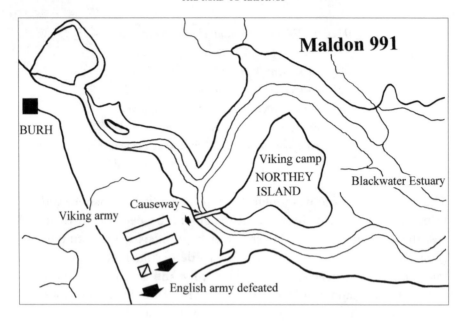

MAP 2 The battle of Maldon, Blackwater estuary, Essex, 991

after the great victory at the battle of Edgington in 878, but this time the English king had lost to the Danes. Whether or not the decision was prompted by the archbishop,[2] Æthelred immediately instigated a policy which would have important ramifications for the future. He raised a tax and paid 10,000 pounds to the Danes. In addition to this, he ordered his ships to fall back on London, a city which would have a pivotal role to play in the wars of the next generation. The army too, needed reorganisation and here Æthelred seems to have suffered either from poor judgement, or just plain bad luck. He chose as the leaders of the army Ealdorman Ælfric of Hampshire and Thored of Northumbria. They were assisted by the bishops Ælfstan and Æswig of London[3] and Dorchester respectively. Together with the fleet, the army would join in a combined operation to bottle-up the enemy in the Thames estuary. But Ælfric, it seems, was a turncoat. He had sent a message ahead to the Danish fleet warning them of what was about to happen and on the night before operations were to begin, he went over to their side. The next day, the Danes set sail early to avoid the trap and although one ship foundered, the others got away. But despite all this there had been a naval confrontation. The English managed to capture the one ship that Ælfric had been aboard and yet it seems that he had fled the vessel before the English boarded it.

Æthelred saw a chance to enter into negotiations with Olaf Tryggvason. The treaty which came from their negotiations was a complex one.

Archbishop Sigeric of Canterbury and two senior figures in Wessex, Ælfric and the learned Æthelweard, undertook the negotiations for the English side. The agreement was essentially that the Viking force should join with the English in keeping the peace towards the king's person and his subjects and be at the disposal of the king if another fleet should fall upon England. Merchant ships from both sides were to be regulated in their activities, too. But the price was high in many respects. All previous raids were to be brushed under the carpet, providing a new legitimacy for the invader:

> Concerning all the slaughter and all the harrying and all the injuries which were committed before the truce was established, all of them are to be dismissed, and no one is to avenge it or ask for compensation.

But more important than this was the colossal payment of 22,000 pounds of gold and silver to the Vikings. In 992 another invasion threat was met by the mustering of an English fleet, but there seems to be no evidence that Olaf Tryggvason's men were ever part of it. In spite of the treaty with Olaf, the eastern seaboard of England continued to suffer. While Æthelred was ordering the blinding of Ælfric's son on account of his father's treachery, both Northumbria and Lindsey (Lincolnshire) were attacked. If the historian ever needed further evidence of the difficulties that Æthelred faced in ruling a culturally and politically divided kingdom, then the *Anglo-Saxon Chronicle* entry for 993 provides it. The ancient citadel at Bamburgh, for so long the pivotal power in the patchwork of northern polities, was broken down and looted by the Vikings, who then went on to harass the inhabitants on the shores of the Humber estuary. A great Northumbrian army was raised to oppose the force, but their leaders, we are told, soon took to flight. This, it was said, was because their commanders Fræna, Godwin and Frithugist had paternal Danish parentage.[4]

What had accelerated the pace of the attacks on England in the early 990s? The king, it seems, was the victim of an unfortunate set of circumstances which had weakened his control on the kingdom. From 990, Æthelwine of East Anglia, Byrhtnoth of Essex and Æthelweard of Wessex were regulars at court. Up until then, for some years the balance of power in England had been held by Ælfhere of Mercia (who had managed the estates of his late brother Ælfheah of Wessex) and Æthelwine of East Anglia, who after the banishment of Ælfric, Ælfhere's successor, seems to have taken control of Mercia until 990. But by 992, things had dramatically changed. Byrhtnoth had met a grisly end on the battlefield at Maldon and Æthelwine in 992 seems to have succumbed to gout. Archbishops Dunstan and Oswald had departed in 988 and 992 respectively and suddenly English politics had become decidedly unstable.

Very soon there arrived a combined force led by two unnatural but potentially devastating allies. Olaf had returned this time with Swein, son of Harold Bluetooth, and between them they had 94 ships and several thousand men. Their sights were fixed on London. It was too much for some Englishmen to withstand. Disaffection with Æthelred was never far from the surface whether he deserved it or not and some leading figures were prepared to see Swein as master of the kingdom.[5] But in this campaign, the resistance of London proved a notable obstacle for the Vikings, a resistance attributed to the divine intervention of the mother of God herself. Their subsequent devastating raid into south-east England brought them 16,000 pounds of tribute, but the force agreed to split after taking up station at Southampton and provisioning itself from there. Swein returned to Denmark, whilst the Norwegian Olaf came to terms once again with the ever-treating English court. The exchange of hostages was negotiated and then bishop Ælfheah of Winchester and Æthelweard brought Olaf to the king at Andover. Here, at Andover, Olaf was confirmed in his Christianity and made a vow not to return to England in war, a vow he seems to have kept. Henceforth, his attentions would be directed towards domestic issues in Norway.

For two years Æthelred may have thought that the art of negotiation by treaty had worked in his favour. Archbishop Sigeric had died in 995 and this peaceful gap was filled by the appointment to the archbishopric of Canterbury of Ælfric, bishop of Wiltshire, a leading reformer and keen intellectual. Another appointment, that of Wulfstan to the bishopric of London in 996 marked the beginning of one of the most notable ecclesiastical careers in pre-Conquest history. In the decades to come Wulfstan would be responsible for drawing up the king's law codes and for delivering some of the most stirring sermons of the age.

There are no recorded raids until 997 when a different but still devastating force returned. Wessex, Cornwall, Devon, Somerset and the coast of South Wales felt its cruelty and this was followed the next year by Dorset, then Hampshire and Sussex where supplies were extorted from the inhabitants. The *Anglo-Saxon Chronicle* has something to say of the raids of 998. When the Vikings were in Dorset, he says:

> An army was often gathered against them, but then as soon as they should have come together, something always started a retreat and they [the Vikings] always had the victory in the end.

English morale had collapsed. Also significant in this year of 998 was the fact that the devastation and extortion of Wessex was carried out by a force which had stationed itself on the Isle of Wight within easy reach of Hampshire and Sussex. Any fleet gathered at the Isle of Wight could not only provision itself from there and the surrounding mainland coastal settlements, but would also have the all important weather gauge against enemy shipping to the east. In the years to come, the Isle of Wight would prove useful to both English and foreign fleets alike.

In the following year, the force sailed from the Isle of Wight up the Medway to Rochester where they were met by the local Kentish fyrd, who fled the field of battle we are told, through lack of support. Brave though the Kentish men apparently were, the Peterborough scribe who recorded the incident once again touches on the heart of the English problem. Even though a giant land and sea force had been raised by the king to oppose the enemy, it seemed unable to fight due to a combination of natural and political obstacles. Bad weather and poor leadership compounded the king's difficulties in what was proving to be an immensely costly exercise. Then, in 1000, the fleet found shelter across the English Channel where it waited for a whole year in the safety of a Norman harbour. The next year the fleet returned from Normandy and raided West Sussex. Then it turned west attacking Exeter, which resisted successfully. To counter the subsequent raid into the West Country, a force was gathered from Devonshire and Somerset which met its foe at Pinhoe. Once again, it gave way too early and lost the struggle. The Viking force ended up back on the Isle of Wight after a successful campaign of plunder. As they provisioned themselves from the southern shires, their presence was felt everywhere. Æthelred and his councillors could think of nothing other than buying the force off to prevent further destruction in Wessex. The envoy who was sent to the Vikings was the successor to Byrhtnoth of Essex, a man named Leofsige. His mission resulted in the payment of 24,000 pounds of tribute to the enemy. But extraordinarily, and for reasons that we do not know, Leofsige murdered Æfic, the king's high reeve and was exiled by the king for his actions.

Only weeks after the payment of tribute to the Viking force, Æthelred married his second wife Emma, daughter of Richard I, duke of Normandy. The famous treaty of 991 in which the Normans and the English agreed reparations towards one another seems not to have remained in force for long. Something more binding – a royal marriage alliance across the English Channel – seems to have been the new approach. Emma's long and fundamentally important political career in England had begun. She was scarcely a teenager.

For some reason, soon after the marriage, Æthelred is thought to have become disaffected with Duke Richard II of Normandy and he sent an English army to the Cotentin to ravage it. Interestingly, the English king made a point of ordering his forces to restrain from attacking the monastic community at Mont-St-Michel, an act which does not seem to have gone unnoticed in later years by his son Edward. It is most likely that the reason for this animosity lay in an agreement made between Richard II and Swein in which they were to share out English loot between them. If this is the case, it reinforces the idea that since the reign of King Athelstan (924-939) English kings were quite able to launch foreign expeditions not just in support of claimants to various thrones, but as a form of punishment too. But if we are to believe a remarkable passage written by William of Jumièges, the English king had good reason to regret his assault on the Cotentin:

> Your serene highness [reports an English survivor to his king], we never even saw the duke, but to our destruction we skirmished with the particularly fierce people of one county. Not only are the men extremely brave warriors, but the women are fighters too. They attacked our strongest soldiers with the carrying poles for jugs and smashed the men's brains out. Be assured that these women killed all your soldiers.
>
> William of Jumièges,
> *Gesta Normannorum Ducum* (5.4)

Yet it was still with the more traditional enemy that Æthelred had the most trouble. The rashness and paranoia for which Æthelred later became famous displayed itself admirably on 13 November 1002 when the king ordered the massacre of all Danes in England on St Brice's Day. He had been told that the Danes had intended to rise up against him and after this, take his kingdom. It might seem that the order was utterly unworkable given that there were literally thousands of Danes in England at the time, many in important political positions and a great number of them had inter-married with the English. Historians often doubt whether any aspect of the order was carried out at all, but sadly, it seems that there were one or two rather notable victims of the king's extremism. Gunnhild, the sister of King Swein of Denmark was living as a hostage in England and was killed in the massacre. And those who doubt that the massacre happened have to refute the word of the king himself. In a renewal of a privilege to St Frideswide in Oxford of nearby lands dateable to December 1004, he has this to say:

...For it is fully agreed that to all dwelling in this country it will be well known that, since a decree was sent out by me with the counsel of my leading men and magnates, to the effect that all the Danes who had sprung up in this island, sprouting like cockle amongst the wheat, were to be destroyed by a most just extermination, and this decree was to be put into effect even as far as death, those Danes who dwelt in the aforementioned town [Oxford], striving to escape death, entered this sanctuary of Christ, having broken by force the doors and bolts, and resolved to make a refuge and defence for themselves therein against the people of the town and suburbs; but when all the people in pursuit strove, forced by necessity, to drive them out, and could not, they set fire to the planks and burnt, it seems, this church, with its ornaments and its books.[6]

Swein did not take the news well. It was as if history was repeating itself. Long ago, in the days of Ragnar Lothbrok, the famous Scandinavian warrior who had landed in East Anglia in the ninth century, another murder had taken place, with Ragnar ending up in a pit of snakes in Northumbria. This paved the way for a legendary revenge attack upon the English by the sons of Ragnar which changed the course of English history. Now, a Danish king would prosecute his desire to gain political power in England and this time it would be at least partially driven by a personal motive.

Swein was not a man with whom Æthelred could afford to play games. Since his return to Denmark in 993 he had become the most powerful man in the northern world. By the time his kinsfolk were meeting their doom at the hands of Æthelred's murderers in England, he had become ruler of Jutland and Scania and was on friendly terms with the notorious Jómsborg Vikings, a fearsome independent fighting force. He was master of the Baltic and an ally of the king of Sweden. Most importantly, he had overcome Olaf Tryggvason and had much of Norway at his command. He arrived in England in 1003 at the head of an impressive army. During this first campaign an event occurred which will have gone some way towards sewing the seeds of English mistrust of the Normans in the next generation. The city of Exeter, which had held out against the Vikings in 1001, was now held in dower by a French reeve of Queen Emma. The Peterborough scribe describes the man as a churl in an early usage of the word as a disparaging term, but he seems to have held a much higher office than that description might suggest. He betrayed the town to the Danes and from here they were able to attack Wessex from the west and went as far as Wilton and Salisbury before turning to the sea. The incident probably represents a Danish attempt to test the strength of the Norman alliance and Hugh's betrayal must have greatly disturbed the young queen and her advisers.

But this year saw the most extraordinary example of Æthelred's predicament laid bare. Swein, the victor at Exeter, would not go unchallenged on his Wessex campaign. A great force was raised against him and it was led by none other than Ealdorman Ælfric, who had drawn men from Hampshire and Wiltshire. The Anglo-Saxon chronicler leaves us in no doubt as to his opinion of the ealdorman:

> Then a very great army was gathered…and were very resolutely going towards the raiding army; then Ealdorman Ælfric should have led the army, but he took to his old tricks: as soon as they were so close at hand that each of them looked on the other, then he pretended to be ill, and began to retch so as to vomit, and said that he was taken ill, and thus deceived the people that he should have led. As the saying goes 'When the commander weakens, then the whole raiding army[7] is greatly hindered'.

With friends like Ælfric, Æthelred hardly needed enemies, yet still he had them. The following year saw the start of an East Anglian campaign which began with the Danish fleet sacking Norwich. Peace was bought from the Danes by the local East Anglian leadership on account of the time it was going to take them to raise a fyrd. The Danish landing had clearly been unexpected. But Swein pushed inland as far as Thetford and sacked this ancient settlement. The Danes were at length met in the field by the local fyrd under a man whose personal history is somewhat shadowy but who is said by the Danes themselves to have been the most ferocious warrior they had ever encountered in England. His name was Ulfkell. Later sources gave him the nickname 'Snilling', or 'the brave'. He had risen to prominence under a somewhat reluctant king who had never allowed him to carry a title above that of 'minister'. Perhaps the old pro-Edward lobby which had such support in East Anglia had affected the king's attitude to the earldom. Nevertheless, the brave Ulfkell ordered his men to break his enemy's ships at Norwich, but this was not carried out, so he had no choice but to face Swein in the field. Ulfkell's movements seem to have been quite clever – he was determined that if the ships could not be broken, the Danes should be denied the chance to return to them. So he positioned his own force at a point where they blocked the Danish route from Thetford to Norwich. After a night of burning and looting in Thetford, the Danes were compelled to face Ulfkell outside the town. The poor morale of the English in recent encounters in Wessex seems to be in stark contrast to the fighting spirit of Ulfkell and his own East Anglians. A fearsome struggle followed. Casualties were high on both sides and the Danes eventually had the victory after some difficulty. East Anglia, for so long a second home to the Danishmen of yesteryear, was proving a difficult nut to crack.

Despite receiving a glowing reference from the Scandinavians, Ulfkell had, of course, lost the battle on that morning outside Thetford, but both he and the Danes realised that there would have to be more sword-play in the future. What the Danes did after their Pyrrhic victory of 1004 is not recorded, but in 1005 they left a country beset by a great famine and a poor harvest and set sail for Denmark. Their departure gave the king an opportunity to look again at the question of domestic government. Here, there would be significant casualties.

2

TREACHERY AND AMBITION

One of the curious features of Æthelred's long reign is the way in which the king organised his governmental appointments by way of promotion, demotion and purges. The king's attitude towards East Anglia and Northumbria are a case in point. However, there was one man who rose to significance in Mercia at the king's behest who seems to have had no scruples at all about what he did for the king.

Æthelred created something which might on the face of it seem unexpected. The Mercian ealdormanry was rekindled. The first new incumbent of an ancient office which had lain open since the driving-out of Ælfric in 985 was a man known as Eadric Streona, son of Æthelric, an obscure thegn from the north-west Midlands. The name he was given is still something of a mystery to historians, who have tried to find its root in the Old English language with varying degrees of success, but it is generally taken to have meant 'grasper', 'acquirer' or 'climber'.[1] His reputation has declined over the centuries perhaps with some justification. It was an unwise appointment. Eadric may well have gained his position from the part he played in a foul deed which he performed for the king prior to his real rise to fame. According to John of Worcester,[2] Eadric had bribed the hangman of Shrewsbury, a man known as Godwin Porthund ('town dog'), to ambush Ealdorman Ælfhelm whilst he was out hunting. The ealdorman was the ruler of southern Northumbria, the son of Wulfrun. More importantly, his sons, Wulfheah and Ufegeat, were blinded at the same time. As if the tale needed another twist, the blinded men's sister who seems to have been unharmed if she was involved at all in the incident, would rise to play an important part in the politics of the

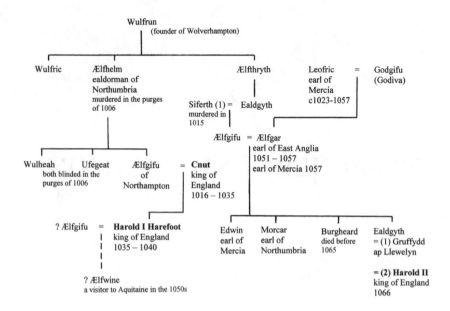

TABLE 5 Mercian Connections
(Names in bold indicate kings of England)

Anglo-Scandinavian world of the next generation. She was the redoubtable
Ælfgyfu of Northampton, a woman whose liaison with the future King
Cnut would bring another dimension into the tangled complexity of Anglo-
Scandinavian politics. The king, it seems, had directly ordered the murder and
the blinding. Anglo-Saxon governmental reshuffles were rarely bloodless.

In the summer of 1006, the Viking force had sailed back to England and
arrived at Sandwich off the Kent coast. The army plundered in Kent and
Sussex, playing a sadly unrecorded cat-and-mouse game with a giant fyrd
called out from Wessex and Mercia combined (a kind of imperial-style
grand army) but 'it did not achieve anymore than it often did before'. In
fact, the inhabitants of Sussex and Kent suffered as much hardship from
the passing of their own army through their territory as they did from
the Danish. By the winter, the fleet was in its dominating position off the
Isle of Wight and it set out on a raid through Hampshire and Berkshire
to Reading, making sure to stop off at carefully prepared supply dumps
along the way. Then it raided across the Chilterns to the great burh at
Wallingford where it burned the town. It struck out along the ridgeway
and arrived at the ancient shire assembly point at Cuckamsley Knob where
it boasted loudly of its achievements[3] before swooping to defeat the men
of Wiltshire near Avebury. It subsequently marched triumphantly past the
shocked inhabitants of Winchester and pushed on to the coast.

Meanwhile, Æthelred had gone to Shropshire for the winter and it was whilst he was in Shrewsbury (with Eadric) that the panic of the whole nation began to dawn on the king. Here he mused with his councillors upon what should be done and, to the surprise of no one, the decision was taken to raise a tax and pay the Danes off. Before leaving England, Swein's army received a further 36,000 pounds in tribute.

In 1008 Æthelred busied himself with the reorganisation of England's fleets in a policy change that would provide warships of 60 oars from every 310 hides of his kingdom. 'A hide in English...' remarked Henry of Huntingdon '... means the land that can be cultivated annually by one plough'. Furthermore, every eight hides of land would provide one helmet and one mailcoat for a warrior.[4] This giant new fleet had great promise, but its leadership would soon let it down. By the next year, it was ready. It stationed itself off Sandwich and awaited its enemy. However, its leader, a Sussex thegn named Wulfnoth was accused of treason against the king by Eadric Streona's brother, Beorhtric. The accusation was described by some as unjust, but Wulfnoth proceeded to seize 20 of the fleet's ships and took to so-called 'piracy' along the south coast. Eighty of the fleet's ships under the command of Wulfnoth's accuser sailed after him, but they were wrecked on the Sussex shore. Worse was to come. The 80 ships were permanently destroyed by Wulfnoth's men. Æthelred and his councillors left for home and the remaining ships of the fleet set sail for London, 'the whole nation's labours wasted' as the Anglo-Saxon chronicler put it. Sandwich, a fine anchorage, was left at the mercy of the invader, and in August 1009 the Danes took the golden opportunity to occupy it. Wulfnoth clearly had a lot of experience in sailing the coastal waters off Sussex and it is interesting that his pursuers, who came from the west Midlands, seem to have been less competent sailors. Wulfnoth, the father of a young and ambitious man named Godwin who would also use these coastal waters to his advantage in the future, was soon exiled by the king and his subsequent fate is uncertain. He may even have joined the Danes, but his son would have his father's Sussex lands returned to him just five years later by the eldest son of the king himself in his will, a document of singular significance.

The new Danish army was larger and better organised than before. It arrived in two waves with the first being led by Thorkell the Tall and the second by his brother Hemming and another commander named Eilaf. The combined fleet was massive. Thorkell was a brother of one of the Jómsborg commanders and had been with Swein on many campaigns. Despite this impressive military organisation and apparent readiness for war, there were no pitched battles for over half a year, with the force being content to raid and provision itself from the land. Canterbury bought its own peace for the price of 3,000 pounds, and then the combined force fell upon the shores of the beleaguered shires of Sussex and Hampshire after stationing itself once again on the Isle of Wight. Another giant fyrd was called out by the king and at one point managed to prevent its enemy's passage to the coast, but we are told in an enigmatic statement that despite the fact that the king was with his army and was prepared this time to do-or-die, Eadric Streona had thrown a spanner in the works, as was his wont, and it all came to nothing.[5] Soon, the fleet was back in Kent and then took quarters in the Thames estuary where it focused its attentions during the winter on the surrounding shires and frequently attacked London which once again bravely withstood its enemy.

The Danes caused great trouble wherever they went. Oxford was badly burned in the new year of 1010 and the Danes returned to their ships crossing the Thames at Staines to avoid London. The spring of that year was spent by the Vikings repairing their vessels back in Kent. But the army soon turned its eyes to the east and towards some unfinished business with the redoubtable Ulfkell Snilling. They sacked Ipswich as soon as they landed and then moved out into the hinterland. Ulfkell had drawn a fyrd together from East Anglia and Cambridgeshire and waited for the Danes whilst blocking access to Thetford which had suffered at the hands of the Danes in 1004. The battle probably took place at Ringmere, 4 miles north-west of Thetford. After a struggle, the East Anglians were routed; their flight started, it is said, by the actions of a certain Thurcytel 'Mare's Head'. The Cambridgeshire men stood firm but could not avoid being overwhelmed. Once again the Danes had the victory, but more importantly, they could now move around the countryside unmolested.

A dramatic and poetic glimpse of the battle at Ringmere Heath is captured in the *Olaf's drápa*, penned by Sighvat the scald, and it contains an interesting reference to the English:

> Moreover once more Olaf brought about the meeting of swords a seventh time in Ulfcetel's land, as I relate. All the race of Ella stood arrayed at Ringmere Heath. Men fell in battle, when Harold's heir stirred up strife.

Ella had been the Northumbrian king allegedly responsible for the murder of the famous Ragnar Lothbrok, whose death was said by some to have sparked the subsequent invasion of the Great Danish Army into England in 865. The scald has dug deep into the past to remind his reader of that famous moment in the mutual history of Englishman and Dane.

After Ringmere Heath, the subsequent raiding was unlike anything in the history of the Viking era in England. They horsed themselves from East Anglian stud farms, burned the land far into the fens and razed Thetford and Cambridge. Oxfordshire, Buckinghamshire, Bedford and Tempsford also felt the heat of the Viking torch, but it was after the assault on Cambridge that according to the reliable testimony of Henry of Huntington the Danes fell back to Balsham and murdered everyone they found there, tossing children on their lances. One local man, it was said, was able to defend himself from the church tower against the whole force to his lasting local memory. But the effect on the already declining morale of the English as expressed in the *Chronicles* makes for depressing reading. Wherever the raiders went, the English force which had been ordered to fight seemed to be somewhere else. It lacked both leadership and conviction. In the end, not even one shire would help another, or so we are told.

Northampton was next to feel the flames on 30 November, followed by another excursion into Wessex, before the Vikings returned to their ships for the winter. There was scarcely a settlement in the whole of the south-east of England which had not been affected by the devastation of 1010. One place in the ancient kingdom of the South Saxons, the settlement at Hastings, had been cruelly burned along with its surrounding district and yet as they peered through the smoke and looked across the unfriendly sea, the poor survivors of the mauling of 1010 could hardly imagine what the waves would bring to their grandchildren. The once glorious kingdom of the English was on its knees.

By September 1011 the Danes were back in Kent and this time Canterbury fell to them through the betrayal of a man named Ælfmær. As a result, the former bishop of Winchester, now Archbishop Ælfheah of Canterbury, who had a long history of diplomatic relations with the Danes, was captured along with Ælfweard, the king's reeve and other notable clerics.[6] If anything could possibly surpass the scenes of 1010, what happened in Canterbury in 1011 did. The Danes simply went wild in the town, plundering Christchurch and murdering the population with the clear intent of sparing no one. They over-wintered in the town and as if by some sort of divine retribution, many of the Danes were struck down with disease probably brought about by polluted water supplies.

By spring of 1012 when Eadric and other English councillors had come down to London, it seems that the English had gathered enough cash from their depleted resources to pay the Danes a colossal 48,000 pounds to leave, but the enemy demanded a ransom for the archbishop as well, said to have been a further 3,000 pounds. The pious and loyal archbishop would not let his countrymen pay the ransom, even if they had wanted to, and for this he was murdered whilst in the hands of his drunken captors, his head pulverised by the butt end of a Dane-axe. This foul deed had taken place at Greenwich. Greenwich and Woolwich were appurtenances of Lewisham, a property which the monks of St Peter's in Ghent had claimed was granted to them in 918 by the daughter of Alfred the Great. It was also a great port and the disruption caused to trade by persistent Scandinavian activity here also made it difficult for St Peter's to maintain their grip on the Lewisham estate. In fact, while the ætheling Edward, Æthelred's son, was in exile in Normandy, the monks made him swear an oath to restore the estate to them if he were to return to his paternal kingdom. The tale of drunkenness and cruelty might seem to be exaggerated, but the fact that the murder of the archbishop took place at the end of the Rouen-to-London wine trade route might explain a great deal. The archbishop's body was taken to St Paul's Minster in London where it wrought miracles until 1023, when it was returned to Canterbury.

High-profile gruesome political murders are hardly unknown in the Anglo-Saxon and Viking worlds, but there was something about this hideous event which seems to have over-stepped the mark, even for some of the Vikings themselves. There was more to the Viking reaction than mere guilt, as well. Back in the ninth century when King Edmund of East Anglia had been murdered by the sons of Ragnar, the leading Danes of the next generation were minting coins in his honour, but that was no sign of a sense of outrage. Here, the deed was carried out against the express wishes of Thorkell the Tall and because his bargaining for the life of the archbishop was ignored, Thorkell's anger turned to thoughts of betrayal, or so we are led to believe. By the end of 1012, he had placed his own fleet of 45 ships at the disposal of the king of the English in a move that gave Æthelred a mercenary force of Scandinavians that would have been the envy of the great English kings of yesteryear who had often sought such an arrangement. This employment by an English king of a sizeable force of Scandinavian soldiery marked the beginning of a new Anglo-Danish veneer in the military organisation of later Anglo-Saxon England that would last for over 50 years.

But the English armies of the age of Æthelred were not those of the age of Athelstan. Confidence had been drained by a series of spectacular defeats and a profound sense of fatalism. The new millennium had brought with it only suffering for the Christian English and this was a sign of God's anger at the sins of the people.[7] The situation was exasperated by the divisions in regional leadership, with some senior thegns openly hostile to the king and others fighting valiantly if not for him, for the defence of their patrimonies. Then there was the king: impetuous, thoughtless and troubled. He must have thought that the negotiation which brought him the services of the disaffected Thorkell, had been something of a diplomatic masterstroke, but he had once again brought the fury of Swein upon him.

King Swein of Denmark had had enough of Æthelred. If we chose to believe the story, there had been the murder of his sister which occasioned his first retaliatory attack on England and now the English king had solicited the services of the Jómsborg Vikings and their leader who was technically the Danish king's own man. This time, Swein would campaign for the ultimate political goal in England. The line of the house of Wessex, which stretched all the way back to the sixth century, would have to be broken. The duplicitous Æthelred must go. England would have a Danish king.

In 1013 the anchorage at Sandwich was once again occupied by the Danes, this time under their king. Then, Swein sailed up the east coast and entered the Humber, a time-honoured entry point for so many Scandinavian fleets in the past. He sailed down the Trent as far as Gainsborough. Here, in the heart of the Danelaw, he could solicit support. The leaders of the Danelaw, whose ancestors had thrown in their lot with the powerful English kings of the line of Alfred, now heard a direct plea from a would-be ruler of all Danish England. Their leaders came to Swein and heard what he had to say and with the exchange of hostages, the local rulers of Northumbria and Lindsey once again horsed the Danes and joined with Swein on a campaign where the stakes this time were very high indeed. But it was not just the Danes of the Danelaw who went over to Swein at Gainsborough. Many English nobles opposed to Æthelred on the grounds that they shortly expected to be disinherited or those who had suffered from the purges of 1006, went over as well. Among these men were Siferth and Morcar, senior thegns who had maintained a close relationship with Æthelred's sons by his first marriage, Athelstan and Edmund. The stage was set for the most extraordinary and unprecedented shift of allegiance in later Anglo-Saxon history.

Under Swein, they poured across Watling Street. Once across this great cultural divide, further agony was inflicted upon a tired and beleaguered population. The morale of the king's men was at rock bottom. Oxford fell without a fight, perhaps its townsfolk remembered only too well the recent burning it had suffered in 1010, but more disastrously for the English king, so did Winchester. Wessex was split down the middle, with Danish dominance cutting the west from the east. The Danes then turned to London, where Æthelred and the fleet of Thorkell were waiting. The

English and their Jómsborg friends had an ally in the river Thames which accounted for many of Swein's men who attempted to ford this most deceptive river. Currents ran as deep then as they do now. Swein, who seems to have had no stomach for a protracted siege of London, instead turned his attention to the Wessex heartlands. From London he went to Wallingford, and then on to Bath. Here, the leading figures of western Wessex led by Ealdorman Æthelmær of Devon gave their submission to him and he left for Gainsborough. He was, in virtually every respect bar the anointing, the practising king of England. Æthelred had little left. According to William of Jumièges, he was in Winchester when he learned of London's surrender. Emma had already gone back to Normandy to her brother accompanied by the abbot of Peterborough and the bishop of Durham and she was quickly followed by Edward and Alfred, the two young æthelings. It was inevitable that Æthelred would follow. He went to the Isle of Wight in mid-winter and, after staying there for the season, he took his ships to Normandy. The king of the English was an exile. Swein now had his kingdom, not just the Danish part, but all the kingdom of the English. But then something happened which changed things dramatically. At Gainsborough, Swein suddenly died in February 1014. The Danes quickly elevated his son Cnut to the position which Swein had occupied among them. There was no immediate campaign, however. Clearly, the death of the first Danish king of England had come as a blow to his supporters, both English and Danish. He had only the time to instigate one kingly act, to raise a tax, much of which was returned to its depositors at his death.

But what happened next was of profound significance for the future of the relationship between monarchy and noblemen in England. Those who had been intimidated into submitting to Swein had their chance to turn to Æthelred once more, even though he was in exile. The plea from the remaining English leaders and churchmen to the descendant of the West Saxon royal line would not come without terms, however, and these were firmly expressed. The English people would have their natural lord back so long as he ruled more justly than before. He would have to forgive people for their previous behaviour and put into action the reforms that they had demanded. The king sent his son Edward, the young ætheling from Normandy who would soon occupy a famous place in English history, to England with a writ in his hand from the king which outlined an offer of friendship which contained the promises of fair treatment in return for the support of the people. In the spring of 1014, Æthelred, the descendant of Alfred the Great, and his Norman wife came home.

Edward and Alfred, who may have stayed a little while in Normandy, soon followed and returned to their paternal kingdom. Meanwhile, a man who might have been king himself, who was behind much of the politicking of these extraordinary years, was drawing up his will as he approached death. His name was Athelstan, and despite his illness, his contribution to English history was far from over.

3

A FLAME THAT DIED

Were it not for the survival of one remarkable historical document, we would know nothing of the deep tensions amongst the English aristocracy around the time of Swein's invasion. In fact things would seem to be perfectly simple – but they were not. The will of Ætheling Athelstan, Æthelred's eldest son by his first marriage, is littered with clues as to where people's loyalties lay. It was drawn up on 25 June 1014. The will stresses the ætheling's legitimacy to the title of his estates by stating that he had either bought them from the king or received them as gifts from other high-ranking noblemen. And there is clearly tension between son and father in that the will makes a direct appeal to the Witan, or high council, that the king should be seen to keep his word. In other words, Athelstan thought that there was every chance that Æthelred would continue to turn his back on him, even after death.

The beneficiaries of the will included Siferth and Morcar, leading thegns from the Danelaw. Athelstan must have known these two very well. He had already given Morcar a mailcoat, a most expensive gift which would have symbolised Morcar's allegiance to Athelstan. Soon, Athelstan's brother Edmund would take Siferth's widow for his own wife. Siferth, as we shall shortly discover, did not meet a natural end. Thurbrand, another beneficiary, had given Athelstan a horse and Leofwine, possibly the ealdorman of the West Mercian region of the Hwicce, had given him a fine white horse. We also learn that Ulfkell Snilling had given the ætheling a silver-hilted sword. The king's attitude to these men and his appointment of Eadric begin to become clearer. Also, we can discern from the will that Æthelwold, the father of Æthelmær, had left a widow when he died and Athelstan had supported her in the meantime. Both Æthelwold and Æthelmær appear to have been victims of the king's purges of 1005-1006. A reference to Bishop Ælfsige of Winchester who was also linked to the shrine of Edward the Martyr at Shaftesbury is interesting in that it may indicate that the bishop had leanings towards the old Edward lobby of the succession crisis which had so divided England in 975. One other man, the son of the Sussex thegn Wulfnoth, had his father's estate at Compton restored to him by Athelstan in the will. This young man, as we shall soon discover, had a long and fruitful career and while he would never quite be king himself, he would be the father of one. His name was Godwin.

Clearly, the two most important people who stood to gain from Athelstan's will were his brothers Edwy and Edmund, in particular Edmund. Edmund's inheritance was both symbolic and impressive: a sword with a pitted hilt, another blade and a trumpet, Athelstan's East Anglian estates and most splendid of all, a sword that had once belonged to an English legend, King Offa of Mercia. The East Anglian connection is of some importance, since it links the ætheling Athelstan with the patrimony of the descendants of his namesake Athelstan 'Half-King' who were firmly committed to the Edward lobby. By inheriting these estates Edmund's immediate political future would have a firm root in the Danelaw. And then there was the sword. A symbol of power, of rightful legitimacy to the throne of England. Passing this treasure to Edmund signified that Athelstan, who considered himself the heir to the throne, was in effect giving the nod to Edmund. It should be he and not Edward, the son from Æthelred's marriage to Emma of Normandy, who must inherit the kingdom. The symbolism is overwhelming. There had once been a great king who led his countrymen in a time of crisis and his name too was Athelstan. He too was the owner of great riches which included a remarkable sword. And it was he who was succeeded by a brother who had fought alongside the king in the great struggles of the day. That brother's name had been Edmund. None of these names are a coincidence.

So, in that eventful and remarkable year of 1014 Athelstan lay on his deathbed knowing that his father had turned away from him, preferring, it seems, to recognise Edward and Alfred as heirs. He and his brothers had made friends with senior political figures across the country who felt aggrieved against Æthelred. They had either been sidelined by the king in his governmental purges or had a background on the Edwardian side in the accession crisis of 975. Few, if any of the beneficiaries in the ætheling's will were neutral. Many of them had even taken the dramatic step of offering their support to a foreign king in 1013.

The year of 1014 ended with another huge payment to the Viking force which lay at Greenwich in the south and an unwelcome inundation from the sea which drowned many people in coastal settlements. It was a difficult time to be living in England. A combination of human and natural disasters conspired to depress a once proud people. Never had the Anglo-Saxon past been looked at so fondly by people who recalled the memories of great warrior kings who had expanded the kingdom, given land and wealth to a growing thegnly class and treated the Church with great favours and gifts. All this had gone. The king, despite his return to his natural office, was still proving to be unlucky in politics. The people of England from the settlement at Hastings to the shores of Lincolnshire could smell only burning and feel only the loss of their children. Then, when they went to church, they were told that these events had come to them because they were being punished for their sins. In a famous sermon of 1014 known as the 'Sermon of the Wolf to the English', Archbishop Wulfstan, the very man who penned so many of King Æthelred's laws told his flock at great length why things had gone so wrong. It is difficult not to agree with the sentiments expressed by the famous churchman, even if they were couched in terms which may seem strange to us:

> For now, for many years, as it may seem, there have been in this country many injustices and wavering loyalties among men everywhere…this people, as it may seem, had become very corrupt through manifold sins and many misdeeds.

Wulfstan, in his lengthy treatise, went on to state that there were in England many people who had become degenerate apostates, that is to say, there were those who had given up their beliefs in Christian ethics and gone over once again to pagan ways. By a strange chance, a fragment of an Old English letter survives from this era and it is written by a woman to her brother Edward. She leaves her unfortunate reader in no doubt as to what she thinks of his moral decline and in so doing gives us a remarkable insight into the relationships between Dane and Englishman at a certain level in contemporary society:

> you do wrong in abandoning the English practices which your fathers followed, and in loving the practices of heathen men who begrudge you life, and in so doing show by such evil habits that you despise your race and your ancestors, since in insult to them you dress in Danish fashion with bared necks and blinded eyes…

Yet for the ordinary people life was somewhat different. They did not have the chance to culturally affiliate themselves with the Dane, nor to borrow his clothes. In fact, since the turn of the millennium these poor people had been living on borrowed time. The problems of the age had a great deal more to do with factional and regional politics than with any sort of racial antipathy, despite what our disaffected woman has to say to her brother. High politics were being played out a long way above the heads of the people of the countryside. It did not seem to matter to them who claimed control of the kingdom, the people continued to suffer. And so, the final years of Æthelred's reign were to be so much different than before his exile. For a start, there was still a Dane with ambition resting in the north with his ships.

Cnut had stayed on the Trent at Gainsborough for some time. He had managed to secure horses from Lindsey, so that his army could go on widespread raids. There must have been some sort of formal recognition of Cnut by the men of Lindsey, because very soon Æthelred brought a large fyrd into Lincolnshire and with an energy befitting a restored king, but not the morality to match, he laid waste the land in much the same way that the Vikings had in the south. Cnut had apparently been caught by the speed of the king's advance into Lincolnshire. There was no military engagement between the two sides. Instead, Cnut left with his fleet and sailed down the east coast to Sandwich where he disembarked the hostages which had been given to his father before his death. This he did with the intention of showing Æthelred what he thought of the king's grand expedition into the Danelaw: he had the hands, ears and noses of the unfortunate hostages cut off before they were put ashore. Then Cnut set sail for Denmark, abandoning Lindsey to an appalling fate at the hands of the king of the English. Lindsey had been the unfortunate victim of a political game. The people felt betrayed by Cnut and angry at the king for the style of his retribution. Somebody would have to lift the spirit of the Anglo-Danish communities north of Watling Street, and in the event, this somebody turned out to be an Englishman and a son of the king. The ætheling Edmund had been watching political developments in the north with great interest and, as the will of his now dead brother Athelstan had shown, he seems to have had many friends there.

But, if the defeatist Abingdon chronicler is to be believed, more darkness would fall. Eadric Streona had not yet finished in his career of treachery and double-dealing. During a meeting of a great assembly at Oxford in 1015, Eadric betrayed and had murdered Siferth and Morcar, the sons of Earngrim and leading thegns in the seven boroughs of the

Danelaw.[1] William of Malmesbury puts the blame squarely on Eadric's shoulders, saying that it was the greed of their estates and the advice of Eadric which caused the deaths of these high-born Danes. In fact, Siferth's estates were the largest in Northumbria. Their supporters were stopped from exacting revenge, we are told, when they were shepherded into a church and set ablaze. Siferth's wife, Ealdgyth, was taken on the orders of the king to Malmesbury and her husband's lands were confiscated. Eadric had once again done Æthelred's dirty work for him. But neither of them had anticipated events. Edmund came to Malmesbury and took Ealdgyth away with him and married her against his father's wishes. By September, the couple had travelled up the Fosse Way and into the heartlands of Ealdgyth's former husband's territory, winning acclaim and recognition from a population tired of war.

Edmund had arrived as the legitimate heir to the territory of Siferth through marriage and because he had defied his father who had laid waste to parts of the Danelaw, his welcome was most enthusiastic. But now Cnut appeared once again with a fleet off the English coast, heading for Sandwich. The Danishman chose not to venture north to the Danelaw where he would not be welcomed by those who had felt betrayed by him, but instead went round the Kentish coast into Wessex and came to the mouth of the Frome and raided into the West Country from there. While Æthelred lay ill at Cosham, his son was gathering an army in the Danelaw and Eadric was gathering another force in Mercia. Logic dictates that together these sizeable English forces might well have crushed Cnut in the field, but we are told of Eadric's desire to betray Edmund, an assertion made by the Anglo-Saxon chronicler with a firmness which we need not doubt. And so, two giant English armies, one led by the son of the king and another by a senior ealdorman, did not come together. Worse was to follow for Edmund. Eadric managed to prize from their allegiance to Æthelred 40 ships 'manned by Danish soldiers'[2] which had been Thorkell's. He then gave his submission to Cnut and in an instant the Dane was in control of Wessex and, through Eadric, the nobility of Mercia.[3]

Treachery, if that is what we choose to believe, had set the scene for an unlikely contradiction. On the face of it, it had seemed that for centuries the power struggles in England had been between the southern kings of the rising house of Wessex and the aspiring imperialists of the northern Viking world. Now, in an extraordinary reversal, a son of the king of the English, a descendant of the line of Cerdic would lead the men of the Danelaw in direct opposition to a Danish challenger to the throne in the south, one who had at his disposal the support of another English leader and his men south of Watling Street. And yet all this was taking place while there was a perfectly legitimate king still living.

Despite all the campaigns which had taken place in the last 30 years in England, nothing quite like those which took place in 1016 would be seen in England again until the fateful year of 1066. It was to be a year of decision of equal importance in the fall of Anglo-Saxon England to its more famous counterpart. The winter of 1015-16 saw Cnut and Eadric march a giant army across the Thames at Cricklade into Mercia where they both subsequently reduced the territory belonging to the ancient under-kingdom of the Hwicce, an area controlled by an ealdorman, Leofwine. Edmund, meanwhile, was struggling to pull together a force of equal proportions in the north. There were two problems for the man who, from his strength of character alone, was known by his men as 'Ironside'. The first of these was that many of the men he led were northern Mercians and they were loathe to take on Cnut's Danes, who had West Saxons in their army, unless the burghal garrison of London would also take part. But more than this, these men wanted the king himself to take to the field with them.[4] Despite having initially set himself up in opposition to his father, it became clear to Edmund that the men of the Danelaw wanted to be sure that the recognised king would support their chosen leader in a time of approaching war against Cnut. There was no immediate resolution to the problem and his men returned to their homes whilst Edmund sent to the king with these demands. Edmund issued a new call-out, this time with the threat of stern penalty, and the king did indeed take to the field in response to the request. But Æthelred was ill and by now was developing paranoid delusions of all around him. He was told that somewhere in the army lurked a treacherous man and this news alone was enough to send the tired king riding back to London.

With Cnut and Eadric still at large in the south, Edmund had to think quickly. Much time had been wasted, but he could not do it all with the men he had. So he rode to Northumbria to solicit the help of Earl Uhtred. There began a giant circle of campaigning where both chief protagonists, Edmund and Cnut, managed to avoid each other for some time. Edmund and Uhtred ravaged the region of Staffordshire and went into Shrewsbury and then Chester, probably in order to punish Eadric by destroying his heartlands. Cnut for his part travelled into the places where Edmund was not. He went through Buckinghamshire, Bedfordshire, Huntingdonshire, along the fen to Stamford, into Lincolnshire and then up the Great North Road towards York. Uhtred got wind of this manoeuvre and had no choice but to part from Edmund and race back to the north to protect his earldom. But he was too late. Out of necessity, we are told, when he got there he had to submit to Cnut. Northumbria would be at Cnut's disposal, but what would he do with Uhtred? The earl's fate has attracted the attentions of a variety of historians. The *Anglo-Saxon Chronicle* says that Eadric had bargained for the murder of Uhtred along with another son of a leading northern nobleman, and it is difficult with what we have already learned about Eadric to dismiss the claim. But later northern sources tell a tale of great complexity and infamy which appears to have resounded down the years to the time of their writing in the twelfth century. The man named as responsible for the murder of Uhtred, allowing Cnut to place Eric, son of Hakon, earl of Hlathir in a position of power in Northumbria, was Thurbrand the Hold, possibly the same Thurbrand who had given Athelstan a horse. It was through Thurbrand's treachery that Uhtred and 40 others were slain by Cnut's soldiers. Somewhere, almost certainly, in this complex web of deceit laid Eadric Streona, spinning and weaving.[5]

With an ally in power in Northumbria, Cnut turned south by a western route. By Easter his army was reunited with their ships in the south. Edmund, for his part, was heading towards London and to the sick king. So too did Cnut with his fleet at hand. London would be the focus of the next stage of the great war of 1016.

However, something happened which was not entirely unexpected. On 23 April, St George's Day, as Cnut was sailing from Poole harbour up the English Channel towards the mouth of the Thames, Æthelred died. The country was split. Those who had been with the king at his death in London, and the leading men of the garrison there, quickly chose Edmund as their new king, but at Southampton, leading abbots, bishops and ealdormen of England met and gave their support to Cnut, denouncing the line of Æthelred, and in return Cnut gave his assurances that he would rule them as a loyal lord before God and the world. The man they called Ironside could not stomach this for a moment. Edmund knew he had the loyalty of London and the men who had remained in the field with him, but what he really wanted was to turn the men of Wessex back to their natural lord, a descendant of the line of Cerdic.

In May 1016 Cnut's ships came first to the long-suffering port at Greenwich and then to London. The ships' crews built a remarkable series of ditches around the town and dragged their ships to the west side of the bridge. So well-enveloped was the city that it was said that no one could get either in or out of it. But this seems not to have been the case. Cnut had certainly succeeded in encircling the town, but his main quarry had escaped with great speed before he arrived. Edmund had gone into

Wessex to recruit for a titanic series of battles. The destiny of England would be fought for between Edmund and Cnut. Both were still keen to see the decision made at the sword's edge. According to some sources, the two æthelings, Edward and Alfred, also managed to slip away, whilst their mother Emma may have stayed in London. Thietmar of Merseburg, who records Cnut's siege of London, but who gets his names hopelessly mixed up, says that the Danes offered Emma something of a Hobson's choice: she was to give up the princes to slaughter and pay a ransom. Finally, she is supposed to have accepted the terms, but in the meantime 'Athelstan' and 'Ethmund' (surely Alfred and Edward, for Athelstan was already dead and Edmund was busy recruiting) escaped in a little boat. Then the princes raised support 'to the defence of their country and the rescue of their mother'. In the battle which follows this episode in Thietmar, 'Ethmund' is killed and when the Danes learn of 'Athelstan's' approach they mutilate their hostages and flee. The problem with this account is that it telescopes a number of events into a short space of time and it is irreconcilable with its naming of the protagonists. But there is a little something to recommend it. It could be the case that Edward and Alfred did indeed flee. They, or at least Edward, had certainly turned up on the Continent by the end of 1016: Edward even made a promise in the form of an oath to the monks of St Peter's in Ghent to restore Lewisham to them when he returned to his rightful kingdom. But when did the two æthelings flee? Why did Emma not go with them? Later Scandinavian tradition reports a curious fact that Edward is supposed to have fought alongside Edmund Ironside in 1016. It would seem improbable, given that Æthelred had already nominated Edward as his heir and had utterly turned his back on Athelstan and Edmund. Why should Edward want to fight alongside the man who was challenging for his rightful throne? The only possible answer can be desperation. England was about to be taken by a man whose capacity for murdering his political opponents would become legendary. Furthermore, he was not a member of the line of Cerdic. We have no record of whether there was an arrangement between Edmund and Edward, but what we do know is that Edward's oath taken on the altar of SS Peter and Paul at Ghent is datable to 25 December 1016. Edmund Ironside died on 30 November. Perhaps Edward and Alfred (accompanied by their sister Godgifu) had indeed stayed in England to fight alongside their kinsmen whilst the light of the line of Cerdic still shone in England.[6]

There is some evidence that Edmund's return to the Wessex heartlands in 1016 was received by the people there with some delight. But it would take him time to a raise a sizeable army. Cnut lifted the siege of London, leaving behind a small force to guard the ships, and went after Edmund in deepest Wessex. With the troops that he had managed to muster there, Edmund met Cnut in the field at Penselwood near the manor of Gillingham in Dorset and won the first English victory over Danish opposition for almost as long as anyone could remember. Very soon after midsummer the two armies met again in another pitched battle at Sherston in Wiltshire. In the *Chronicles* compiled at Worcester, we see a clear idea of what it was like to fight in the English shield wall of the period, a formation which was time-honoured and which would be used again on Senlac Ridge in 1066. We also see what the compiler thought of a certain Eadric:

> Drawing up his army as the nature of the ground and the strength of his force required, he [Edmund] posted all his best troops in the first line, placing the rest in reserve…
>
> The battle was so hard fought and bloody that both armies being no longer able to prolong the fight for very weariness, drew-off of their own accord.
>
> But the next day the king would have utterly defeated the Danes had it not been for the stratagem of Edric Streon [*sic*], his perfidious ealdorman. For when the fight was thickest, he struck-off the head of a man named Osmær whose features and hair were very like Edmund's, and holding it up, shouted to the English that they were fighting to no purpose: 'Flee quickly', he said 'ye men of Dorsetshire, Devon and Wilts: ye have lost your leader: lo! Here I hold in my hands the head of your lord, Edmund the king: retreat with all speed'.[7]

This thrilling account is given further drama by William of Malmesbury who says that, after taking off his helmet to prove to his troops that he was still alive, Edmund threw a great spear at Eadric, who dodged it. The weapon was hurled with such ferocity, however, that it impaled two warriors nearby.

Sherston had cost a great many lives, but ended in something of a draw. Cnut returned to besiege London and Edmund licked his wounds. Both armies had fought each other to a virtual standstill on that western field, but there would be more fighting to come. Edmund knew that he had to call out another fyrd. With his new force he headed for London with the intention of relieving it. He chose an unexpected approach to the city, coming north of the Thames and around through Clayhanger near Tottenham. The stealth of his approach clearly surprised the Danes and they were driven from their positions to their ships. London was relieved. But Edmund still needed a decision in the field. He headed with his army to cross the Thames at Brentford just two nights after his strike on the besiegers and here, at the water's edge in West London, he caught the Danes and inflicted great losses. Unfortunately, many of Edmund's men fell in the subsequent excitement during the rout, some of them running after their enemy's baggage train and drowning in the Thames along with the vanquished. Edmund, despite these notable victories, could not achieve his goal of completely crushing his enemy. He knew that he needed yet more men from Wessex and so he turned back to get them. Cnut returned to London to re-establish his position there. Yet still London held out. Cnut was getting desperate. With supplies running out and London still holding, he decided to launch one final assault on the city, but it came to nothing.

The Danes left London and sailed north to the Orwell. From here they went into Mercia and provisioned themselves in the usual devastating fashion. Providing mounts for themselves, some of the Danes continued to harry the Mercian countryside, whilst their infantrymen took their supplies and ships and headed for the river Medway in Kent. Another nationwide fyrd was raised by Edmund. He took it once again to Brentford and crossed the Thames and went into Kent. Here he found his enemy again and fought against it at Otford. After an impressive victory, he overtook many of the escaping Danes who were heading with their horses to Sheppey and killed them. But then something happened which King Edmund should have expected. With Cnut clearly on the back foot, Eadric Streona crossed the Medway at Aylesford and brought his men to join with Edmund, to the great consternation of the *Anglo-Saxon Chronicle*: 'there was no more unwise decision than this was', it dryly recorded.

The Danes still had the sea and they used it to good effect. They sailed back to Essex and raided inland again. This brought the fifth royal fyrd call-out from King Edmund, all inside the same tumultuous year. With another giant army, Edmund, gaining in support and popular admiration every day, marched back across the Thames and over into Essex, shadowing the Danish force until he overtook it at Ashingdon in south-east Essex on 18 October. The writer of the Canterbury version of the *Anglo-Saxon Chronicle* had hinted that Eadric's arrival at Aylesford had not been quite what it seemed. It had been a ruse, a kind of trap for Edmund. This may have been the case, but what happened at Ashingdon amounted to the greatest of all betrayals, just as it looked like the new king was about to rid himself a fearsome enemy. Eadric, fighting on Edmund's side, started a flight with his men from the west Midlands and it became a domino effect in the English lines. Cnut had a signal victory after what had been a number of conspicuous defeats. Just when it looked like the brave King Edmund would keep alive the line of his ancestors on the throne of England, another Englishman betrayed him on the field of battle and this one act would provide for a very different future for the English. The casualties were significant. Among them on the English side was the bishop of Dorchester, the abbot of Ramsey, Ealdorman Ælfric of Hampshire, Godwin of Lindsey, Æthelweard son of Æthelwine of East Anglia, and the famous Ulfkell Snilling of East Anglia. Edmund himself may have been badly wounded in the struggle.

Edmund had no choice but to flee the field. He must have wanted to pursue Eadric for his sedition. He headed west and went into Gloucestershire. Here Cnut followed him. As ever, Eadric was the player in the drama. He and other councillors advised both Cnut and Edmund to mediate. On a small island in the river Severn, the two men met, face-to-face. Legend has it that Edmund challenged Cnut to a single-combat duel, but it is not known for certain if this was the case. The duel was an Anglo-Norman way of settling such affairs by revealing the judgement of God and it is in the Anglo-Norman texts that we find the legend. These two men however, had chased each other across England for a whole year. Each had commanded sizeable armies and each had won significant battles, but neither of them had completely defeated the other. The men agreed a mutual pact of friendship. Payment was set for the Danish army and the kingdom was split between Edmund and Cnut. Edmund, as natural heir to the house of Cerdic, would have Wessex. Cnut would have all of England north of the Thames. Significantly, John of Worcester tells us that '...the crown of the kingdom, however, remained with Edmund'. It is a point worthy of note. Cnut, when he became king, would claim that he had 'inherited' it from King Edmund. Henry of Huntingdon even puts words into the mouth of Cnut by claiming that he had said that the two of them should be brothers 'by adoption'. So, Edmund's line, who had conquered all Britain in the tenth century, were back where they had begun it all, in the deep south, although the crown was still with the Englishman. But the control of London was denied to Edmund, with the Danes taking winter quarters there and securing payment from the hardy citizens who had fought them off for so long. Ashingdon had been a watershed for England and a severe blow for Edmund.

We may never know how or why Edmund ended his days on 30 November that year. The wounds he received at Ashingdon may have been the reason. Surely the grasping ealdorman had not committed the final act in his bid for infamy? Some said Edmund died while he was in London, so it seems that, if he died of his wounds at all, he survived long enough to travel the width of the country and back again before he departed this life. But there is a darker reason given by William of Malmesbury, who tells us that Edmund was murdered by trusted servants who had listened to the seductive promises of Eadric. Although he assigns no source to the story, he says that Edmund was dispatched whilst at his toilet in the most gruesome manner. Henry of Huntingdon suggests that Eadric's son performed the foul murder himself. Dare we believe such treacherous tales?

Whatever the reason, the brave Ironside, who it seemed could not be defeated in war without being betrayed, passed away and with him went a curious accolade: he was the last truly English king of England from that day to this. Wessex soon recognised Cnut as ruler. The war was over and England would be ruled by a Scandinavian monarch for some time to come. The political aspirations of a new class of Anglo-Danish nobleman would be rather different than they had before.

Early in 1017, Cnut succeeded to the whole kingdom of England. He set about a grand division of the kingdom, dividing it into four regions along historical lines, but with new leaders in some places. Edmund's Wessex was to be the new king's domain now, the jewel in the crown which he could never have held while Edmund still drew breath. Thorkil would receive East Anglia, all of Mercia would go to Eadric who had done so much to bring about the downfall of his countrymen and Eric would stay with Northumbria. Much blood would be spilled at the highest political levels in this year as purges were carried out by the new regime. Æthelred's son, Edwy, his only surviving son by his first marriage now that both Athelstan and Edmund were dead, was driven from England on the king's orders by Eadric Streona. In fact, if the chronicles of John of Worcester are to be believed, it was a certain Æthelweard who was put forward by Eadric Streona and presented to the king as the would-be assassin of poor Edwy. Cnut is supposed to have said to him 'get me his head and you will be dearer to me than my own brother'. Æthelweard agreed to do the deed, but had no intention at all of carrying it out, so he quietly slipped away and forgot about it. After a secretive return to England Edwy, however, was discovered and killed.

A more curious fate befell the sons of Edmund Ironside, Edward and Edmund. They were sent to the king of the Swedes who did not fulfil the murderous end of his agreement with Cnut. In fact, John of Worcester tells us that it had been Eadric who had advised that the brothers could be dispatched by the Swedish king, a not unlikely scenario. However, we should bear in mind that, whenever Eadric's name appears in the texts of John of Worcester, it is always accompanied by an invective of some sort. There then began, for Edward at least, an extraordinary life in exile which saw him appear in many courts in Europe before eventually arriving at the court of King Solomon of the Hungarians where both he and his brother found a home. The brothers' journey is difficult to reconstruct. It is thought that the king of the Swedes harboured them for some time, perhaps until Cnut's agents came too close for comfort when the Danishman conquered Norway. After this, they may have gone to Denmark and to the house of a nobleman named Walgar, or more likely to Russia, before finally coming to Hungary perhaps as late as 1047. Edward would make another brief but fundamentally important appearance in English history on his return to England, but this would not be until 1057.

To the relief of one of the Anglo-Saxon chroniclers though, Eadric Streona was himself a casualty of the purges. He was killed 'very justly' on the orders of his former ally the new king and his body unceremoniously tipped into the Thames at London. John tells us that Cnut had Eadric killed '… because he feared to be at some time deceived by his treachery'. A reasonable enough argument, one would think. So much for Machiavellian manoeuvring. It is difficult even for the most broad-minded observer to feel sympathy for the man who solicited the downfall of Europe's most ancient royal line. In fact, the statement by Henry of Huntingdon that Eadric's head was stuck on a pole and displayed on London's highest tower might sound like hyperbole, but probably has much to recommend it.[8]

Many leading thegns who had opposed Cnut during the war of 1016 were dispatched with equal ugliness, including the son of Leofwine of the Hwicce and Æthelweard, son of the ealdorman of the western provinces. But there is one tantalising reference in the *Anglo-Saxon Chronicle* to another political exile, another Edwy, a man known as 'the churl's king'. He too was driven out by the agents of the king, but his identity remains uncertain. There is the possibility that he was a 'people's choice', some sort of popular hero about whom Eadric had been suspicious, and John of Worcester says that he was later reconciled with the king, but his history has been neither discovered nor told.

Cnut, in 1017 is supposed to have 'ordered the widow of Æthelred, Richard's daughter to be fetched as his wife'. This has often been seen as an attempt by Cnut to recall Emma from Normandy and rekindle the old Norman alliance to keep England safe from invaders. But Emma was important to Cnut, so important in fact, that it is very likely that she did not go back to Normandy but was held in England until 'sent for'. Furthermore, Cnut had to give up his relationship with Ælfgifu of Northampton, a woman he had previously formed a relationship with in the Midlands. Emma was an immensely powerful woman. By marrying her, he would indeed hold the cards if she bore him a male child. Emma had been very young when she came to England to marry Æthelred and

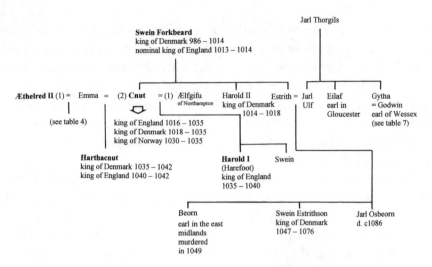

TABLE 6 The Danish kings of England

(Names in bold indicate kings of England)

so for Cnut, she was the perfect choice. On the face of it, it may seem that Richard of Normandy was comfortable with the arrangement. One eleventh-century source says that the marriage had taken place with his approval.[9] Others even point to the fact that Cnut was trying to make peace with Normandy, whilst William of Malmesbury suggested that Cnut's purpose was to get Richard to support Cnut's line from Emma as opposed to the line which came from her union with Æthelred. William was right. The union between Emma and Cnut would indeed bring a new candidate for the succession into the argument, but as for the notion that the marriage represented a Norman alliance reborn, there are two elements which we should remember: Edward and Alfred. They were under Norman protection and Edward was considered by the Normans now and for evermore as the rightful heir to the throne of England. For now, the price Emma paid for marrying Cnut would be that she would have to distance herself from the æthelings. The price the new king paid was in having to distance himself from Ælfgifu of Northampton whom he had taken as a sort of temporary wife in the Danish style. History would show that Cnut still had a role for Ælfgifu, with some unfortunate consequences for the people of Norway. Far from being an alliance which reconciled the English with their Danish monarchy, and far from being an olive branch of peace across the English Channel, this union between Cnut and Emma represented the creation of yet another political fault line which would split the new Anglo-Danish aristocracy and bring into the fray one of Europe's most hungry predators.

4

HOUSE OF THE KING-MAKER

There are some strange-sounding tales which surround the early history of the career of England's most remarkable pre-Conquest nobleman. They seem to be partly legendary, but they are interesting nonetheless. One story has it that Godwin was the son of a cowherd who rescued Æthelred when he was lost in a forest. Another equally amusing tale tells of a young Godwin directing the lost Jarl Ulf to Swein's camp during the Danish wars. Swein was so pleased at the help of the young man that he gave him his sister's hand in marriage and a place in the royal household. Certainly, Godwin's characteristics seemed to recommend themselves to the new Danish king of England and Godwin's rise would indeed be inexorable. But there had been no cowherd. Instead there had been an experienced and hardy thegn who had known the Sussex coast like the back of his hand. Perhaps this is why Godwin, son of Wulfnoth found his fortune during the reign of Cnut.

The ætheling Athelstan's will however, had hinted at the political realities of Godwin's background. It might not appear to have been a mention of serious consequence, for so much would pass before Godwin, the father of the future king of England, would ascend to the highest political offices of the land without actually being king himself, but for what it is worth, let us remind ourselves of the wording: 'And I grant to Godwin , Wulfnoth's son, the estate at Compton, which his father possessed'. If this Godwin was the Godwin who became earl of Wessex and whose partisan approach to high politics brought him into conflict with Edward the Confessor, then it ranks as the earliest mention of the man in history. He was one of the men who gained his position during the reign of Cnut and whom the author of the *Vita Eadwardi Regis* calls the 'new nobles'. He seems to have found favour in the entourage of Prince Athelstan and had clearly begun to retrieve some of his father's confiscated estates by 1014. Later Anglo-Saxon society was not so rigid in its structure that it did not allow for the rise of this class of super-thegn. Godwin would become both the king-maker and king-breaker of English history. His story at once reflects the strengths and the weaknesses of contemporary society.

Godwin's relationship with Edward the Confessor would become quite complex and his power would be immense. He had many children with his wife Gytha, one of whom, Edith, would marry the king in an attempt to bring two competing factions closer. But it was with Cnut that Godwin founded his career in both national and international politics.

And yet it seems that there has always been some confusion surrounding the man who would turn English history on its head almost without knowing it. According to the *Vita*, a document more or less commissioned by his daughter, Godwin had been 'Earl and Office Bearer of all the kingdom', occupying the 'first place among the highest nobles'. But there is evidence to suggest that he had not achieved this position quickly and more likely had it only towards the end of his career. He may well have been for most of Cnut's reign a very powerful soldier of the king.

One would have thought that such an important man's history would have been easy for medieval historians to recall, but we must remember who took the kingdom of England in 1066 and what they thought of the house of Godwin. Godwin's marriage to Gytha, the sister of Jarl Ulf Sprakalegson, is at least one matter not in question. And yet it has been noted that a certain Godwin is supposed to have married in the presence of Cnut himself, the daughter of Bryhtric or Beorhtric, the probable brother of Eadric Streona who had accused Godwin's father Wulfnoth of treason in 1008.[1] The resulting political fiasco in 1008 had paved the way for a Danish sea-borne landing after Wulfnoth had taken to sea with a significant portion of the king's fleet, whilst the remainder foundered on the shores of southern England even as they were giving chase. If this marriage did take place at all, it might have been a union designed to reconcile two competing families. But it was with Gytha that Godwin produced a potentially formidable dynasty.

The story of Godwin's early career reads like that of a professional soldier, similar perhaps to that of Thorkell the Tall. By 1018 he appears in a charter as 'Dux', indicating that his political standing was as important as his military role. The fact that he was an Englishman from the south-east of the country

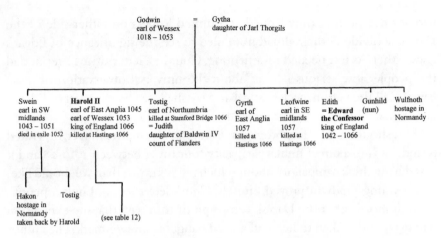

TABLE 7 Descendants of Godwin, earl of Wessex
(Names in bold indicate kings of England)

and not a Dane should not confuse us necessarily. His activities throughout his career showed him to be a man whose dynastic and personal ambitions were tied very closely with the Anglo-Danish world and his performance as a military man in the service of Cnut is our key to understanding the nature of the man and the things he subsequently tried to do.

Cnut's approach to the governance of England was energetic, but he knew that, after dismissing the fleet which had brought him to England, he had to rule the kingdom fairly and as the chosen king of a Christian people. Soon the king would have a minster built at Ashingdon for the souls of those who had fallen in the great struggle of 1016, which he gave to his own priest, Stigand. There then began the career of one of England's most notorious churchmen whose later reputation was not entirely deserved. Stigand came from an Anglo-Scandinavian background based on estates held in East Anglia. It is probably this which recommended him to the king, but he was also closely associated with Emma. In fact, their political fortunes would become quite closely tied to one another; for now Stigand would continue at Ashingdon until he had the chance to hold the bishopric at Elmham some time before 1043. What happened to him after that is a matter to which we shall return.

In 1018 Cnut reached a settlement with the English at Oxford, drawn up by the great churchman Wulfstan, who had also presided over the consecration of the minster at Ashingdon. It was an agreement which made a direct and symbolic appeal to the laws of Edgar (959-975). This was to be the benchmark. Edgar had been the ideal king at a time of peace and of great royal power and his laws were clearly viewed as just ones. They had at once both acknowledged and united leaders on either side of the Danelaw divide. Æthelred had not failed to see the significance of Edgar's laws, either. As if it needed re-affirming, Cnut in a letter of 1020 reminded the people how serious he was about the universal observation of these laws: '…all the nation, ecclesiastical and lay shall steadfastly observe Edgar's law, which all men have chosen and sworn to at Oxford'.

Yet it should not be forgotten that Cnut ran an empire. In fact, he visited Scandinavia in a direct military capacity four times between 1019-28 and it was during these campaigns (about which less is known than we should like) that a young Godwin proved himself. Cnut's letter to the English people, written shortly after the Danish campaign of 1019, says that the expedition had been undertaken to head off a great danger from Denmark. The author of the *Vita* goes further, suggesting that Godwin was taken along with Cnut in order to punish certain 'unbridled men' who had challenged his authority in Denmark. Certainly, the king would have been concerned that his family's hold over Denmark might weaken following the death of his brother King Harold of Denmark in 1018. This concern must have played a role in the motivation for the campaign, although there was probably more than one reason for the launching of a campaign which saw the young Godwin put to the test. Although some people have assumed that the lack of direct royal rule in Denmark after Harold's death led to a resurgence of Viking westward wanderlust,[2] it should be noted that both Adam of Bremen and Henry of Huntingdon suggest that the reason for the voyage was trouble at the borders of Denmark with the Wends. This sounds a more plausible reason for the campaign. Moreover, Henry says that Godwin led a night attack on the Wends which greatly pleased the king.

The force which Cnut took to Denmark was said only to have been nine shiploads in strength, not a force capable one would think, of putting down any sizeable rebellion from within the country without significant aid. Perhaps it was intended that this small force should meet up with other troops in Denmark in order to then make a move against the Wends.[3]

Meanwhile, it seems that Thorkell was given the important job of governing England while Cnut was away. Somehow, by November 1021 he had fallen foul of the king and was banished from the kingdom, along with his wife Edith, the widow of Eadric Streona. What happened next is not clear, but it may be that the old warrior went back to the bosom of the Jómsborgs of which he was once a commander. Wherever he had gone, it seems that Cnut found good reason to follow him there. In 1022 the king went out to the Isle of Wight with his ships probably as a defensive measure against an expected attack on the southern shores of England, but soon he was campaigning once again in Denmark. Godwin was with him and again he impressed the king. Cnut entered into an agreement which amounted to a reconciliation with Thorkell which involved the latter ruling in Denmark in Cnut's name and taking into his household one of the king's sons in return for offering one of his own to the king. The well-known recruiting power of this famous old Viking commander must have been a significant factor in these negotiations.

However Thorkell was soon dead and a new arrangement was needed in Denmark; it seems that Jarl Ulf was appointed regent there. Godwin's marriage to Ulf's sister Gytha would appear to have the hand of Cnut behind it. By linking the new regent of Denmark and guardian of Harthacnut, the king's son by Emma, with the house of Godwin, Cnut hoped he would secure some degree of obedience from Ulf. The marriage is a testimony to the speed at which Godwin was rising through the ranks of English society. He was by now the powerful earl of Wessex.

Cnut's hopes it seems, were ill founded. Olaf Haroldson, a Norwegian nobleman, had managed to gain a great deal of political power in Norway while Cnut's attentions had been turned to affairs in England and Denmark. Olaf is a curious figure. He had lived in the shadow of the family of Eric of

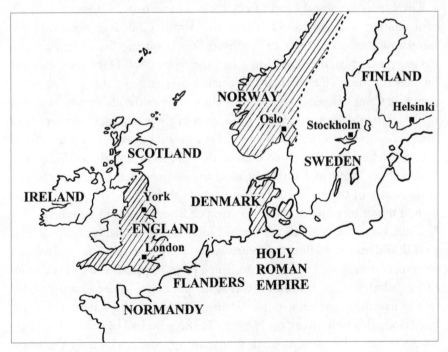

MAP 3 Cnut's Scandinavian Empire

Hlathir for some time and is thought even to have joined with Æthelred in 1013 at around the time of Swein's invasion of England. He appears to have stayed with Æthelred in exile and fought for the duke of Normandy in 1014 against Odo, the count of Chartres.

Olaf had seen his opportunity to gain further power in his Norwegian homeland while Eric of Hlathir was out with Cnut in England during the wars of 1016. He found great support around the Oslo fjord where Cnut's power was felt the most and he soon was able to convince the men of Trondheim in the north to come to him too. Cnut was loosing his grip on Norway. To make matters worse, Olaf defeated the brother of Earl Eric of Hlathir in a major sea engagement near Nesjar. Although he had several internal enemies in Norway, Olaf had one important ally in Anund, the king of Sweden, who had good reason to keep Danish ambition in check. Worse was to follow for Cnut. Jarl Ulf and his brother Eilaf, whom Cnut had made an earl in Gloucester in England, saw an opportunity to join the alliance. Their motivation is unclear but their involvement is elevated by Danish tradition to a point where they are actually held responsible for bringing together the forces which finally met Cnut at the famous battle of the Holy River in 1026.

The battle was an odd sort of engagement and many sources which tell of it conflict with one another over the details. Cnut had sailed into the mouth of the Holy River in southern Scania on the Swedish mainland having pushed back a naval force belonging to Olaf. Here they met the Swedes and their allies in a battle which either ended with the sinking of many of Cnut's English and Danish ships due to the deliberate bursting of a dam, or the enticement by Ulf's men of their enemies over a rickety bridge which subsequently collapsed. However it ended, Cnut had suffered a signal defeat. We are led to believe that Godwin was there. William of Malmesbury is not the only historian to have claimed that Godwin was at the battle of the Holy River. Gaimer said that it was here that Godwin gained much treasure '... from the king of Sweden whom he killed'.[4]

Cnut, however, was a sore loser and soon his agents had caught up with Jarl Ulf and murdered him. But Norway was by no means secure and in 1028 he returned to it with an impressive force of 50 shiploads not of Danes, but of Englishmen. Olaf Haroldson was again the target of the exercise and is said to have been driven south without offering an engagement. Cnut had been doing his homework on Norway. Those who had opposed Olaf there on account of his austere Christianity, an approach which in the event brought him sainthood, were ready to throw in their lot with Cnut. The English ships were soon joined by a large Danish fleet and Olaf knew the game was up. Godwin was there again, this time unwittingly leaving a mark in the archaeological record. A runestone commemorating the passing of a Bjor Arnsteinson 'who found death in Godwin's host when Cnut sailed [back] to England' is a striking example of Godwin's wide-ranging military activities and perhaps of the cosmopolitan make-up of his army.[5]

At Nidaros in the northern district of Trondheim a triumphant king, ruler of an Anglo-Danish empire, held a council to decide how he was to rule his kingdoms. His son Harthacnut was to be king of Denmark. Hakon, the son of the late Earl Eric, would rule in Norway in Cnut's name but would keep the title of earl. That country however, would continue to provide Cnut with more problems. In fact, the king may well have sent Hakon and his wife, along with the king of the Wends, on an ambassadorial mission at one point just to keep them out of harm's way since their political enemies were still very active in the country. King Olaf, not prepared to give up his claim to Norway, returned in 1030, but met stiff resistance from the men of Trondheim who had thrown their support behind Cnut. At Stikelstadt they confronted Olaf and killed him in battle. It was a crushing defeat and it led to the exile of a young man who had fought at the side of his half-brother at just the tender age of fifteen. That boy was Harald Sigurdsson. Harald's eventual return to Norway would have profound effects on the course of events in England's darkest year.

Olaf had seen his chance when he had learned of the premature death of Hakon who had apparently perished at sea, possibly while coming back from England. The details of the jarl's death are obscure, but John of Worcester adds that 'some say he was killed in the island of Orkney'. However it happened, it left Cnut with a power vacuum which he determined to fill with issue from his own line. Cnut's choice in fact, left a lasting impression on the Norwegians. Swein, his son by Ælfgifu of Northampton, would rule Norway with his watchful mother beside him. Her overbearing attempts at punitive legislation, many of which were based upon Danish customs, coincided with the rapid rise to prominence of Magnus, son of Olaf. It led to a period of Norwegian history which few in that country were keen to remember fondly. Instead, they looked back to the days of the pious Olaf and perhaps naturally, they turned to Magnus. By 1035 they had driven Ælfgifu and her son from Norway and established Magnus as king there. The refugees both found a home in Denmark.

Back in England, Godwin had much to occupy him. Towards the end of Cnut's reign the earl had begun to assume a more wide-ranging role in the governance of the country, closest perhaps to that of a viceroy. His presence in royal administrative circles is evidenced by the consistency with which he, along with Earl Leofric of Mercia, attested the king's charters. But throughout 1035 Cnut was growing weaker and his health finally failed him on 12 November that year. He died at Shaftesbury and was taken to Winchester where he was buried. Of Cnut's legacy, twelfth-century historians could point out that never had a king of England held such a wide-ranging power base encompassing so much of Britain and the Scandinavian world. Historians would also remember the marriage of the king's daughter Gunhild to the future Emperor Henry III which was of such splendid proportions that it was remembered in popular song. Nor would they forget the king's journey to Rome and his successful reduction of the French taxes levied on travellers passing through that kingdom. But it is perhaps for one extraordinary tale that we remember this remarkable king today and it is to Henry of Huntingdon that we mainly owe the pleasure of its recollection:

> ...when he was at the height of his ascendancy, he ordered his chair to be placed on the sea-shore as the tide was coming in. Then he said to the rising tide, 'You are subject to me, as the land on which I am sitting is mine, and no one has resisted my overlordship with impunity. I command you therefore, not to rise on to my land, nor to presume to wet the clothing or limbs of your master'. But the sea came up as usual, and disrespectfully drenched the king's feet and shins. So, jumping back, the king cried, 'Let all the world know that the power of kings is empty and worthless, and there is no king worthy of the name save Him by whose will heaven, earth and sea obey eternal laws.' Thereafter King Cnut never wore the golden crown, but placed it on the image of the crucified Lord, in eternal praise of God the great king. By whose mercy may the soul of King Cnut enjoy rest.
>
> Henry of Huntingdon. *The History of the English People*. 1000-1154. II 17-20

A masterful eulogy from one of England's finest Anglo-Norman writers does not mask the fact that there would be great danger in the years following Cnut's departure from this life. Across the English Channel a political storm was brewing. Not long before his death, there is reason to believe that Cnut genuinely attempted to reach out to the Norman court by trying to arrange a marriage between his sister Estrith, the widow of Jarl Ulf, and the Norman duke, but nothing came of it.[6] The king's desire to reconcile the English and Norman courts would have been governed primarily by his fear over the impending succession crisis in England. The æthelings Edward and Alfred had been in Normandy for some time. William of Jumièges tells us that they were 'treated with such honour by

Duke Robert…that bound them by the closest ties of affection, he adopted them as brothers'. In fact, Duke Robert (1027-1035) was their cousin.

The strength with which the Normans were to support Edward's claim to the throne perhaps reflects a deeper dynamic at work in Normandy than mere power politics, something which we shall examine in the next chapter of this book. Unquestionably, Emma's boys by Æthelred were favoured as candidates by successive dukes of Normandy over Harthacnut, her son by King Cnut. The suggestion made by Emma's own encomiast that Edward and Alfred had been sent to Normandy so that Cnut and Emma could bring up Harthacnut is at best an over-simplification of the matter.

Edward and Alfred's time in Normandy was not spent idly. In fact, it was while Edward was in Normandy that he gained a reputation for practising the art of the miracle cure. The two were clearly no embarrassment to the Normans. Their sister, Godgifu, who had gone with them, was married to Drogo, count of the Vexin where she seems to have taken the name Emma. This union shows that the family of Emma and Æthelred was taken very seriously indeed at the Norman court. So much so, that Godgifu could be used in the same way that a Norman duke might use his own daughter or sister. The marriage of Godgifu to Drogo would in fact produce a child Ralph, who before the Norman Conquest would play a key role in the regional politics not of Normandy but of the marcher area of England and Wales. Godgifu's second marriage would be to an even more important figure, that of Eustace of Boulogne, whose colourful involvement in English politics in the heart of Godwin's patrimony we shall explore.

Had Cnut ever expected trouble from Normandy? Perhaps he should have. When the king took his ships out to the Isle of Wight in 1022, he must surely have been expecting a threat to the southern shores of England. That island had in the past proved to be the classic station from which to both protect and attack England. The threat seems not to have materialised and so the king then sailed on to Scandinavia to pursue his goals in that theatre instead.

At least three medieval historians have suggested that towards the end of the reign of Cnut, Duke Robert attempted a large-scale invasion of England, designed to restore Edward to his paternal kingdom. This one episode in the history of Normandy and England is often brushed over since the developments of the 1050s had so much more to do with the eventual Norman Conquest of 1066. And yet it is of vital significance because it tells us precisely how the Normans viewed the English succession crises from the mid 1030s to 1066 and it demonstrates beyond all doubt the lengths to which they were prepared to go to see Edward, son of Emma, on the throne.

The statement by William of Jumièges is the most straightforward account of it. He says that Duke Robert had sent envoys to Cnut to demand the restoration of the æthelings, but Cnut refused. Consequently Robert mounted an expedition to invade England to force the issue. A fleet was assembled at Fécamp but when it set sail it was blown off course and ended up at Mont-St-Michel on the Cotentin peninsula, the very area in which Æthelred's ships had landed so many years ago. Robert then ordered his troops to ravage Brittany instead. William of Malmesbury, writing later in the twelfth century, recalling oral tradition says that in the river at Rouen could still be seen the rotting hulks of this invasion fleet many years later. William, whose capacity for assigning credence to the spoken or sung word of history is part of his attraction, need not necessarily be dismissed on this matter. It had clearly been a major exercise and it presents the historian with the fascinating likelihood that three decades before the Norman Conquest actually occurred, there had been a clear attempt by the Normans to cross the English Channel in force. It would not be the only time before 1066 that it would happen, either. The next 30 years of Anglo-Norman history would be dominated by Norman interest in the English succession.

There are several aspects of this crucial episode in 1033–34 which have been skilfully brought to light.[7] A number of charters survive which appear to coincide with the times and positions of Edward and the Norman forces

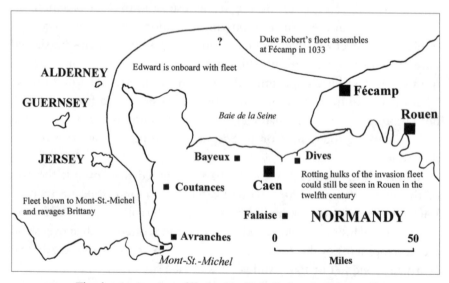

MAP 4 The abortive invasion of England by Duke Robert I of Normandy, 1033

during this event. In fact a pair of charters, one relating to the awarding of Arques church to the community at Saint Wandrille and the other to restoration of lands to Fécamp, may have been drawn up at Fécamp – a possible ducal chancery – whilst the invasion fleet was waiting. Both the charters refer to Edward and Alfred, but more significantly in two other charters arguably drawn up when the fleet arrived at Mont-St-Michel, the references to Edward are as 'king'. The Normans were serious about Edward's claim.

In 1035 both Cnut and Robert died. There are claims that Cnut had announced shortly before his death that he was ready to restore half the English kingdom to the sons of Æthelred in order to establish peace for his lifetime. He had clearly been worried about rumblings across the Channel. It was not an arrangement which would ever see reality, however. In England the scene was set for yet another of those famous factional splits which so characterised later Anglo-Saxon history. Ælfgifu of Northampton and Harold Harefoot, her son by Cnut,[8] were ranged in one camp and Emma and Harthacnut, her own son by Cnut, were ranged in the other camp. Harthacnut was still in Denmark trying to deal with the tangled affair caused by the rise of Magnus, son of Olaf. What would Godwin make of all this? When Emma was in Winchester that year, we are told that Harthacnut's housecarles were there too and that Earl Godwin was her most loyal man. But soon, the Witan had chosen not Harthacnut, but Harold Harefoot to rule the country and worse for Godwin, it seemed that Emma was waning in her support for Harthacnut. In fact, Edward and Alfred, long ago 'abandoned' by Emma, seem to have become the new focus of her attention. The lobby, which had decided for Harold Harefoot and his mother to preside over England as a sort of regency until the Danish situation was resolved by Harthacnut was headed by Earl Leofric of Mercia. He was the son of the ealdorman Leofwine who had featured in the wars of Edmund Ironside a generation earlier. The agreement was made at Oxford early in 1036 and meant that Emma would wait in Winchester accompanied by Harthacnut's soldiers. Shortly after this, in the same year as Harold's grip on the country was tightening with the aid of his mother, the exiled æthelings made another attempt to return to England. Godwin, who was not entirely comfortable with the arrangement brokered by the ealdorman of Mercia, was even more alarmed at developments across the Channel and at Emma's apparent abandonment of Harthacnut. He quickly went over to Harold.

There then followed an incident which lived in infamy for hundreds of years and its recollection was the clarion call for all those who had felt then and indeed still feel now that the Norman Conquest of 1066 was in some way a morally justifiable campaign. Both Edward and Alfred set sail for England in 1036, but by far the most significant of these journeys was made by Ætheling Alfred. He travelled from Normandy to Wissant in Flanders and from these continental shores he left for Dover in England, bringing with him some men from Boulogne, a town whose count would soon feature in the local history of Dover to some considerable degree. 'This some men in power, bore with indignation and concern', wrote John of Worcester. '... because though it was not right, they were much more devoted to Harold than to him [Alfred]; and especially, it is said, Earl Godwin.' While travelling across the south of England to visit his mother in Winchester, Alfred arrived with his men outside Guildford in Surrey. Guildford is on the time-honoured route from Dover to Winchester via the North Downs and it was here in Surrey that a famous betrayal would take place. It would never be forgotten by the Normans. Godwin intercepted Alfred and his entourage and allowed the men of Harold to arrest the prince and take him away. Earl Godwin would probably have claimed that he was simply doing the king's bidding, merely showing loyalty by following instructions, but he knew very well what was about to happen to one of the two men who could seriously damage his own career prospects by returning to England. Alfred was spirited away to Ely and was brutally blinded. So brutal was the assault that the ætheling died of his wounds shortly afterwards.[9] For his part in the deed, a part which can hardly be disputed, the Normans never forgave Godwin. Moreover, the incident coloured the way they looked at Godwin's heirs. One of the princes, a son of Emma, whom the dukes had cared for since 1016 had been betrayed by the House of Godwin. Bad blood would forever flow between the houses of the duke and the earl. What made matters worse for the Normans was that Harold's grip on the throne of England was tightening still further. His rule was beginning to be widely accepted in England as something of a *fait accompli*. To rub salt into the wound there was the rumour that Harold, who claimed that he was the son of King Cnut, was in fact, nothing of the sort but was instead the son of a shoemaker, something which even the Anglo-Saxon chronicler hinted at.

Godwin's culpability is further evidenced by the quill of the Anglo-Saxon chroniclers in their entries for 1036. Version E of the *Chronicle*, written at Peterborough, is generally taken to be pro-Godwinist in outlook. It does not mention this dramatic episode in its entry for that year at all. The Abingdon scribe, along with others, is perfectly clear on the matter and he breaks into an alliterative verse:

But then Godwin stopped him [Alfred], and set him in captivity,
and drove off his companions, and some variously killed;
some of them were sold for money, some cruelly destroyed,
some of them were fettered, some of them were blinded,
some maimed, some scalped.
No more horrible deed was done in this country
since the Danes came and made peace here.
Now we must trust to the dear God
that they who, without blame, were so wretchedly destroyed
rejoice happily with Christ.
the ætheling still lived; he was threatened with every evil;
until it was decided that he be led
to Ely town, fettered thus.
as soon as he came on ship he was blinded,
and blind thus brought to the monks.
And there he dwelt as long as he lived.
Afterwards he was buried, as well befitted him,
full honourably, as he was entitled,
at the west end, very near at hand to the steeple,
in the south side-chapel. His soul is with Christ.

But what of the other ætheling, the one who would be king? More than a handful of medieval historians have said that Edward too had come across the Channel. William of Jumièges says that he came with a sizeable fleet of 40 ships to Southampton but met resistance and turned back, whilst others said that Emma had managed to get word to Edward of Alfred's fate and that he had turned back to Normandy on her instructions. Emma's encomiast, who does not even mention Edward's journey at all, has something very sinister to say about Harold Harefoot's role in the death of Alfred. Harold, he says, had forged a letter to Alfred from his mother suggesting that he came to England. In other words, it had all been a devious plot.

For Emma, the episode had been a disaster. The agents of Harold had thrown her out of Winchester 'to face the raging winter' and she fled into exile, travelling not to Normandy, but to the court of Count Baldwin V of Flanders. The chroniclers tell us that Harold's rise was now complete. He had been 'chosen everywhere as king' and Harthacnut had been forsaken. Whatever Emma had in mind in 1036, she had no choice but to think again. From the relative comfort of the court at Bruges, Emma contacted Edward in Normandy and called for his presence. He did not come. Harthacnut, however, did indeed join his mother at Bruges in what must have been a long-awaited reunion, despite the impression we get of Emma turning her back on him. He had had some important business to attend to which had kept him in Denmark during the English succession crisis and it would seem by 1039 the Danish kingdom's relations with Norway were finally settled by mutual agreement. It was in the nature of that agreement that further problems would arise. Magnus and Harthacnut had agreed a pact whereby if either of them should die without an heir, his kingdom should pass to the survivor.

Joined by her son from Denmark, things began to look slightly better for Emma. The winter of 1039 was beset by gales and poor weather generally. Harold's health was failing. By March 1040 he was dead. His death would not be the end of his story either.[10] Whatever the truth of the rumour surrounding his true parentage, Harold was not liked by Harthacnut who considered himself the true son of Cnut and the rightful heir to the empire of his father. Emma's son finally came to England on 17 June 1040 with a significant fleet of 60 Danish ships for whose crews he raised a punitive tax in England, a burden which people found difficult to bear. Rightful heir or not, Harthacnut must have been expecting trouble.

Harthacnut's rule was relatively short and harsh. He disinterred Harold's body and had it flung into a fen and then later into the Thames where it was evidently fished out and buried by the Danes in their London cemetery. He was chiefly remembered for the taxation which he levied in order to pay his ships' crews and keep them as a fighting force. He used his housecarles, well-armed retainers, as tax collectors and in a famous episode in Worcester two of them named Feader and Thurstan were murdered by the townsmen who had cornered them in the tower of the minster. Harthacnut was not impressed by the incident and ordered a large-scale ravaging of Worcestershire which saw the population flee to a small island in the Severn to escape death. It is a measure of the king's power that he was able to call upon all the earls of England to help in this action, but it was not a measure which endeared him to history. Nor were the chroniclers particularly triumphant about the way in which the king had betrayed Eadwulf of Northumbria who had been killed on the king's orders by Siward of York while under supposed 'safe conduct'.

Godwin, on the other hand, who had at one time supported the Harthacnut camp, was given good reason to regret his fickle politics. He will also have regretted the infamous incident regarding the ætheling Alfred for he was to be held to account for it. Harthacnut, for all his harshness had regarded Edward and Alfred as his kinsmen, which indeed they were. He and Emma even invited Edward to England to live at court with them and there is every reason to believe that being childless himself, he had nominated Edward as his heir. There is a great significance in the chronicler's statement that Edward, despite his long exile, had in fact been sworn in as king of England a long time ago. This would account for the numerous references to Edward as 'king' or 'king of the English' in Norman charters which were drawn up during his exile. The heir to throne of England had at last returned peacefully to his paternal kingdom where he was to live with his mother and his half-brother until such time that he inherited his kingdom. It might seem to us to be a natural and logical conclusion to a very long tale of exile, planned invasion, murder and hardship, but we should not forget that these sorts of arrangements often have something deeper at work beneath them than that which appears on the surface. William of Poitiers tells us that the man who had a lot to do with brokering the return of Edward to England, was William II, duke of Normandy.

Godwin and Bishop Lyfing of Worcester and Crediton, whom Harthacnut also held responsible for the murder of Alfred, stood trial for their deeds. Worcester, perhaps predictably, was taken from the bishop but the arrangement with Godwin was of more interest. Harthacnut knew very well that Godwin had become the most powerful man in England. He could not punish him too hard but he could, in front of all the chief figures of the kingdom, make him explain himself and extract pledges from him and this is what he did. Godwin gave to the king a fine warship manned with 80 crewmen, an act which demonstrates not only the earl's wealth, but his military standing in the kingdom as a whole. The gilded sail of the ship was decorated with images of great naval battles of the past and was by all accounts a sumptuous vessel. Godwin swore that he had not wished for the blinding of Alfred and that he had just done what the king had told him to do. Both Lyfing and Godwin may well have been made to support Harthacnut's designation of Edward as heir too. If this was the case, it may account for the fact that they are often held responsible for the elevation of the ætheling to the throne. The truth is that Godwin, whose house would produce a king, probably had no choice in the matter and we must treat the claim made by the author of the *Vita* with some degree of scepticism:

When by God's gracious mercy there came for the English, who had suffered so long under the yoke of the barbarians, the jubilee of their redemption, that Earl Godwin... took the lead in urging that they should admit their king to the throne that was his by right of birth.

Harthacnut, who was only in his twenties, must have had an inkling that he would not live a long life. There is a hint in the sources that he was not in good health. We may never know quite why he seems to have been anxious to secure the succession issue at such a tender age and his curious death does not really shed further light on the final act of reign. He had been attending the wedding of Gytha, the daughter of Osgod Clapa, to the Danishman Tofi the Proud at Lambeth. The Chronicle's account of it would suggest that the proud Tofi had unexpected reasons to forever remember his wedding day:

> Here Harthacnut died as he stood at his drink, and he suddenly fell to the earth with an awful convulsion; and those who were close by took hold of him, and he spoke no word afterwards, and he passed away on 8 June. And all the people then received Edward as king, as was his natural right.
>
> Anglo-Saxon Chronicle.
> Abingdon manuscript (C) entry for 1042

The proximity to London of this incident probably had something to do with the swiftness of the subsequent election of Edward as king there. But there does seem to have been a tide of popular feeling flowing toward the son of Æthelred. The line of Cerdic was once again restored to the throne of England and no amount of cattle plague and poor weather could dampen the spirits of a nation who waited patiently for the king's consecration by Archbishop Eadsige of Canterbury at Easter of the following year. William of Malmesbury tells of the role of Earl Godwin in the promotion of Edward to the throne, a fact which other sources support. As a descendant of the ancient royal line, Godwin knew that Edward had a perfect right to rule. Godwin revealed his power as a king-maker:

> 'There is nothing in the way', said Godwine [sic], 'if you are willing to trust me. My authority carries very great weight in England, and on the side which I incline to, fortune smiles. If you have my support, no one will dare oppose you, and conversely. Agree with me therefore for true friendship between us, undiminished honours for my sons, and my daughter's hand. As a result, you will soon see yourself a king, who are now shipwrecked on the sea of life, exiled from the world of hope, and a suitor for the help of others.'
>
> William of Malmesbury, Gesta Regum Anglorum, vol. I para. 197.3

The Normans had their charge back on the throne of England, but what would they want in return for years of help? What would the most powerful man in England do about Norman aspiration? To understand what happened next in the tangled history of Norman relations with England, we must turn back the years and examine what it was which made the Norman duchy so successful and why its rulers seemed to be above all else, hungry for power.

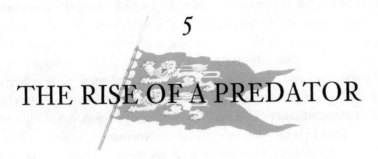

5

THE RISE OF A PREDATOR

Rollo was unwilling to kiss the king's foot, and the bishops said:
'He who accepts a gift such as this ought to go as far as kissing the king's
    foot.'
And he replied:
'I will never bow my knees at the knees of any man, and no man's foot will
    I kiss.'
And so, urged on by the prayers of the Franks he ordered one of the
warriors to kiss the king's foot. And the man immediately grasped the king's
foot and raised it to his mouth and planted a kiss on it while he remained
standing, and laid the king flat on his back. So there rose a great laugh and
a great outcry among the people. Apart from that, King Charles and Duke
Robert and the counts and nobles, bishops and abbots, swore an oath on
the Catholic faith to the patrician Rollo, on their own life and limbs, and
by the honour of the whole kingdom, that he should in addition hand on
to his heirs the appointed territory as he himself held and owned it, and that
the lineage of his sons and grandsons should hold and cultivate it through
the course of all time.

Dudo of St Quentin, The History of the Normans (29)

Notwithstanding this curious and amusing tale, there is something odd
about Norman history. Before the middle of the tenth century there
was no mention of such a place. A little over 100 years later the duke
of Normandy commanded one of the largest power blocks in Western
Europe which had at its heart the kingdom of England. The inexorable

and impressive rise of Normandy cannot have been a tale of sheer good fortune. Something unusual governed the way in which the people who came eventually to call themselves 'Norman' rose to such a dominant position in medieval Europe. Just like the English story, the main answers to our questions are to be found in the nature of the relationships of competing families, in the tales of shifting allegiances, empire building and warfare. However, the notion of inheritance in Normandy became significantly different than it was in England. And there were other more subtle differences which, when carefully considered, show themselves to be of vital importance. The very landscape of Normandy holds all the clues we need to understand the secret of Norman success.

Normandy on the eve of its greatest moment stretched roughly from Dieppe in the east to Mont-St-Michel and the borders of Brittany in the west. To the north was the natural boundary of the English Channel which would prove in the end to be no barrier to Norman ambition. To the south of the duchy were a series of rivers forming natural boundaries along with the political ones already imposed by other power groups which included that of the king of France himself. Seven dioceses comprised the archbishopric of Rouen; a further six suffragan bishoprics at Evreux, Lisieux, Sèes, Bayeux, Coutances and Avranches. On the secular side we must add to these dioceses 12 administrative districts known as 'Pagi' of which only two, the Vexin and Mèresais, shared some of their territory and government with other polities.

And yet it had not always been this way. The treaty which the French king Charles the Simple made with a ferocious Viking raider named Rollo in 911 gave to the Scandinavian certain Pagi in northern France on the sea coast along with the city of Rouen. This agreement, often referred to as the treaty of St Clair-sur-Epte, certainly did not give to the Norwegian anything like the territory which later became the famous duchy, but its beginnings can be clearly seen. What sort of agreement had it been? For the French king, it was an insurance policy. Northern France had been devastated by Viking raids throughout the late ninth and early tenth centuries. Brittany, famous for its relics and religious houses, had been so thoroughly wrecked that both secular and religious life had been turned completely upside down. The leaders of Brittany found refuge in England at the court of King Edward the Elder, and famously in the court of his son King Athelstan who directly intervened on their behalf in their own country in order to help restore the balance of power there. Along with the political refugees into England came a flood of Breton relics and pilgrims, greatly enhancing England's medieval equivalent of a tourist industry. Like

Brittany, the region which became Normandy was devastated. From 862 the bishopric at Avranches had been without an incumbent. Bayeux had been vacant from 876 and Sèes from 910. Religious life was not the only casualty of the Viking attacks, but we must acknowledge why the assaults on monastic communities received so much attention. It was not just because these institutions educated the men and women who wrote the history books. There was something else about the monasteries; across northern France, monasteries along with royal estates were well known for their horse breeding. The Vikings knew this only too well and would frequently demand horses as part of their tribute. It is easy to wreck a stud farm and difficult to rebuild it. All one has to do is steal the key stallion, or a number of the selected mares and the breeding programme will have to be started from scratch once again. In fact, so delicate is the job of horse segregation and selection that a simple hole in a fence can lead to disaster. And yet here in the ideal horse breeding country, perhaps there was hope for the future. The descendants of the Scandinavians who settled in Northern France in the early tenth century would quickly become the most feared horsemen of the western world.

The French king knew that he needed protection along the northern littoral and Rollo was the man to whom he entrusted the task. On the face of it, the agreement seems simple. Rollo would become Christian and would pay homage to the French king and in return he would get a small power block of his own. The agreement, it was said, had been made for the safety of the French kingdom. As with so many of these agreements which seem to oil the machinery of government in medieval times, a spanner would soon be thrown into the works and it would come in the form of some great political opportunities for the descendants of Rollo.

The first dukes of Normandy were nothing of the sort. They were, in fact, counts of Rouen. This title applied to Rollo (911–c.925), William Longsword (c.925–942) and Richard I (942–996). In fact, the title of duke is not mentioned in any sources until the year 1006. A name by which the Scandinavians of Rouen and their descendants were sometimes known, was 'pirates' and in this our observers were quite accurate. When we trawl through the references to the early history of Normandy, it becomes clear that this epithet greatly bothered the well-educated Christian men who wrote down the history of the duchy in the eleventh and twelfth centuries. One gets the sense that the Normans of the late eleventh century were trying to reinvent themselves, trying to find a legitimacy for their polity and for some observers this obsession went as far as creating the myth of a race of militarily superior people. The Scandinavian background of the Normans can hardly be denied, despite the best efforts of some contemporaries, nor it seems in all fairness can the overt martial nature of their history. Ordericus Vitalis says that up until the time of William the Bastard (Duke William II of Normandy 1035-1087 and King William I of England 1066-1087), the Normans devoted themselves to war rather than to the reading of books.[1] And yet once again, the plain truth about their background seems to have bothered the Normans. Take, for example, how they appear to have been perceived abroad. A letter of 1050-1054 written by Abbot John of Fécamp to Pope Leo IX refers to 'gens illa Northmannorum bellica', a warlike race. The writer of the letter then goes on to complain about being attacked in the Roman suburbs simply because he was a Norman.

It is to Dudo of St Quentin who wrote between 1015 and 1026[2] that we owe so much of our material for the early history of Normandy and yet here there are grounds for concern over the accuracy of his work and the motivations behind it. His 'On the Manners and Deeds of the First Dukes of Normandy' contains in its very title a blatant anachronism considering what we already know about the origins of the office of the count of Rouen. Similarly, we owe to Dudo the amusing story of the homage ceremony and numerous other tales besides. William Longsword, he tells us, had to send his son to a school in Bayeux to learn the Scandinavian language since it had fallen out of use in the district of Rouen. But William was only a second generation Norman. There must have been hundreds upon hundreds of men and women who were still alive from Rollo's first wave of Scandinavian speakers. Dudo is clearly trying to deny that the Scandinavian background had a lasting effect, by suggesting that Longsword's son had to be taught the language of his grandfather. Try as he might, his attempts were not very successful. It is an aspect of Norman history which never fully disappears. But even in Dudo's wildest ramblings about Norman prowess, we find an attitude which continually returns. He suggests that 'the English are obviously subject to him [Duke Richard II of Normandy] and the Scots and Irish are ruled under his protection'. How outrageous is this claim for a mere duke? We must not forget that Dudo was probably writing at the time when the English æthelings Edward and Alfred were resident in the Norman court. The Normans seem to have regarded Edward as the rightful heir to the English throne and as we have seen, they attempted to prosecute their conviction in 1033. Rather than displaying our first instance of Norman delusions of grandeur, this interesting and extraordinary claim might reflect a prevailing attitude that the dukes of Normandy, by harbouring the heir to the throne of England, had a right to feel haughty about themselves.

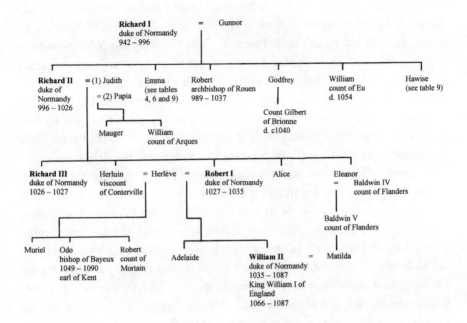

TABLE 8 The dukes of Normandy

(Names in bold indicate dukes of Normandy)

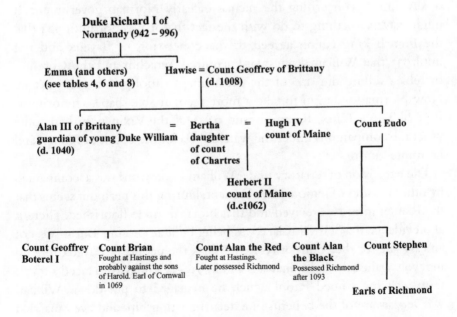

TABLE 9 Emma's French connections

Other, more reliable writers who clearly had a reason for talking-up the so-called Norman achievement, include William of Poitiers, William of Jumièges and OrdericusVitalis. Poitiers' *Gesta Guillelmi Ducis Normannorum et Regis Anglorum* is invaluable for the detail that it provides upon events up to and during the battle of Hastings and Jumièges' *Gesta Normannorum Ducum* and Ordericus's *Ecclesiastical History* are also indispensable. But what none of them fully explain is why the Norman version of its own history is so extraordinarily triumphant. For this, we need to examine how Normandy grew and explore the motivation behind its early leaders.

Nothing is known of Rollo's government. This is because there is not a single surviving charter from his time. Nor for that matter are there any governmental documents from the reign of his son William Longsword (*c.*925–942). There are only four charters relating to the long reign of Richard I (942–996), none of which are original and two of which are dubious in many of their characteristics. We might be forgiven for thinking that early Norman government was illiterate, but this is surely taking things too far. Medieval government needed a literary arm. The people who drove this machinery came from the monastic communities. Indeed, there is every reason to believe that William Longsword coveted churchmen to a degree and was responsible for the restoration of Church lands to a number of monastic communities, some of whom were even based outside of his patrimony. And yet there remains a certain amount of discomfort concerning the silence of early Norman government. It might have something to do with the fact that it was not until 924 that the French king Ralph agreed to the concession of Bayeux and not until 933 that William Longsword acquired Avrachin and the Cotentin thereby swelling the size of the Norman patrimony to a great extent. Now Normandy began to take a more recognisable shape. The original Pagi of Talou, Caux, Roumois and parts of the Vexin now had some welcome companions under the watchful eye of the count of Rouen and he wanted more.

The expansion of territory under William Longsword was accompanied by other features of regional government. During this period it seems that the Rouen mint was revived and that Norman trade flourished. There is also evidence that a royal palace was being built at Fécamp. But it was not an easy rise for the count of Rouen. In 925 the people of Bayeux rose up in revolt against the Scandinavians and in 933–34 Longsword faced a revolt from a Viking named Rioul which he managed to put down. William was very aware of the benefits of external relationships and even married Leutgarde, the daughter of Count Herbert II of Vermondois. But politics

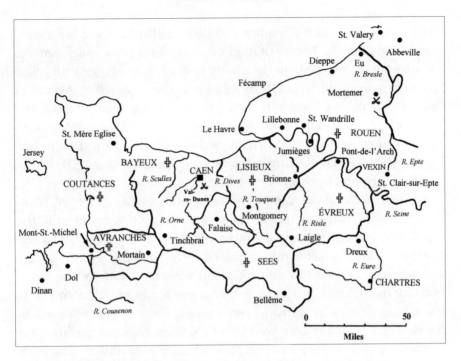

MAP 5 Normandy on the eve of the Norman Conquest of England
(Names in large capitals indicate bishoprics)

would cost him his life. He was assassinated in 942 on the orders of Count Arnulf of Flanders. It was a feature of the politics of northern France from this time right the way through to the twelfth century that out of the great power blocks of Flanders, Normandy, Blois-Chartres, the French king, Anjou and countless small border polities, as soon as one power began to get too powerful and expansionist, then the others would seek to combine in order to check it. The counts of Rouen, although they did not yet know it, would one day have a reason to look across the English Channel for the fulfilment of their natural predatory urges.

William Longsword was followed by his son Richard I whose long reign saw an initial period of crisis followed by a long one of consolidation. The crisis period of the 940s and 950s was inextricably linked with the fortunes of a Carolingian monarchy which was going through its death throes, but which still wagged its tail in the face of the count of Rouen. In 944, Louis IV who had spent a great deal of time in exile at the court of King Athelstan of England, launched an attack against Rouen and was supported from another thrust against Bayeux by Hugh, 'duke of the Franks', the king-maker of his time. There is every possibility that King Edmund (Athelstan's brother) provided more than just a token support for this enterprise, as his brother had done in Brittany and we should bear in mind that the history of Anglo-Norman animosity which came to the attention of the pope in the Viking raids of the early 990s may have had its origins in this episode. By 945 Louis was captured by Harold of Bayeux and ransomed back into the captivity of Hugh. Hugh and Richard I seem to have had an understanding at this time. Harold was very much a thorn in the side of Richard here in the heart of his own patrimony and Hugh, who married Richard's daughter, campaigned against Harold in 954, helping to rid Richard of his rebel.

Richard's subsequent campaigns against Theobald, count of Blois-Chartres brought the counts of Anjou and King Lothaire into the fray and led to a fierce struggle on the outskirts of Rouen. Richard I had to defend himself against the combined forces of three separate groups and apparently found this difficult to do without calling for the aid of Scandinavian friends in a move which some might say gives the lie to the notion that such ties had been severed. The struggle was won by Richard and the subsequent years of his reign saw Normandy consolidate its territory and advance its claim to an identity as an almost completely independent power block in northern France.

Clearly, these campaigns of the mid-960s had been a turning point in Norman fortune. Richard is described by the relatively quiet sources of the later period of his reign, written outside of Normandy, as taking only a subsidiary role in the military campaigns in northern France in the later period. But there was much which was going on behind the scenes. Richard clearly had a hand to play in the accession of Hugh Capet to the French throne in 987 and in 991 he fought for him against Count Odo of Blois-Chartres. Although Richard's loyalties would change once again in favour of Odo against the count of Anjou, it is clear that he was far from inactive in the later years of his reign.

It is in 966 where we pick up a clue as to how the former count of Rouen now wished to view himself. The re-foundation of the monastery at Mont-St-Michel is recorded in a document which uses the title *marchisus* or *marchio*, a term which means that Richard saw himself as a marquis, someone who ruled over counts, a way perhaps of legitimising his control over the lands once ruled by William Longsword. Nor does it seem to have been a self-imposed title, as at least one diploma of King Lothaire refers to Richard in this way. But the Carolingian monarchy was on its way out of French political life. It would soon be replaced by the Capetian dynasty and although they fought hard for their power, nothing like the days of Charlemagne would be experienced for a very long time.

Regional identities were being created at an unnerving pace. The counts of Poitou were the dukes of Aquitaine by 965 and the count of Flanders was a marquis by the end of the tenth century. By 1006 the Norman marquis had risen to the status of duke.

Behind this increasing tendency towards separatism a number of dynamics were at work across France. The revival of the monasteries was a slow affair, but it was there nonetheless. In Normandy, St Ouen of Rouen and Jumièges were re-established by 942 and the communities at Mont-St-Michel, St Wandrille and Fécamp all saw a revival in fortune during the reign of Richard I. By 996 the canons of Mont-St-Michel had been replaced by monks and a similar history is reflected at Jumièges. But to what extent the secular leadership was responsible directly for revival is open to debate. The community of St Ouen of Rouen received aid not from the Norman marquis, but from King Edgar of England and the late tenth-and early eleventh-century grants awarded to Mont-St-Michel came from Brittany and Maine, not from Normandy.

But perhaps the most compelling and significant changes in France were in the secular aristocracy. It is hard to imagine the extent to which society had broken down in the decades following the Viking incursions. At least in England there was still a central authority, a king with law-making powers stretching more or less from coast to coast. Also in England the nature of the ties of lordship remained more or less intact and unchanged, whereas in France these ties and obligations were being redefined. One can argue about the limitations of English royal power and of the dangers of a cancerous factionalism in the ranks of the English aristocracy, but in Normandy it seems that it really was every man for himself. Here in the hills, woods and fields of a fertile horse-breeding country a predator was born.

Put simply, there were two chief characteristics of the new French aristocrat from about 1000. The development of a new form of defended home, the castle, and the notion of the single eldest son inheriting all of his father's estate, no longer to be divided among his heirs. The powerful families which rose in Normandy in the early eleventh centuries also frequently endowed monastic institutions or colleges of canons. So, from his well-defended castle the Norman controlled a territory of his own. In a world of alarming instability rose the famous Norman knight, a militaristic class called *milites*, a group which in many cases appears to have had quite humble origins. The nature of the lordship ties were changing rapidly in France at this time, sometimes to the confusion of even the counts themselves.[3] Within the remit of the castellanry existed the right to judge and the right to tax. Along with this the Norman would have his own private military following. This was as true for the knight as it was for the counts, and so it was to be for the duke himself. The only way some sort of political normality could be achieved within each area was to be constantly aggressive outside one's immediate patrimony. It was a form of expansive self-protection at which the Normans excelled.

The political environment in which Richard II (996-1026) came to power was no more stable than it had been earlier. In the beginning, there had been a popular grass-roots uprising which needed to be suppressed by the duke's own noblemen in his very first year at the helm. Contemporaries saw Richard as something of a peacemaker for his time, although it was noted that he was skilled in the art of warfare. Peaceful or otherwise, there were dark whisperings in the year after his death when he was succeeded as one might expect by his son by Judith the Breton, who became Richard III. He lasted just one year before he died on 6 August 1027 and there were rumours implicating his brother Robert, who some say was behind a poisoning. Robert quickly became Duke Robert I (1027-1035) and the memory of the way in which he came to power might well have haunted him.

Robert's reign was not particularly good for the new Norman polity, especially where relations with outsiders were concerned. However, in 1031 King Henry I found it necessary to flee to Normandy during a period of great upheaval in France. Although Henry would prove to be most grateful to the Normans for the help they gave him, the duchy was thrown into chaos once again not just by Robert's unexpected decision to go on pilgrimage to the Holy Land, but by what might appear to be his appalling sense of timing. He died at Nicæa on his way back. William of Malmesbury implicates a servant of the duke in this, another murder involving the use of a poisoned chalice. The servant he says, was immediately exiled on his return to Normandy.

The fact remains that powerful secular leaders do not go on pilgrimage for no reason at all.[4] What was Duke Robert atoning for? Ordericus Vitalis simply states that it was the 'fear of God' which 'drove him to renounce worldly honours'. It may well have had something to do with the whispering campaign surrounding the death of Richard III, or it might have to do with the famous attraction which Duke Robert had felt for Herlève, the daughter of a tanner from Falaise.[5] Lustful liaisons were nothing new amongst the nobility of medieval Europe[6] but the Church invariably took a dim view of it all, at times voicing its disapproval loudly. Nevertheless the union between Robert and the tanner's daughter brought a boy into the world and his name was William.

Whatever the chemistry between his parents, William the Bastard was made of steel. He was probably not even ten years old when his father had died and his subsequent teenage years were to be dogged by jibes about his parentage. This, it might be argued, was enough to provide the foundation for the personality of a man who would change the history of England in one single day.

So a mere boy, the bastard son of a duke, entered into his minority as Duke William II of Normandy. It was essentially a life on the run from internal enemies for the boy, at least for the first few years: a time of narrow escapes from attempted assassinations and midnight flights into the Norman countryside on horseback which left a bloody trail of dead friends. In fact, William of Malmesbury, part Norman himself, said that after the death of William's guardian, Count Gilbert 'it was fire and sword everywhere'. Perhaps without realising it, William's internal and external enemies were creating the ideal medieval politician. William would trust only himself and never seems to have allowed anyone to get to him. But when it came to the test for William in his early years, it seemed that for now at least he did indeed have one very important friend.

The battle at Val-ès-Dunes in 1047 marks the coming-of-age of William in terms of open warfare. The rebellious ambitions of Guy de Brionne were drowned in the river Orne just a few miles south of Caen by William with the aid of the French king himself. But the extraordinary thing about the battle is that far from making him firmly indebted to the French king, it seems to have given the young duke the confidence to project himself almost everywhere within Normandy and sometimes even out of it. The predatory instincts which appear to have lain dormant during the long reign of Richard II were reborn when the river ran red at Val-ès-Dunes. If it had not already been a reality in Norman history, then something approaching total warfare was about to make an appearance in northern France and it would be spearheaded by Duke William.

A confident duke is not necessarily an untroubled one. Further developments in Normandy would see a complete reversal of fortune in William's relations with the king who openly opposed the duke in 1052. And there was the creeping problem of private castle building, a phenomenon which would be repeated with serious consequences in Anglo-Norman England during the twelfth century. The upshot of this meant that the duke was almost permanently in the saddle and it must have been a strain on the apparatus of Norman government. There were also Mauger, the archbishop of Rouen and the 'treacherous and fickle' William, count of Arques to contend with. These two were the duke's uncles and they had thrown in their lot with the French king. All these dilemmas are often given as the reasons why William could not possibly have come to England to formally receive his nomination as heir to the throne of England.[7] Indeed, in 1054 William had to fight another battle at Mortemer to throw off his rebellious enemies once more and in a crushing victory he managed with profound implications, to secure the support and obedience of one of the vanquished leaders in the form of Count Guy of Ponthieu. Danger, of course, was never far away for the duke and there would be much to occupy him in the late 1050s with the attentions of the Angevins and the French king playing a great part in his troubles, but it is to the early 1050s that we must return, for it seems that there was something occupying William's mind above all other things. To find out what it was, we must explore the peculiarly English history of the wishes of a king.

6

A KING'S WISHES

He [King Harold II] remembers that King Edward at first resolved to make you heir to the kingdom of England and that he himself gave you his pledge in Normandy. Equally, he knows that this kingdom belongs to him by right, because the same king, his lord, gave it to him on his deathbed. Now, since the time when Saint Augustine came to this land, the common custom of the nation is that a donation made by a dying man is held valid. He therefore asks you and your men to leave the land which is his by right. Otherwise he will break the oath of friendship and the articles which he confirmed to you in Normandy, and the responsibility will be entirely yours.

William of Poitiers, *Gesta Willelmi ducis Normannorum et Regis Anglorum*

These were the words of King Harold's messenger as spoken to Duke William before the battle of Hastings. The work quoted here, written by William of Poitiers, reliable though he is as a contemporary writer on the issue, does not fully reveal the tangled web of complexity which was the English succession issue either in 1066 or before then. It does, however, hint at the nature of the problem.

The single most important thing in the transition from one king to another in Anglo-Saxon times was the publicly stated wish of the existing monarch as to who should succeed him. Usually the successor would be a blood relative, not always the first son, but perhaps the product of a later union between the king and a recognised queen, as we have already observed in our account of the reign of Æthelred II. We will see that the succession issue, which had always been near to the surface of

Harold swears his oath. *Bayeux Tapestry*

English politics, was in Edward the Confessor's reign a most dominant and overwhelming influence. To understand why the issue so dominated the age, we must turn our attention to the way in which kings were chosen in Anglo-Saxon England. There were very few rules governing the matter, but the actions of a series of kings of England towards the end of their reigns seem to have placed an emphasis squarely on the final or most recent choice made by the reigning monarch. Therein lay the strength of Harold Godwinson's argument in 1066. But let us look again at how kings had claimed their rights to rule before then.

Edward the Martyr (975-979) had the blessing of his father Edgar. This much however was not strength enough to defend himself from the challenge of Æthelred's supporters. A country's aristocracy had been split over the succession and had remained divided throughout the short reign of the king. In the end, it was the act of regicide which tilted the balance in favour of Æthelred, an act which he was never allowed to forget.

Æthelred's own descendants fought long and hard for their rights. Athelstan, who had expected to succeed to the throne, had been forsaken by the king in favour of the sons of the line of his second marriage to Emma of Normandy, but Edmund, a surviving son of the king's first marriage, managed through sheer force of personality and energy, together with a cleverly contrived marriage, to successfully prosecute his claim at a time of war with the Danish pretenders to the throne. He had commanded armies and had inherited huge amounts of land by 1016. Despite the fact that Æthelred seems to have nominated Edward to succeed him, the nature of the crisis at hand in 1016 meant that only one man could possibly lead the kingdom in a time of war, and that man was Edmund. Æthelred, on his deathbed, probably had no choice but to acquiesce with the general feeling in London at the time. When Edmund died after the great struggles of 1016, Cnut succeeded to the kingdom, but made special efforts to point out that he had done so with the agreement of the former king. His extraordinary coup was carefully engineered, but was made to look legitimate by referring to the wishes of a former king. Cnut even referred to Edmund on more than one occasion as his brother. Cnut's real reason for prosecuting his claim, however, had been the fact that his father Swein had managed to secure the support of a huge number of Anglo-Saxon and Anglo-Danish noblemen who for the first time had promised their allegiance to a would-be king not of the house of Cerdic. Swein had even been recognised as king for a short time before his death.

The novel experiment of a regency had been tried after Cnut died in 1035 and the guiding force behind the decision was the Witan or high council of England who knew that the dead king's wishes were in favour of a candidate whose hands were tied in a serious political struggle in Denmark. The Witan, which comprised the senior most noblemen and prelates of the age, was in this case dominated by Earl Leofric of Mercia and, with the Witan's support, Harold Harefoot and his mother had set about strengthening their grip on the kingdom until Harold died in 1040. Harthacnut, whose short reign marked the belated fulfilment of his father's wishes, seems to have nominated an heir in the form of his half-brother Edward, who shared the same mother with him and who it seemed, to the English at least, was far and away the most appropriate candidate. He had even spent his years in exile being treated by the Normans as a king-in-waiting.

So, we arrive at Easter 1043 witnessing the consecration of a king of England whose right to sit on the throne went unquestioned. He was of the traditional royal line of England, and he had the support of his noblemen and some time ago had been chosen to succeed his father by the king himself, and if we are to believe the *Anglo-Saxon Chronicle*, he had even been sworn in before his exile. Surely this was the dawn of a new golden age for Anglo-Saxon England; the ancient royal line was restored, its right to rule unchallenged. But not everyone was happy in Edward's England, not by a long way.

If there were any rumblings of discontent in England at Edward's accession then they were drowned out by the noise generated by the tumult in Denmark. That country was about to suffer the consequences of Magnus's treaty with Harthacnut. The two of them had agreed to give the other his kingdom if one of them died first without heirs. In the event, it had been Harthacnut who died first. Although he seems to have nominated Edward as his heir in England, he could not have done the same in Denmark. Magnus viewed Denmark as his rightful inheritance by the terms of his agreement with the former king. He had outlasted Harthacnut and felt it was only right that he should claim his inheritance. Denmark, under the leadership of Harold, son of Throkell the Tall and Swein Estrithson, son of Cnut's sister and Jarl Ulf, waited to see what Magnus would do. It did not take long as Magnus launched an invasion and soon Harold had been murdered by Magnus's brother-in-law, the duke of Saxony. But Swein Estrithson stood firm and to him fell the task of campaigning for Danish independence from its hungry neighbour. As for Magnus, there is every reason to believe that until his death in 1047 he had set his sights on that other possession of Harthacnut's, the kingdom of England.

The seriousness with which Magnus regarded the English question is perhaps illustrated by the rumour that Queen Emma had promised a great deal of treasure to Magnus if he were to invade the country. It is certainly the case that King Edward turned against his mother at this time. In fact, the Anglo-Saxon chronicler tells us that on the advice of earls Leofric, Godwin and Siward, the king, accompanied by his advisers, rode to Winchester and deprived her of her treasures 'because earlier she was very hard on the king her son, in that she did less for him than he wanted before he became king and also afterwards'. In addition, we learn that her lands were also confiscated by the king.

Quite what Emma's motives were, or why there seems to have been such a deep rift between mother and son, who appeared to have been reconciled, is not recorded. She may have been aware that the house of Godwin had achieved its meteoric rise and was threatening to rise still further now that the male heirs were coming of age. A Norwegian invasion might drive a wedge between Edward and Godwin, her former man. But then she must have been aware that despite appearances to the contrary, Edward's relationship with the earl, who was responsible for the arrest of the king's brother, was not as sweet as it seemed. This fact notwithstanding, it would not be long before the king himself accepted Edith, Godwin's daughter as his bride. The king-maker was coming closer to realising his ambition.

That same year (1045) saw Edward adopt a defensive posture to counter the Norwegian threat. If Magnus should extricate himself from the struggle with Swein Estrithson and sail to England, he would have to contend with a massive fleet of ships pulled together by the English king, to which he had added his own 35 ships off the Kentish coast. There were rumours of great fleets at large in the North Sea in that year and clearly there were grounds for English concern. As for Swein Estrithson, his Danish troubles were about to get worse. Magnus was still intent on driving him out of the kingdom which he thought should be his, and despite pleas to England for assistance which did not arrive, Swein had to flee Denmark in the face of Magnus's overwhelming force, arriving after a time in Skaane. Magnus finally had his kingdom. The promise had been realised. Alarm bells rang loud around the halls of Edward's palaces. What if Magnus should now turn his attention to the one unfulfilled part of his promise, Edward's England, for which he, Edward the Confessor, had waited so long to rule? Why had Edward not responded to Swein's plea for help, despite the best efforts of Earl Godwin, who urged the king to send a fleet in assistance?

As it turned out, fortune favoured the nervous English and for that matter Swein Estrithson too. Magnus, shortly after his Danish triumph and to the dismay of his loyal followers, died unexpectedly, leaving his army with no good reason to be in Denmark. The grief with which Magnus's death was met by the Norwegians was matched only by the relief which Swein and his followers must have felt. Swein, perhaps even by a deathbed arrangement with Magnus, returned to his kingdom. But the dismay of the Norwegians was palpable and is captured in the words of an obscure court poet, thus:

> Tears were shed when the good
> King was carried to his bier:
> A sad and heavy burden
> For those whom he had given gold.
> Grief-stricken, his courtiers
> Could scarce keep back their tears;
> And sorrowing, his people
> Have mourned him ever since. [1]

In England these few uncertain years were marked by curious natural phenomena including an appalling winter, poor harvests and even an earthquake in the Midlands. But despite all this the chroniclers of the age did not foresee doom and gloom in these natural events, as they had in the past. Perhaps they should have done. Norway was about to embark upon a glamorous period of its history under the leadership of a man whose legend spread across the whole of Christendom to the Byzantine east. His name was Harald Sigurdsson, uncle of the late King Magnus. His appearance on the English stage would come at just the wrong moment for the presiding king of that country and, as it turned out, for Sigurdsson too. Harald had been with Magnus when he attempted his Danish coup. Harald had also been at Stikelstadt in 1030 when his half-brother Olaf was killed. After that battle, he chose exile. For much of his illustrious and colourful career, Harald had been in service with the Byzantine emperor where he put his military skills to good use in the Varangian Guard. But now, this new king of Norway, the man whose sobriquet 'Harðraði' ('the ruthless') would echo down the ages in the form of the name Hardrada, wanted the same as the late Magnus: he wanted Swein's Denmark.[2] A bitter and protracted struggle with Swein Estrithson of Denmark would for the time being prevent Harald from turning his attentions to the west. He seemed to understand that he was in for a long haul with Denmark and so he sent an embassy to England which stressed his peaceful intentions. When it finally came, his legendary campaign in Northumbria in 1066 should have surprised no one and yet it seems that in that year England was full of surprises.

Perhaps it was the arrival off the shores of England of a Scandinavian fleet led by two mysterious figures called Lothen and Yrling, which kept Edward from sending help to Swein Estrithson in Denmark. The fleet took men and treasure from the coasts of Kent and Essex before returning home, but little is known about its true intentions since it was stoutly resisted wherever it tried to land and failed to penetrate inland. Certainly, Earl Leofric of Mercia and many other leading English nobles were against sending ships to Denmark to help Swein Estrithson, leaving only Godwin in favour of an expedition to support his own nephew at a time of crisis. We may never know what might have been said between Swein Estrithson and Edward the Confessor before this year. There remains a possibility that the English king may have entered into an agreement which granted Swein the English throne after Edward's death. The English king was now in his forties and childless, but more to the point, why was Godwin so keen to help his nephew against the Norwegian threat? Could it be that Godwin's Danish leanings went as far as promoting Swein to the kingdom of England? If so, this might explain the continuing rise of the house of Godwin in the early years of Edward's reign. The king of England may well have sought to purchase the loyalty of England's most powerful family by awarding land and titles to the sons of Godwin who were now rapidly reaching an age where they could exercise political influence effectively. In fact as early as 1043 Godwin's eldest son, himself named Swein, received an earldom of his own from the king centred in the west Midlands near the Welsh border. His subsequent depravity would cast a shadow on his troubled period in office there.

And yet there is reason to believe that the nervousness of the English nobility in 1048-49 was matched almost everywhere on the Continent. The young Duke William had just defeated a serious rebellion at Val-ès-Dunes and his eyes must have been fixed on developments further to the east in Flanders where things were happening on a truly international scale.

The Scandinavian fleet which left the shores of England in 1048 had sold their booty in Bruges on their way home. This news had been met with great consternation in England though there would continue to be complications. Baldwin, the count of Flanders, the man who had strained Anglo-Flemish relations by allowing the sale of English treasure and slaves in the markets of Bruges, had also joined a powerful alliance of low country rulers in direct opposition to the Emperor Henry III. As it turned out, the alliance had not been a very good idea but the threat to Henry III did not pass very quickly. Baldwin personally led a force against the Imperial palace at Nijmegen and burned it to the ground, incurring the wrath of the emperor. The army which Henry gathered against the recalcitrant count was spectacular in many respects. It even attracted the admiration of contemporary observers. It included the soldiers of both the pope and the patriarch and at the head of the Danish contingent was none other than Swein Estrithson, king of Denmark, who had taken the step of making himself the emperor's own man so that he might have protection against the Norwegian threat in the absence of English assistance. It was a huge force, but it needed some naval back-up and to this end messages were sent to the king of England for his help and this time it came. Henry had feared that Baldwin might sail from Bruges and escape his clutches, so he needed a naval deterrent to stop him from doing so. Edward took to the sea himself and provided the emperor with what he wanted. Baldwin was effectively blockaded. Edward stationed himself at Sandwich and waited. It bought enough time for the emperor to demonstrate to Baldwin that the game was up. Fairly soon the count submitted to Henry.

This was hardly the end of Edward's entanglement with Flanders. In fact, developments of both a domestic and international nature were going on all around the king while he lay at Sandwich. On the domestic front, having already outlawed Osgod the Staller in 1046, the king had cause to revisit an offence committed by one of Godwin's own sons, Swein.

Swein Godwinson, the eldest of the many sons of the house of Godwin had risen to power in 1043 when he had been appointed by the king to an earldom in the west Midlands. This appointment, so close to the Welsh border had inevitably led to the earl's involvements in marcher politics. He had joined with Gruffydd ap Llewelyn, king of Gwynedd and Powys in a punitive campaign in South Wales, but it was not for this that he fell foul of the English king. On his way back from the expedition he appears to have taken an unhealthy shine to Eadgyfu, the abbess of Leominster and ordered her to be brought to him. Whether he was truly smitten or simply took a liberty we shall never know, but he is recorded as wanting to marry her, something which was apparently denied to him. The great majority of the noblemen of England saw it entirely differently; Swein had crossed the line. He had effectively abducted a woman of Christ and if love had anything to do with it, then it was secondary to the eyes of the law. For him the penalty would be exile and an abandonment of his earldom, the spoils from which others were to benefit. But he was not out of the picture, not by a long way. Swein Godwinson sailed to Denmark and took refuge in the court of his cousin Swein Estrithson, king of Denmark.

It is not clear why Swein Godwinson left Denmark after a short stay, but there were rumours of another crime being committed, something which does not paint a positive picture of this most senior of Earl Godwin's sons. Nevertheless, he took to the sea again with seven or eight ships' companies and arrived eventually at Bosham on the Sussex coast, having probably met up with Edward and his fleet still anchored at Sandwich. His attempts to offer peace to the king seem to have been strenuously opposed by his own brother Harold Godwinson and by a man named Beorn, both of whom had stood to gain from the redistribution of Swein Godwinson's wealth when he was sent into exile. Beorn held an earldom not unlike Swein's, but this one was in the east Midlands. More important than this, Beorn was Swein's cousin and the brother of Swein Estrithson, the very man who had sheltered the son of Godwin in his darkest hour. Beorn's opposition to Swein Godwinson's reinstatement will have come as an unpleasant surprise to Swein and it seems that he was unwilling to quickly forget it.

Swein Godwinson decided to pay Beorn a visit. Despite the fact that Beorn had opposed Swein's reinstatement along with Swein's own brother Harold, the eldest son of Godwin seems to have thought that there may have been something in the rumour that Beorn was still willing to help him in some way, as is suggested by one of the Anglo-Saxon chroniclers. But events would show that Swein Godwinson, true to character, had treachery in mind. When Edward became aware that there had been a settlement between Baldwin of Flanders and the emperor, he let some of his fleet go, remaining with his own ships for a while at Sandwich. Earl Godwin, who had been with the fleet all the time with a powerful force of his own was ordered to take his ships to the west. He took Beorn with

1 The field of Ashdown from the Danish position. In 871, a young prince named Alfred led a division of Englishmen up a slope to soundly defeat the Danish Great Army. The heptarchy of English kingdoms would soon be dismantled by the Vikings, but this battle and that at Edgington in 878 set the tone for the next two centuries. Wessex, England's remaining Anglo-Saxon kingdom, would rise from the ashes to dominate the country and its rulers traced their line back to the sixth century

2 Aerial view of Wallingford. This important burh on the Thames was sacked in 1006 by a Viking army, passed through by King Swein on his campaigns a few years later and once again, in 1066, William of Normandy came to this important strategic town before pressing on with his campaign after the battle of Hastings. *Crown Copyright.* 1951 / *MOD. Reproduced with the permission of the controller of Her Majesty's Stationery Office*

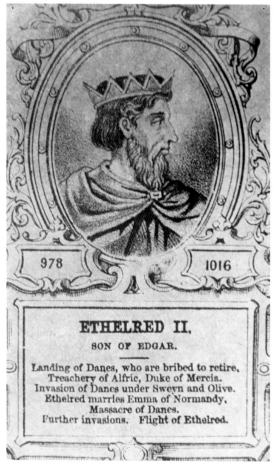

3 The name of Eadweard the Martyr is inscribed on the plinth of the coronation stone at Kingston upon Thames in Surrey. Edward's short reign (975-979) would demonstrate very well the divisive factionalism of Anglo-Saxon England. And yet, when he emerged from the succession crisis of 975 as king, he did so at the head of Europe's longest-reigning royal house

4 A Victorian drawing of Æthelred II. The king's image has suffered greatly over the years, but the problems during his reign were profound. However, he was prone to making rash judgements and appointing dubious characters to positions of power in the kingdom

5 *Above left:* An Anglo-Saxon thegn, *c.*990–1016. *Photograph: Julie Wileman*

6 *Above right:* A Viking warrior, *c.*990–1016

7 *Below:* The Anglo-Saxon camp at the battle of Hastings re-enactment in 2000. *Photograph: Lise Farquhar*

8 *Left:* The walls of York. A city which was the centre of the northern world saw considerable activity in the eleventh century. It was at the heart of the struggle between Harold Sigurdsson and King Harold II of England and later became the focus of a northern rebellion in 1069-70. *Photograph: Julie Gilbert*

9 *and* 10 *Left and above right:* Richard's Castle, near Ludlow. This castle was one of the earliest Norman-style castles in England, pre-dating the Conquest by some years. Situated in the marcher areas on the borders of Wales and England, the castle also had a commanding view of the local English countryside, particularly relevant to the family of Earl Godwin, which held land in the area. A castle's command of the landscape is rarely an accident. *Photographs: Richard Hill*

11 *Right:* The secret of Norman success. Deep in the heart of the Norman countryside lie the perfect horse-breeding fields, with grass rich in calcium and plenty of woodland to aid segregation in the breeding programmes. By the eleventh century, the studs of Normandy had managed to regain their breeding programmes after the Viking attacks of the previous era. The result of the Norman equine achievement soon expressed itself in the creation of a formidable war machine. *Photograph: Katie Pegler*

12 *and* 13 *Left and above:* Arms and armour: The Bayeux Tapestry shows how the Norman army transported its armour. The most efficient way to carry mailcoats is to thread a stiff pole through the armholes. Here, two re-enactors demonstrate the technique using the haft of a Dane-axe. In some scenes from the Bayeux Tapestry, warriors of both sides are shown wearing separate mail coifs, or head-pieces, in preference to the more prevalent integral coif. Here, the coif is displayed to show what might have been a method of fastening at the back. *Photographs: Julie Wileman (12) and Martin Pegler (13)*

14 *and* 15 *Below:* An Anglo-Saxon housecarl with Dane-axe and Norman warrior with sword and shield based on a depiction in the Bayeux Tapestry. William of Malmesbury said that the English axe and the Norman sword were the main weapons of the two armies which clashed at Hastings, but in all probability the most popular weapon on both sides was the spear

16 *Above left:* Fécamp Abbey. Here on the northern coast of France, the dukes of Normandy had in all probability a ducal chancery. The community at Fécamp had a long involvement with the claiming for and administration of estates in England in the era before the Conquest

17 and 18 *Above right and below left:* The tower of the church of Saint-Etienne, Abbaye-aux-Hommes at Caen. Here beneath the crossing under the lantern tower, William the Conqueror was initially buried. Only his thigh bone survived a later Huguenot ransacking. Several other places within the church concealed the remains of William before they finally came to rest in 1802 beneath the marble slab which marks the spot today. William's body was taken from Rouen to Caen by sea. At his own orders he was buried in the abbey which he had founded. As his body was lowered into the sarcophagus, the flesh tore, emitting a foul stench which put some of those present to flight

20 *Above left:* Battle High Street, looking north from the abbey gatehouse. The ground falls steeply away to the east and west, either side of this picture. The High Street is on a narrow neck of land. Along this route came Harold's warriors from Caldbec Hill on their way to form a shield wall on the constricted ridge at Senlac

21 *Above right:* The Abbey-Aux-Hommes dominates the city skyline at Caen. This proud and beautiful city carries the scars of the appalling traumas of the Second World War and yet its medieval past continues to influence the visitor

22 Several historical sources describe the English army at Hastings as 'emerging' from a nearby wood. Here, re-enactors show what this might have looked like

19 *Opposite below, right:* Re-enactors climb the lower slopes of Senlac ridge for the 1995 Battle of Hastings show

23 Norman cavalry move out on the field of Hastings. Such units were given the name *Conroi*. Many had a great deal of difficulty in pressing home an advantage against a tightly packed infantry line

24 Norman bowmen in a preparatory assault on the English lines. In reality, according to William of Poitiers, some of them may have come too close to the English lines for their own safety

25 A slow march from the field of battle for some tired re-enactors cannot reflect the carnage of the real battle, but the mud may still be the same

him and between them they may have been asked to take care of a threat posed by a fleet from Ireland which was causing trouble in Wales and the West Country. They moored in becalmed seas at Pevensey in Sussex and here Swein Godwinson took his opportunity. This ancient coastal bastion, the site of the old Roman Saxon shore fort which would feel the soles of Norman feet in years to come, was witness to another treacherous act perpetrated this time not by the father but by the son. Swein came from Bosham to Pevensey and asked Beorn to accompany him to Sandwich to help plead his case with the king there. And so, the two of them set out apparently for Sandwich but very soon Beorn was diverted to the west and towards Bosham where a cruel fate awaited him. He was bound and silenced and thrown aboard one of Swein's ships. From here he was taken to Dartmouth and murdered. He had been horribly deceived. It was an act committed by a man who already had incurred the displeasure of the king and the noblemen of England and now he would have to be punished again, this time by the laws which pertained to the military caste of Anglo-Danish England. Swein was declared a 'nithing', utterly disowned by his military brethren, unfit for office. The murderer knew he could not defend himself.

Clearly, King Edward had had enough of Swein Godwinson. Quite what he said to Godwin about the matter is not recorded, but it remains a fact of great interest that another son of Godwin, Harold, seems to have been so moved by the murder of Beorn that he went to great lengths to travel west and fetch the dead earl's body from a small church and bring it back to Winchester where it would be more properly buried alongside Beorn's uncle, King Cnut.

Swein Godwinson's act of treachery greatly troubled his crewmen, many of whom raised anchor and parted service with him. Those who chose to sail past the Sussex coast near Hastings were permanently reminded of their part in the deed. A fleet of sailors from this extraordinarily resilient coastal settlement intercepted some of Swein's ships and boarded their vessels, murdering virtually everyone on board. Then they took the ships and gave them to their king. All this had come from the heartland of Swein's ancestors, the shire which had given rise to Wulfnoth the wily sailor and Godwin the aspiring and successful housecarl. But now Swein Godwinson, the murderer and outlaw, would have his men stopped in their tracks by the sailors of the south coast. As ironies go, it was an impressive one. Bigger still was the fact that Swein soon turned up on the other side of the sea, mooring with just two ships at Bruges where Baldwin greeted him with open arms. English royal opinion of the Flemish court must now have been at an all time low. As if Swein's reception there was not enough ignominy for the English king, there was still the case of the exiled Osgod the Staller. He had been driven from England in 1046 and was now anchored with 39 ships off a small island north of Bruges. His threat to England was credible enough for the king to recall much of his fleet to Sandwich and after dropping his wife off at the Bruges court, Osgod decided to run the gauntlet and sent some of his men to raid the Essex coast where a mixture of bad weather and appalling odds confounded him. Few of his ships returned home.

Apart from the problems with Flanders, it was the increasing Norman influence in Edward's England that would be the catalyst for the next stage of Anglo-Saxon England's date with destiny. The importation of a number of senior ecclesiasts, the appearance across England of Norman warriors entrenched in their castles, one dangerous promise and the actions of a very angry English family were all factors which would conspire to produce the most extraordinary stand-off in the country's history. The road to Hastings was to take a curious detour to a field near Tetbury in Gloucestershire.

7

A VERY ENGLISH REVOLUTION

England in 1050 was no stranger to crises of royal succession and internal political tensions based on the conflicting interests of competing families. But what happened in the few short years between 1050 and 1052 went a long way towards sealing the fate of a kingdom which had already begun its journey to Senlac Ridge. At the heart of the great crisis of 1051 was Earl Godwin. It seemed to many observers, both contemporary and later, that the earl had decided to make a stand against the increasing influence of Normans in the running and management of the kingdom of England. Everyone knew that Edward had grown up in Normandy, had a Norman mother, spoke French as well as he spoke English, distrusted Denmark and was openly hostile to Flanders. He even had a French chef named Theoderic. Thus it was only natural that there should be an anti-Norman reaction in England spearheaded by the family who stood to lose the most from increasing Norman influence. If only it really were this simple, we might be able to see the eventual Norman Conquest as an obvious case of 'them and us', a case of the proud English being overrun by mail-clad mounted warriors who hid in their castles and oppressed the once free English churl. The truth of the matter is that the continental influences in England before the Conquest were in fact quite cosmopolitan. The fact that Edward was half-Norman had little bearing on it. Harthacnut, we might recall, was half-Norman too. The point is that Edward grew up in Normandy and so his open accommodation of French officials, scholars and churchmen is perhaps understandable. It was not these men with whom Godwin had a problem. The threat to Godwin was far more direct than any form of creeping French influence.

Godwin's anti-Norman stance has even been seen by some as the first recorded revolution by a patriotic English statesman, the forerunner perhaps of the baronial complaints which surrounded Magna Carta and so forth. These views owed much to the influences of the time of their writing[1] and despite the seductive simplicity of an Englishman's view of events, we should not in the modern age be deceived by such things. When we dig deeper for the real motives behind the struggles of the year 1051, we find once again that straightforward power politics played the greatest role in the drama. However, William of Malmesbury writing much closer to the events in question, but with no fewer tendencies towards emotion than the passionate E.A. Freeman, told us that even in his day – the middle of the twelfth century – people were still occupied by the rights and wrongs of Godwin's stance against the king. It had clearly been a crisis of national proportions. There is only one thing to say in support of the simplistic argument that Godwin was an English nationalist and it is this: for a man whose political career and dynastic aspirations were tied up in the Anglo-Danish world and for a man to whom the greatest dangers posed had come from Normandy, his view of the Frankish world was bound to be jaundiced. One cannot help but muse upon the likelihood that, for all we have said so far about the anachronism of an overly nationalistic view of the Norman Conquest, Godwin simply did not like the Normans.

By 1050, despite Swein's departure to Baldwin's court, the house of Godwin was a very powerful entity indeed. Godwin's Wessex stretched from Cornwall to Kent beneath the Thames and his second son Harold Godwinson was earl of East Anglia, commanding also Cambridgeshire and Huntingdonshire. In a quite remarkable reversal of fortune, the family's share of England was about to be restored again to its former glory. The *Anglo-Saxon Chronicle* glibly records in its entry for 1050 that Earl Swein was reinstated. After having been outlawed for one crime, declared 'nithing' for another and having probably committed yet another in exile, the eldest son of Godwin was allowed to return to England. How had it come about? Had Godwin campaigned for his son's reinstatement? If so, what had the king asked of the earl of Wessex in return?

Whatever royal promises had been made in the past, the king of England was quite entitled to change his mind. As a childless man in his mid-40s, Edward's chief concern in 1050 was to secure a peaceful succession which would take into account the very real threats from Flanders and Denmark with whom relations were somewhat strained. Edward the Confessor was not in the least bit an insular king. His life had been spent observing continental politics at first hand and it seems that developments abroad around this time were playing heavily on his mind. The news that Edward's kinsman Duke William – who had brilliantly risen from a difficult minority – was about to marry Matilda, the daughter of Baldwin of Flanders, must have raised a few eyebrows at the English court. The danger for England would be that it could tie Edward's ancestral Normandy into a relationship with a court which had brought trouble to the English coast and which had harboured all sorts of exiles from England in the past. It is therefore entirely probable that Edward decided at this point to nominate Duke William as his heir in order to distance the duke from the count of Flanders by offering William a prize bigger than anything Flanders had at its disposal. But to pull off this piece of international statecraft successfully, Edward would need the acquiescence of Godwin, without whom no peaceful Norman succession could possibly be achieved if the whole of the south coast of England was controlled by a man opposed to it. The reinstatement of Swein to his midland earldom is therefore most likely to have been a way of coercing Godwin into accepting Edward's decision to nominate William as his heir. If this was the case, Godwin must have nearly bitten his lip off. If blood was already bad between Wessex and Normandy, it was about to curdle.

The promise to William was probably made in the summer of 1051. The news of the king's decision was brought to William by Edward's new appointment to the archbishopric of Canterbury: Robert Champart of Jumièges, or Robert 'the Frenchman' as one Anglo-Saxon chronicler stated. Robert had been appointed in preference to one of Godwin's own candidates for the archbishopric and Robert and Godwin were to have a foul relationship in which the former ceaselessly brought up the affair of Alfred and his untimely death. Robert, who had formerly been the abbot of Jumièges and then the bishop of London, travelled to Rome to fetch his pallium, an ecclesiastical vestement and symbol of office.[2] It is most likely that he visited William with the king's news at this time. He took with him Wulfnoth, a landless son of Godwin and another of Godwin's grandsons, probably Swein's son Hakon to be held hostage in Normandy. This, Edward thought, should secure the arrangement and keep the earl in order. To what extent Edward's decision came as a surprise to William is open to question. The two of them must have discussed the English succession issue at great length in the later years of Edward's exile, but quite what was said will remain a mystery. Although many years separated the two men, we must not reject the idea that they will have spoken to each other frequently.

It is generally thought that the spark which lit the flames of Godwin's revolt was the infamous visit to England of Eustace of Boulogne, the brother-in-law of Edward the Confessor, in the autumn of 1051. Certainly as we shall see, it was an incendiary moment, but the flame was already burning. William of Poitiers tells us that Godwin had been made to swear an oath to Edward. The terms of this oath completely confounded Godwin's ambitions. It was an open secret by now that the king was afraid of the power of his wife's father. Historians have agonised over what might have been Godwin's obligations to Edward at this time and some have cleverly sought to find the answer in the oath sworn not by Godwin, but by his son Harold in the fateful year of 1064 when he met Duke William in Normandy.[3] Indeed, it is even suggested by William of Poitiers that Harold's oath to William of Normandy was simply a repeat performance of that which had been given by his father to Edward in 1051. So what was it? In 1064, it is said, Harold was to serve as the duke's agent at the English court, a sort of *sub-regulus* during Edward's lifetime. On the death of the king he was to use his wealth and influence to secure for William a peaceful succession to the throne. But perhaps the most significant thing of all in the 1064 agreement was that Harold, who by then had become the earl of Wessex after his father's death, was required to fund the presence of Norman knights at Dover and establish at William's pleasure other garrisons of the duke's soldiers at other locations in the kingdom. Harold's response to all this is fully accounted for later in this volume but for now we must look at the course of events of 1051 to see if they indicate that a similar arrangement had been thrust upon Godwin. The implications are quite profound. There seems to have been a real attempt by Duke William to secure the Norman succession in England with at least some degree of military persuasion between 1051 and 1052. Events showed that he had a powerful enemy but William, the short-term loser in the struggle of the early 1050s, would never forget what had been denied to him.

Shortly after Robert of Jumièges returned to England from Rome, the fur began to fly. It was September 1051 and William was keen to secure his position as heir to Edward's throne so he sent Eustace, the ludicrously moustachioed brother-in-law of the king, to England. The rest, we might argue, is history.

And then Eustace, came from beyond the sea [from Wissant] soon after the bishop, and turned to the king and spoke with him about what he wanted, and then turned homeward. When he came east to Canterbury, he and his men had a meal there and then turned to Dover. Then when he was some miles or more this side of Dover, he put on his mailcoat, and all his companions, and went to Dover. Then when they came there they wanted to take quarters where they themselves liked; then one of his men came and wanted to lodge at the home of a certain householder against his will, and wounded the householder, and the householder killed the other [ie. the Frenchman]. Then Eustace got up upon his horse, and his companions upon theirs, and travelled to the householder and killed him upon his own hearth, and then turned up towards the town and both inside and outside killed more than 20 men; and the townsmen killed 19 men on the other side and wounded they knew not how many. And Eustace escaped with a few men, and turned back to the king [who was in Gloucester] and gave a one-sided account of how they had fared; and the king became very angry with the townsmen; and the king sent for Earl Godwin and ordered him to go into Kent with hostility to Dover, because Eustace had informed the king that it must be more the townsmen's fault than his; but it was not so. And the earl would not agree to the incursion because it was abhorrent to him to injure his own province.

Anglo-Saxon Chronicle. Peterborough Manuscript (E) entry for 1051

What had the king's brother-in-law discussed with Edward? Why had the men of Dover, who were surely no strangers to continental military traffic in their town, been so irked at what had happened? The answer lies in the implicit statements in the *Anglo-Saxon Chronicle* and in the words of John of Worcester and in the bumps in the English countryside which represent pre-Conquest castles.

Eustace's visit to the king, despite their familial relationship, was not a social one. He will of course have been received warmly as was the custom of the day in England but evidently when they spoke the count informed the king 'about what he wanted'. Then Eustace set out for Dover via Canterbury where he and his men rested and ate. There are no records of any trouble at Canterbury. But outside Dover, this small continental army put its armour on and entered the town, making a point of settling where they pleased. This is not the sort of thing anyone would do without the permission of the king unless he wished to risk a confrontation with the forces of the king or the earl for that matter. Eustace would not have mounted his horse and donned his armour unless he had been asked to do something in Dover. It is more probable than possible that Eustace was in fact attempting to set up a Norman garrison in Dover in order to comply with the wishes of the king, the same wishes that Godwin had to submit to. When the townsfolk realised exactly what was about to be thrust upon them, they took exception to it and a huge fight broke out. But if we are to believe John of Worcester, the actions of the men of Eustace were even more aggressive than the Anglo-Saxon chronicler makes out. He suggests that women and children were murdered and strongly hints that the people were suffering an attempt to subjugate them, but they bravely sent some of Eustace's men packing, not to Boulogne but to Gloucester. When Eustace presented his case in Gloucester to the king, Edward grew angry at the townsmen of Dover because they had thrown a spanner in the works of his grand design for a peaceful handover to William. The king needed to get Earl Godwin to force his men in Dover to acquiesce; understandably Godwin would have none of it. Yet it seems that Godwin was bound by oath to do just that and so the path to a dangerous confrontation between the king and his most powerful earl had begun.

It seemed to the king that he was being met with open defiance from a man who he had tried to control in the past through a variety of means. Marriage alliance, political bargaining, oath swearing and the open threat of the king's force had not prevented Godwin from standing his ground. So, Edward ordered a meeting of the national council, the Witan, to be gathered at Gloucester on 8 September. But exactly a week earlier, before this council had met, Godwin had called together an army of huge proportions. It consisted of his own men from Wessex, those of Earl Swein from Oxfordshire, Gloucestershire, Herefordshire, Somerset and Berkshire and Earl Harold's men from East Anglia, Essex, Huntingdon and Cambridgeshire. At Beverstone, near the meeting place of the Longtree hundred not far from Tetbury, the force came together. Just 15 miles away in Gloucester sat a very worried king.

We must not underestimate the anger which Godwin felt. His anti-Norman feelings were well known and he'd had disagreements with Robert of Jumièges and made his feelings known about those Normans who he felt had treated the people of the countryside with contempt. But what happened at Dover suggests a deeper, more personal problem to Godwin than a mere appeal to English national identity. Godwin had been made to swallow a bitter pill when it was decided that foreign garrisons should be set up in his earldom, but what was beyond all toleration for him was the fact that his loyal Dover men had been murdered as a result. Despite Eustace's flight to Gloucester, the count had indeed left a garrison in the coastal port at Dover where he had set up a castle. This was not the only source of Godwin's anger. His eldest son Swein had to suffer a similar ignominy in his own west Midlands earldom. A Norman colony had been carefully placed in Herefordshire under the command of Earl Ralph 'the Timid' who was the son of the king's sister by her union with her first husband Drogo,[4] the count of the Vexin. After she had lost her first husband, Goda then went on to marry none other than Eustace, count of Boulogne.[5] As if this was not enough for Swein to have a Norman earl breathing down his neck, there was a castle near Ludlow known as Richard's Castle, which held a continental garrison who may be the men described by the Anglo-Saxon chronicler as those 'who inflicted every injury and insult they could upon the king's men thereabouts'.[6] Any visitor to the atmospheric, remote and overgrown Richard's Castle, founded by Richard, son of Scrob, should be struck by an interesting fact about its position. Most castles built after the Norman Conquest in this important marcher area on the borders of Wales were cleverly coordinated to control the landscape relating to ingress and egress from Wales. Some even commanded considerable views to the west. Richard's Castle does nothing of the sort. In fact, it is overshadowed by rising hills to the west, so much so that one might imagine that a Welshman would spot the castle before the castellans spotted the Welshman. Instead, Richard's Castle commands a quite spectacular view for up to 20 miles into England and is placed at the borders of Earl Leofric and Earl Swein's patrimonies. England was being strategically secured for the Norman succession by the emplacement of castles garrisoned by foreign soldiers. This is not to say that Richard's Castle did not have a role to play in the defence of the marcher area.

So, there stood the house of Godwin on a flat and muddy Gloucestershire field in early September 1051 ready, if necessary, to send their men into a battle that would surely be catastrophic for the whole country. Godwin sent a message to the king which went thus: there will be a war unless the king hands over Eustace and his men to Godwin including 'the French who were in the castle'. Not Richard's, nor Ralph's, but the garrison which had set itself up in Dover.[7] Edward wobbled; nothing quite like this had ever been demanded of him by a subject before. Godwin was really raising the stakes now. And then through the door of the royal hall in Gloucester walked Earls Leofric of Mercia and Siward of Northumbria. Edward's spirits must have lifted. But his earls had come for a meeting of the Witan, not for a war. They had brought only their personal retinues with them. When the king told them of the gravity of the situation, the two loyal earls immediately sent to the north for reinforcements and stayed resolutely at the side of their troubled lord. Soon, the king was accompanied not only by those reinforcements, but by the mounted knights of Earl Ralph. Now the king was set for a military confrontation, should it come.

It would have been an interesting battle if it had happened. Norman knights on a level playing field with supporting infantry would have been quite something to behold, a forerunner perhaps of the great Anglo-Norman hosts of the twelfth century. But it did not happen. The

Witan realised that if the cream of English soldiery destroyed itself in that Gloucestershire field, it would spell disaster for a country that was far from safe from continental predators. Norway and Denmark would have taken a keen interest in the casualty lists from the battle of Tetbury, a battle prevented by last minute diplomacy. Struggles between aspiring noble houses and the monarchy are well known in Anglo-Saxon history, as we have seen from the remarkable reign of Edward's father, but how often had the entire nobility of the country and the king, complete with their armies, looked each other squarely in the face and threatened to fight it out? There had been no large-scale encounters like this for 45 years. Few, if any, of the men arrayed against each other at Tetbury would be able to remember Ashingdon, except of course for Godwin, the old campaigner, but they will all have known the trouble that it led to. If Edward had been nervous about the possibility of a military encounter, then there are indications that despite Godwin's indignation, the leading men of the rebellion thought that it was abhorrent that they should have to take arms against their lord, the king. A very English settlement would be the result of a very English revolution.

Hostages were exchanged in the usual manner for security and then the king ordered that the whole Witan should meet again on 24 September this time in London. Godwin would have time to present his case in a more formal setting. The earl of Wessex went into his earldom and the king went to London, both of them fuming. Edward must have been continually advised now by those who had been with him at Gloucester. Leofric and Siward may well have spoken of their distrust of the house of Godwin and perhaps told the king that they expected the great earl to come to London heavily armed. Whatever was said, Edward made the best of these few short weeks. He called out a national levy, an army whose loyalty by definition would be to the king. It was a move which will have utterly confounded Godwin. These men, some of whom of course would have been at Tetbury, were called from Northumbria and Mercia, but also from the lands of the house of Godwin. Edward, who is never properly recognised for his political wisdom, had done one of the things a king could do which an earl could not. He had found himself just about enough time to raise a national army. The next Witan at London would be a very interesting affair indeed.

Godwin, Earl Swein and Earl Harold arrived at Southwark with forces which were apparently still of a reasonable size, but many of their thegns were torn. Their loyalties were being tested. They would not want to face a national host anymore than they had wanted to face a smaller and more vulnerable force in Gloucestershire. Many of them drifted away from their lords, the three earls. Perhaps they knew what was coming, perhaps they knew that the house of Godwin was about to meet its Waterloo.

At Southwark, Godwin received word that the king had officially summoned him; he was worried. He asked for a guarantee of safe passage, something which we might recall he never granted to the king's brother on the road outside Guildford in 1036. Eventually, he set out with just 12 of his own men. He would already have learned that his eldest son Swein, perhaps now through force of habit more than anything else, had earned himself yet another declaration of outlawry and that his other son Harold had been required by the king to hand his thegns over to the king so that they would become his men and no longer be the earl's. Godwin must have entered the room knowing that he did not have a chance. It is likely that he was judged as a soldier as well as a nobleman. There had been a militaristic tone to his whole career since the days when he campaigned for Cnut abroad and there are hints that he was outlawed in London by the same sort of Scandinavian-style military tribunal which had declared his eldest son 'nithing' years before. What is clear is that Edward had had his fill of the Godwin family. It had not been Edward who had promoted Godwin in the first instance. In fact, Godwin had been part of the pro-Athelstan and Edmund lobby in 1014. Edward had simply had to work with him when he took the throne but now the king had won a great showdown. He gave Godwin and his whole family just five days to leave England. A ship was prepared for them in Chichester harbour and members of a family who had risen to extraordinary power from lowly beginnings on a few Sussex estates, began to load their ship with as much treasure as they could carry. Godwin and his wife Gytha stared back at the Sussex coast as they set sail. And with them aboard a cramped vessel were Swein and two of their younger sons Gyrth and Tostig. Their destination perhaps, should come as a surprise to no one. Young Tostig had recently married Judith, half-sister of the count of Flanders and she was with him on that ship. Once again, Baldwin would host notable English exiles. Clearly, there had been no improvement in the relationship between Flanders and the English king.

Harold Godwinson did not follow his family to Flanders. Instead, he chose to ride with his youngest brother Leofwine to Bristol to find one of Swein's former ships which would take the brothers away from England. After a difficult crossing the two of them arrived in Ireland where they were accommodated by the king of Leinster and Dublin. Here they would spend the winter months.

Godwin had played a dangerous game with Edward. The strength of the king's Norman connections had bothered him, but so too had the fact that ruthless and unwelcome foreigners had been placed in garrisons in the earldoms of his family. Then there had been the outrage at Dover. Some of Godwin's complaints do indeed sound like those of a passionate Englishman decrying the Normanisation of the country and few can argue that the Dover incident should be seen from Eustace's point of view. But much of what Godwin did and said gave the impression that this was a man who would be king, a man who was not reluctant to question the king's succession policy, or his political appointments. In fact, Godwin's arguments with Robert of Jumièges are known to have been heated. Of the fall of the house of Godwin, the Anglo-Saxon chronicler had this to say:

> It would have seemed remarkable to everyone who was in England, if anyone earlier had told them that it should turn out thus, because he was formerly very much so raised up, as if he ruled the king and all England; and his sons were earls and the king's favourites; and his daughter was married and espoused to the king.
>
> *Anglo-Saxon Chronicle* Worcester Manuscript (D) entry for 1052

One final insult to the banished earl took place in his absence. We may never know quite why Edward the Confessor and Edith, Godwin's daughter, never had children. Some have put it down to the probable homosexual tendencies of the king, while the possibility remains that it might have been a quite deliberate policy given that the king had already nominated an heir and wished to hedge his bets with Edith until the Godwin affair was properly resolved. Nonetheless Edith was robbed of all she owned and sent to Wherwell nunnery in Hampshire. The final link between Edward and the house of Godwin had been broken. He could now turn his attention to running the country with loyal earls and seeing to it that the preparations for the transition of his throne to William went well. For his part, William now knew that England was relatively safe enough for the duke to pay a visit to the king and, despite a thousand historians' protestations to the contrary,[8] that is exactly what William did next.

8

AN EARL'S VENGEANCE

Then soon Earl William came from beyond the sea with a great troop of
French men and the king received him and as many of his companions as
suited him and let him go again. This same year William the priest was granted
the bishopric in London which was earlier granted to Sparrowhawk.

Anglo-Saxon Chronicle Worcester Manuscript (D) entry for 1052

It was a golden opportunity for William to come to England. There are
those who insist that the meeting between the king and his nominee never
actually took place. The argument presented by these people bases itself
around the notion that William had some very pressing domestic issues in
his troublesome duchy. Yet Normandy was always like this; William had
known scarcely a day of peace in his whole tempestuous career to date.
Now he was given the opportunity, with Godwin out of the way, to come
to England and formally accept the confirmation of a very special gift. He
was to be a king, not a duke.

However, the problems in Normandy were no small concern and
William indeed gave them close attention. In fact, they probably explain
why William in the first instance employed others to negotiate and deliver
the king's wishes in England, particularly while the drama of Godwin's
revolution of 1051 was still being played out across the Channel. By the
autumn of 1051 Geoffrey Martel, who had established himself in Maine, was
rattling his sabre at the Norman court and, as we have observed, there was
also a revolt of William's uncles – the count of Arques and the archbishop

of Rouen – to contend with. But all this was the very essence of Norman political life. Little wonder that the dukes of that duchy gained such a reputation for their martial prowess. If military tradition in Anglo-Saxon England ran deep into society at all levels as the career of Godwin shows, then in Normandy it was a positive necessity. The young duke, his retainers, their subordinates, their enemies and their enemy's enemies were scarcely out of the saddle. But William wanted to be a king, a ruler of a country whose wealth had attracted the attentions of virtually every predatory force in northern Europe, a country whose capacity for rewarding his own followers was immense. And so he set sail for this strange land that he had heard so much about, to hear what he had always wanted to hear from his kinsman, Edward the Confessor, the king of England.

Just like the visit of Eustace, William's was not a social one. He had brought with him a small army. It was not that he had done so in anticipation of trouble. His chief enemy was cooling his heels in Flanders and the other sons of Godwin who might have objected to William's visit were being entertained way to the west in Ireland. It remains a likelihood that many of the knights whom William brought over stayed in England to garrison the newly founded castles that were appearing now at quite a pace, a phenomenon which had behind it the policy of the king himself. William did not stay for long. He returned to Normandy at least comfortable in the knowledge that a relatively elderly king had promised him a title with which he, like other men before him, could make his name immortal.

At about this time in England there was a noted increase in the number of Norman appointments in positions of influence in both secular and ecclesiastical circles. When Robert of Jumièges had left his position at London to take the archbishopric of Canterbury, he had been replaced by an Anglo-Danish man with the delicious name of Sparrowhawk (really 'Spearhafoc'), the abbot of Abingdon. As far as Edward was concerned, the character was less palatable than the name and before he was even ordained the bishop of London was dismissed. Edward, perhaps with a new found confidence in his policies or perhaps by dint of a close relationship with his own priest, appointed William, the king's priest to the bishopric. The new bishop of London would of course be ordained by the archbishop of Canterbury. It was a very Norman affair. Two of the most influential ecclesiastical appointments in the whole kingdom had gone to the king's Frenchmen. Had the earl of Wessex been there, he would surely have tried to prevent it.

Edward was making the most of the absence of his enemy. An Englishman, Odda, was appointed to an earldom comprising Devon, Somerset, Dorset and Cornwall and, in a move which rewarded the house of Leofric of Mercia for its years of loyalty, the former earldom of Harold Godwinson, centred on East Anglia, was given to Leofric's son, Ælfgar, who had now the chance to become a very powerful man indeed.

The winter of 1051-52 was spent by the members of the Godwin family in their respective refuges. Godwin, although seemingly inactive, had been talking with Baldwin about his options. Although the earl's dynastic aspirations might appear to have been in tatters, there were still some avenues to explore. What mileage could there still be in Godwin's promotion of Swein Estrithson, the Danish king and the earl's own nephew to the throne of England? Could that be backed with the force of the men of Flanders? Perhaps not. What about his eldest, Swein Godwinson? There could surely have been no other candidate in Europe less palatable to the English aristocracy than him. Anyway, he had gone on a barefoot pilgrimage to Jerusalem probably to atone for a life littered with unsavoury incidents, in particular the infamous murder of Earl Beorn. Besides, he would give up his life on his return from that journey, dying cold and broken in Constantinople. Some said that he had even succumbed to wounds inflicted upon him by the Saracens themselves. Nobody knows what was said over the winter months in Flanders, but it is clear that Godwin wanted his English earldom back and his own choice of candidate on the throne. His eldest surviving son, now that Swein had died, was by all accounts a far more agreeable man than Swein had ever been. And there he sat in a hall in Dublin with his younger brother and an amicable Irish king waiting for news from Flanders.

As winter slowly gave way to spring, the English king awoke one morning to the news that his mother Emma had died in Winchester. That morning was 6 March 1052. Emma of Normandy was one of medieval Europe's most remarkable women. She had been a pivotal figure in national and international politics for half a century, having arrived in England at the tender age of 12. The daughter of a Norman duke and his Danish wife, in her long career she had raised two kings, fathered first by an English and then by a Danish king of England. She had suffered imprisonment, isolation, disloyalty, exile and appropriation. She certainly incurred the wrath of her son Edward shortly after his long-awaited accession to the English throne, the accusation against her being that she had done little for the king during his exile, but we must see this incident in its proper context. For most of her life Emma was caught in the middle of a bewildering web of loyalties and alliances and she seems to have coped with it better than any of the multitude of players on the stage of England's greatest drama.

Biographies were written about her, stories told and songs sung. She was a woman of courage and strength, but in the end her legacy was that she unwittingly led England down the road to Hastings. It is difficult to see how the dukes of Normandy could ever have got themselves quite so involved in English internal politics without her.[1]

In the same year in which Emma departed, one of Edward's Norman appointments was put to the test in a struggle which he might well have expected. Thirteen years earlier the Welsh had killed Edwin the son of Earl Leofric in an encounter against the Mercians near Welshpool. Now, the aspiring king of Gwynedd and Powys, the redoubtable Gruffydd ap Llewelyn, launched a penetrating raid into the vital area of Herefordshire which Earl Ralph the Timid had now been detailed to defend. The casualties were quite uncomfortable for the king to bear. Gruffydd had come as far as Leominster and the local Englishmen were soundly defeated by him as well as those who the Anglo-Saxon chronicler describes once again as the 'French men from the castle'. The aggression of these raids would have serious consequences for the immediate and long-term future of the marcher territories. Wales, which had hardly been quiet in the past, would become a positive tumult for the English king on the eve of his greatest crisis.

The weather was improving. Somehow, Godwin had got message to his son Harold in Ireland. The time had come. Godwin knew that whatever he did next in his quest for the restoration of his English power base, it would have to be done with a credible threat of force. He would have to do to Edward what Edward had done to him; he would have to show his adversary that he had no room for manoeuvre. How could an earl in exile possibly manage such a coup? Godwin was nobody's fool. He knew precisely what to do. In the first instance he must employ a reconnaissance-in-force. He must touch base with Harold who would be coming from Ireland and then they must test the strength of the convictions of the men who had formerly been theirs on the south coast of England. This is what Godwin, the son of a skilled sailor, did next. It was a masterpiece of brinkmanship.

The king knew very well what the wind would bring from Flanders and he had expected it in the spring. He placed a fleet of 40 longships at Sandwich for interception duty. His mistake was to give the joint command of this force to Odda and Ralph the Timid. No match for the son of the man whose naval skills off the shores of Sussex had confounded all of his enemies in one remarkable voyage. Godwin left the mouth of the Yser on 22 June with a handful of warships. We must remember that he had arrived at Bruges in just one ship. These were Baldwin's men and they, like him, were superb sailors. They managed, through judgement more than through luck, to evade the royal fleet at Sandwich and made landfall near Dungeness on the Kent coast. Conditions had been choppy in the Channel and the prevailing winds and brewing storms had kept the Sandwich fleet from intercepting the earl's small fleet. Godwin then embarked upon a remarkable naval recruitment campaign among the coastal men whose leaders he will have known personally. The men of Kent came to him and offered their support. So too did the 'Butsecarles', dedicated sea warriors of Hastings, the very men who had taken it upon themselves to intercept the fleeing vessels of Earl Swein Godwinson when he had returned to England and had Earl Beorn killed. A welcome addition to the force. Sussex flocked to the banners of Godwin and so too did Surrey, which does not even possess a coastline. Something extraordinary was happening. Many modern observers have portrayed this event as an outpouring of popular support for a national hero, but this is surely stretching the case too far. But it is certainly the case that their support was secured. Other exiles appear to have had a far harder time securing support on their first contact on return to their homeland, so why had Godwin met with such initial success? Dare we believe that there was a genuine sympathy with Godwin's stance against the seemingly pro-Norman policies of the Confessor?

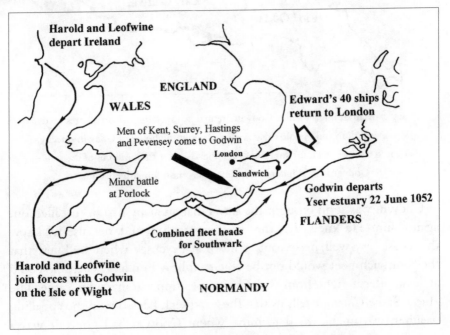

MAP 6 The return of Earl Godwin and his sons from exile, 1052

MAP 7 Map of England after Godwin's return, 1052. Godwin's partially restored Wessex earldom and Harold's East Anglia, brought the house of Godwin directly back into control of a huge stretch of coastline. By 1060, the earldoms of the sons of Godwin would incorporate almost the entire English coastline

Godwin was soon brought the news that an army had been called out against him. He knew that the weather was foul and, because he knew that coast very well, he set out to moor at Pevensey where he knew that the Sandwich fleet would not be able to follow him and where he could at least offer a fight from a defensive position to any who came. The *Anglo-Saxon Chronicle* tells us that the Sandwich fleet, due to the appalling weather, was unable to determine where Godwin had gone. It was a dreadful embarrassment for the king and the news that the redoubtable sailors of the south coast had gone over to Godwin, with the remarkable promise that they should 'lie and live' with him, must have hit the king like a thunderbolt. Indecision and inertia characterised the royal response to this crisis. The fleet eventually had to return to London. Meanwhile Harold had been keeping his side of an agreement which must surely have been arranged during the cold winter months of his exile. He had sailed to England with Leofwine and landed on the coast at Porlock on the borders of Somerset and Devon. Like his father, he had been assisted by his host and brought some Irish-based sailors with him. Here at Porlock he managed to take provisions on board but was quickly met by the local militia who were now technically the men of Odda. Thirty of these unfortunate warriors were dispatched by Harold's men before he decided to embark again and sail around Land's End to join with his father. Godwin could scarcely believe how well it was all going. The news that the Sandwich fleet had returned to London prompted the earl to take up station at the Isle of Wight and provision himself from the population there. Harold soon joined forces with his father and between them they provisioned themselves from the south coast and brought more people to their standards. The next goal, now that the fleet under Godwin's command had swollen to a remarkable size, was to sail to Sandwich via Dover where hostages were taken and ships requisitioned and then on to Southwark, being careful to keep to the southern bank of the Thames. He sent messages promising the Londoners many things and reminded them that the south coast, his natural homeland, had joined with him in this expedition. As the tide came in, Godwin's fleet raised anchor and sailed through London Bridge unopposed. It was yet another tense moment in the long history of relations between king and earl. Both sides of the river bank at London were now lined with troops loyal to each side in the argument and on the watery centre stage Godwin's vessels sailed over to the north bank and surrounded the king's fleet. It was much like an amphibious Tetbury. The men of the army of the king, which was arriving in London, were once again loath to fight against men of their own country at a time of potential trouble from abroad. In fact this is explicitly stated by the chronicler of the incident. And so another council was organised and the armies ordered to put down their arms. This time the impetus was entirely with Godwin and the nature of the subsequent agreement certainly reflected it. Godwin was given back almost everything he had previously owned; likewise with his sons and the rest of his family, including Edward's queen. All, that is, except Swein Godwinson, who had met his fate in the east.

But there was something else which Godwin, the champion of the anti-Norman movement, wanted. He wanted the Frenchmen out. The *Anglo-Saxon Chronicle* has this to say:

they affirmed complete friendship between them and promised complete law for all the people; and then outlawed all the French men who earlier promoted illegality and passed unjust judgements and counselled bad counsel in this country, except for as many as they decided that the king liked to have about him who were faithful to him and all his people. And Bishop Robert and Bishop William and Bishop Ulf [Norman-born former chaplain of the king] escaped with difficulty with the French men who were with them, and thus came away across the sea.

Anglo-Saxon Chronicle. Worcester Manuscript (D) entry for the year 1052

But John of Worcester has something even more revealing to add:

William, however, was, for his worth, soon afterwards recalled and reinstated in his bishopric. Osbern, surnamed 'Pentecost', and his companion Hugh surrendered their castles and being allowed by Earl Leofric to pass through his territories in their way to Scotland, received a welcome from Macbeth, king of the Scots.[2]

In fact, Robert had realised the game was up as soon as he observed that the king and the earl had made a pact of friendship. He could not get out of England fast enough. Some say he went to the pope to present a case there but whatever he did, he would die soon in his native Jumièges having paid a heavy price for being England's first Norman archbishop of Canterbury; of course, he would not be the last. Robert's career as a prominent pre-Conquest Norman churchman in England had been full of events. We learn of many of his deeds through William of Jumièges who must have known Robert.[3] It is this which gives a certain amount of validity to the story of Robert's carrying of the promise of the throne to William during his journey to Rome.

Robert's replacement was no less controversial. He was a man who had sat at the side of the king throughout this crisis, gently advising him. His name was Stigand, the king's handpriest, or chaplain. He had been around for quite some time. We might recall him at the minster at Ashingdon and his associations with Emma and Cnut. He had risen to become bishop of Elmham by 1043 but had fallen foul of King Edward at the same time as Emma was expelled, only to return in 1044. In August 1047 Stigand became bishop of Winchester and began to be more active at court. Stigand was many things: a friend of Godwin and, significantly, a spectacularly wealthy man. His appointment to Canterbury would be shrouded in controversy. He took the see from a man who had been driven out by secular forces and who was not yet dead at the time of the appointment. It was a most uncanonical affair. Moreover, Stigand held Canterbury in plurality with Winchester. In the long term, the pro-Norman lobby would have something to shout about at this their darkest hour. A case could be made against the English Church that it was an institution in dire need of reform and this was exactly the case which would later be presented to the pope himself.[4]

But what of the flight of the castellans? Of course it had been a triumph for Godwin to see these men flee from the safety of their fortifications from which they had daily wreaked havoc and alarm on the countryside, but there is something else of significance in their flight. Had they been men who had owed their direct allegiance to the king of England, then their fall would have been different. They would have been required to return home to the Continent. They would not have had to ask the Mercian earl for passage through his patrimony. These men were looking for another job. They were mercenaries and they found employment in Scotland. Furthermore, they were William's mercenaries. This is why they had treated men so badly in the marcher areas. Their paymaster was in another country and they were not answerable to the king, or at least if they were, then they behaved as if they were not. But interestingly it was Richard, son of Scrob, the man whose castle was near Ludlow, who was allowed to stay in England. His father-in-law Robert the deacon was another and a man called Alfred, another Norman whose important job as a marshall involved the management of the king's horses, was yet another.[5]

Godwin had demonstrated several things in his vengeful campaign of 1052. The king could be persuaded to do an earl's will, although it had been a tremendous struggle which nearly brought the country to its knees. The leaders of the great earldoms had displayed an interesting sense of national unity and identity in the face of foreign threat, despite their differences. But most importantly for the future of England, an incandescent duke had learned something, too. A well co-ordinated naval expedition could confound a royal fleet of England. The notion that by the end of 1052 William had realised that if he were to secure his accession to the throne of England, then it would have to be through overwhelming military might, is one which cannot go ignored. Of course there would be more diplomacy, more promises, more reminders of grievances past and present before two giant armies met each other on rising ground along the road to Hastings, but the strength of the retaliation of the house of Godwin presents us with a signpost along the road that we dare not fail to read. If Godwin had shown his anger, his cunning, his seamanship and his brinkmanship, then so too could the man who was told that he was to be king.

9

RESTLESS KINGDOMS

The winter of 1052 brought with it the kind of weather that people in England were beginning to grow used to. And yet nothing quite like the awful storm which descended upon the country on the eve of the feast of St Thomas just a few days before Christmas had been seen by Englishmen for years. Church roofs were torn off, trees uprooted, livelihoods wrecked and homes devastated. But as Godwin lay at his fireside in one of his regained manors his concerns were not with the weather. He had been recovering from an illness which is unspecified, but which seems to have temporarily incapacitated him after his great victory of the autumn. Godwin was getting on in years and he knew it.

Naturally, the continuing activities of the restored earl, whatever his condition, will have been a key concern of the king's but for now Edward would turn his attentions to matters in the west. Whatever it was that Rhys, the brother of Gruffydd the South Welsh king had done, he would soon pay for it with his life. From his hall in Gloucester, the king sent orders that this young Welsh prince should be dispatched. There is only the enigmatic reference to the 'harmful things' he had done, which may have been something to do with a recorded attack on an English frontier garrison at Westbury on the Welsh side of the Severn. In Gloucester on 6 January 1053, the twelfth day of Christmas, Edward the Confessor was given a gift by those of his men who had paid Rhys a visit at a place called Bulenden. They had brought to their king the Welshman's head. It was a brutal act tacitly acknowledged by an English king who had not been able to bring himself to do this sort of thing to his own earl who had recently undermined the very power of the throne. But it was not the last struggle Edward would face from an increasingly confident Welsh kingdom.

After a hectic few months at the end of 1052 and the beginning of 1053, the weeks up to Easter were comparatively quiet. Godwin had recovered from his illness and must have been enjoying the fruits of his success as he rode to Winchester across an earldom more or less devoid of Norman intrusion. Harold, Tostig, their father Godwin and the king and his entourage had all gathered at Winchester that Easter, reconciled and yet wary. On the second night of Easter, at dinner with the king, Godwin collapsed and fell like a stone by the side of his footstool. His sons carried him to the king's chamber. As he lay on the king's bed, the court was told that this seizure would soon pass. He had been ill recently; there was no reason for alarm. But whatever words Godwin had spoken at the feast before he fell, they were to be his last. Speechless and unmoving he lay for several days before he gave up the ghost. Earl Godwin of Wessex, at once statesman and scoundrel, was dead.[1]

There is little point in musing over what Edward might have thought of the demise of his dinner guest as he watched him being buried in the Old Minster at Winchester. The earl's replacement was Harold. The senior surviving son of Godwin would rule his father's territory. One is tempted to think that Edward knew that the appointment he was about to make was inevitable. And so Harold Godwinson, while genuinely grieving for the loss of his father, comforted himself with the knowledge that he had just become the most powerful man in England apart from the king himself. But his earldom of East Anglia, which he had only recently regained, was given back to the man who he had displaced: Ælfgar, son of Leofric. The late Swein Godwinson's earldom was shared out. Somerset and Berkshire were appended to an enlarged Wessex. Oxfordshire and Herefordshire were given to Earl Ralph who was gaining a reputation at court for being something of a specialist in the organisation of frontier shires, although his real test was yet to come.

Edward's problems at the borders of his kingdom were not, of course, restricted to trouble in the west. Scotland had entered a period of notorious instability when Macbeth had defeated King Duncan in battle in 1040. There is some evidence to suggest that Earl Siward had been Edward's shuttle diplomat to the Scottish king's court in the early years of the reign of Macbeth, but it would all end in a bloodbath for that usurping monarch. To be fair, although he came to the throne of Scotland through intrigue and murder, it seems that Macbeth and his wife Gruach ruled their kingdom reasonably well, giving gifts to a number of churches.

William Shakespeare, drawing upon Raphael Holinshed's chronicles, has given us the most memorable and celebrated version of this Scottish political drama in the form of *Macbeth*. Despite the telescopic sequence of events and the inclusion of some necessary anachronisms, the famous tragedy still has vestiges of real historical events and characters. It was the nature of the Northumbrian earl's inheritance, as it had been with countless English and Scandinavian kings of Northumbria and with the Lords of Bamburgh in the past, that there would always be a pressing Scottish issue in this, the most restless border earldom in England. Now, the old Earl Siward, a loyal warrior of King Edward, was given reinforcements by his king and told to head north with his charge, the exiled Malcolm, son of King Duncan. He would take a combined land and sea force into Scotland where Macbeth sat in his hall confident that with his ranks now swollen by the men of the Norman castle garrisons who had fled from England, he would be able to resist aggression at least until Birnam Wood came to Dunsinaine. And in the summer of 1054 a forest of spears did indeed move against the fabled Scottish monarch. There was a pitched battle between the forces of Macbeth and the English. It was a huge struggle with significant casualties on both sides. John of Worcester tells us that the Norman castellans were all killed in the battle, but the loss of these infamous mercenaries had already been acknowledged by the English crown. Far more important for the future of Northern English politics was the fact that Earl Siward's eldest son Osbern and his sister's son Siward perished on that Scottish field. The old earl, despite the English success in sending Macbeth into flight on behalf of the English king, had been deeply moved by the experience. Henry of Huntingdon places Siward's son in the thick of the fighting with the news of his death being brought to the Northumbrian earl back at home:

Around this time Siward, the mighty earl of Northumbria, almost a giant in stature, very strong mentally and physically, sent his son to conquer Scotland. When they came back and reported to his father that he had been killed in battle, he asked 'did he receive his fatal wound in the front or the back of his body?' The messengers said 'In the front'. Then he said, 'That makes me very happy, for I consider no other death worthy for me or my son'. Then Siward set out for Scotland, and defeated the king in battle, destroyed the whole realm, and having destroyed it, subjected it to himself.

Henry of Huntingdon, *The History of the English People*. 1000-1154. II. 22-23

Macbeth and Malcolm would continue to fight it out until 1057 when Malcolm defeated and killed his nemesis but, on the orders of Edward,

Siward had already promoted Malcolm as candidate to the Scottish throne and Macbeth's grip on power was waning. For Siward, there remained only a very young Waltheof to inherit control of England's most challenging earldom and, although there were candidates for the job from the line of the lords of Bamburgh who certainly knew how to hold their own in a colourful and dangerous northern world, it was not to them that the English king looked when Earl Siward, his proud warrior, passed away at York in 1055. It might seem to us quite extraordinary that one of the Godwinsons should get to rule in the earldom furthest away from their ancestral lands, but the appointment of Tostig to Northumbria in 1055 can at least be viewed as the promotion of a man whose mind the English king was well acquainted with. But Edward was not the only man with an eye on developments in Northumbria. Harald, King of Norway, was keeping himself informed. Sooner or later, he would surely prosecute his claim.

Later in 1055 the king called a Witan in London. Here a decision was made which has puzzled historians. Earl Ælfgar was outlawed. Contemporaries seem to have been quick to point out that he was blameless in the charges of treachery which had evidently been brought against him, but it did not seem to matter. He must go. So Ælfgar went where Harold had gone before him, to Ireland. He seems to have acted very quickly, because he was able to add to his one ship the force of 18 more ships' companies packed with Irish warriors and he sailed to Wales to parley with Gruffydd. The Welsh king received him warmly. With a combined force of Welsh and Irish warriors, the exiled earl headed for Hereford. On 24 October, a few miles outside of the city, the allies stopped. Earl Ralph, whose job it was to deal with such matters, raised a force from his own Normans, Frenchmen and English fyrdsmen. The subsequent encounter has been variously interpreted. In the *Anglo-Saxon Chronicle*, we are told that before there was any spear thrown, the English people had already fled, 'because they were on horse' and a great slaughter then followed to the tune of four or five hundred men on Ralph's side. The victors then moved on to Hereford which was subsequently burned and sacked. Now, let us turn to John of Worcester and see what he says. Earl Ralph had ordered the English to fight on horseback, 'contrary to their custom'. But Earl Ralph, for reasons which are not given to us[2] fled the field and 'seeing which the English with their commander also fled'.

If there has ever been a passage in the *Anglo-Saxon Chronicle* more consistently misunderstood than this, then it has yet to be brought to light. It has been assumed by countless historians, on the grounds of John's statement, that the English were unaccustomed to fighting on horseback, that the failure of Ralph's army was down to the calamitous attempt by him to force the Englishmen to fight mounted against their instincts. But it was not the Englishmen who precipitated the flight. Ralph's own men did that. The English, because they had indeed turned up to the battlefield prepared to fight on horseback, were able, under their own commander, to hastily follow suit after spotting the flight of their Norman allies.

There is no dispute that the mounted Anglo-Saxon did not usually charge at the enemy. It is abundantly clear from 300 years of sources that the English thegn usually got off his horse and fought on foot. He used his horse to gain a strategic advantage in the landscape, not a local tactical one. Ralph had clearly asked something special of the Englishmen in his ranks, but it was no dangerous experiment. These were perfectly consummate horsemen, each of them owning their own horses, each of them obliged under their obligations to their own lord, to bring horses as part of their military service.[3] Any army in flight is at the mercy of its pursuers. The rout is when the casualties truly pile up. It is this more than anything else, which will have accounted for the losses sustained at Hereford. The widespread usage of mounted infantry by Anglo-Saxon armies is one of the most misunderstood aspects of early medieval military history. It has been obfuscated by the well-known and rather different way in which the Normans used their horses, trained as they were, to charge home on the battlefield. That is the difference. The fact that Ralph had decided to ask the Englishmen to adopt this relatively new tactical-level idea, points to the obvious fact that he thought that they were perfectly capable of doing it. In the event, Ralph fled the field before these horsemen were put to the test in fighting in the Norman style. Had they engaged the enemy, history might have been very different.

Hereford suffered appalling devastation and desecration: the minster was burned and looted, seven canons were killed at the gates of the church and innocent market folk murdered or taken away. Ælfgar had blood on his hands. So too did Gruffydd, who was probably behind the campaign plan. The royal response was to gather a regional army of some considerable size. It was not led by Ralph, but by England's most senior earl, the earl of Wessex. Harold had his chance to show his king what he was made of. Through Gloucester he marched and then out to Straddle, 7 miles south-west of Hereford. Harold ordered the wholesale refortification of Hereford. The kingdom could not afford to have these Welsh penetrations cause so much catastrophic damage at a time when military resources might be required anywhere from east to west coast. In fact, the ditches and palisades built by Harold have even left their mark in the archaeological record, so great was the rebuilding. No one quite knew why there was then talk of peace, but Harold moved to his manor at Billingsley and there it was decided, presumably on the advice of Edward, that the recalcitrant earl should have his earldom back. Only three years ago Harold had himself been the returning exile seeking to re-establish his position by force of arms. Here he was, after showing great determination in his approach to a campaign which never really got going, finding himself as the king's man, having to negotiate a reconciliation with an earl who had brought desecration on a minster church.

Ælfgar was allowed to sail to Chester where he paid his fleet off as he had promised them, and many of them returned to Ireland. Once again, as Harold's family had shown a few years earlier, the exile of an earl was not enough to prevent him from coming back and exerting his will with a credible threat of force. That episode and this most recent one, demonstrate the limitations of royal policy in action. Whoever would succeed Edward the Confessor would have to be utterly ruthless with those who crossed him, lest royal authority be deemed a sham.

10

ECCLESIASTICAL AFFAIRS

The ecclesiastical affairs of Hereford at this time have an important bearing on secular events. The bishop who had the misfortune to experience the plunder of Hereford lived on through an uncomfortable winter, assisted at first by his Welsh deputy. Bishop Athelstan had in fact been blind for 13 years. He had put his heart and soul into the running of his bishopric, but his increasing illness had meant that Tremerig, his assistant had to run the show. Now, on 10 of February the following year, Bishop Athelstan died and was buried in the town he loved. Tremerig had failed to survive the winter and is said to have perished soon after the horrors of late October. Harold's own mass-priest was given the role. His name was Leofgar and he was an odd sort of a fellow. In fact, the Godwinsons' capacity for attracting clerics from the fringes of canonical acceptability was already a moot point among their critics. Leofgar, against canon law, wore his fashionable droopy moustache like his own secular lord until his ordination. Then, after his ordination, he seems to have retained a keen eye for the battlefield. Off he went on campaign into the west, upon whose orders we can only guess. There, in a field near Glasbury-on-Wye, he was killed along with many Englishmen who could scarcely be spared. The man responsible for Leofgar's end was a certain Gruffydd. The casualties had included the sheriff of Herefordshire, and numerous of Leofgar's priests. The campaign, although little is known of it, is supposed to have been appalling. It was midsummer, but it was arduous and gruelling, costing a great deal of losses amongst the English horses. Leofgar had held his bishopric for just 11 weeks and four days, before he impaled himself on a Welsh spear. It was once again time for Harold to intervene. Both he and Earl Leofric of Mercia came to Gruffydd. They gently persuaded him that it would be wise if he would declare himself to be the man of King Edward and a loyal underking. The words in this conversation must have been carefully chosen. Accompanying Harold and Leofric was a man who masterminded the terms of their agreement and who, as bishop of Worcester, had undertaken a very important continental journey just 18 months earlier. Bishop Aldred would now be bishop in Herefordshire as Leofgar's replacement. But the journey he made might well have changed English history were it not for a curious twist of fate.

Edward's Celtic preoccupations had not kept him from thinking about the English succession issue any more than William's troubles had prevented him from doing so in 1051. Bishop Aldred's journey, however, reveals to us that the king had completely changed his mind on the matter as was his privilege, but Aldred's remit strongly suggests that there was the guiding hand of a certain son of Godwin behind it. In fact, in 1056, Harold is known to have made a journey to Flanders where he almost certainly asked the count for his assistance in getting Edward the ætheling back to England from Hungary. The bishop sailed across the Channel and arrived in Germany where he was received by the Emperor Henry III and Heriman, the archbishop of Cologne. The reception was notably warm and the message he brought with him was clear. On behalf of the king of England, the emperor was asked to send messengers to Hungary. In that strange land, whose people spoke a language closer to Finnish than to any of its neighbouring languages, lived a prince. He was an Englishman of royal stock who had fled England in 1016 when King Cnut had initiated his purges. In Hungary Ætheling Edward, son of Edmund Ironside, had found a home. He had learned to speak Magyar, ridden with the cavalry of the famous armies of the country and married a relative of the emperor, Agatha.[1] Despite the desperate flight from England during his early years, when he went from court to court, he had found a country which had recognised his status. Edgar, Margaret and Christina were his children and the sound of their names for centuries would strike a chord of approval with those who saw the Norman Conquest of England as an unjust phenomenon. In fact, this particular Edward had spent even more years in exile than his namesake who had at least managed to realise his royal ambition with the help of the Normans. But Edward, son of Edmund, had no Normans behind him. The political aspirations of the Magyar nobility were completely different from those of the tempestuous and expansionist French Vikings. Theirs was a history which had brought them into conflict with the Ottonian Empire and which saw them look east too. The Magyar people who eventually gave rise to the Hungarian state had always felt different from their neighbours, misunderstood and surrounded. Edward had spent at least 10 years with them. There was very little he did not know about European politics in the heart of the Continent but he was old when he answered the call to return home to England.

The calamities of 1016 must have played heavily upon the mind of the son of Ironside as he disembarked on the shores of England in 1057. One can only imagine how he felt when he mounted his horse and began his journey to see the man who he had last seen when they were both very young and when Edmund Ironside's flame was still burning strong in the hearts of Englishmen. In fact he never saw the king. The scribe at Worcester who compiled one of the *Anglo-Saxon Chronicle* manuscripts seems to have had a soft spot for the grand old man from Hungary. In fact, he was not at all sure that there had not been foul play behind the untimely demise of the unfortunate prince:

> We do not know for what cause it was arranged that he might not see his relative King Edward's [face] Alas! That was a cruel fate, and harmful to all this nation, that he so quickly ended his life after he came to England, to the misfortune of this wretched nation.
>
> *Anglo-Saxon Chronicle*. Worcester manuscript (D) entry for 1057

If it was the unhappy case that Edward had been murdered, then who had the motive? The obvious answer to the question has absolutely no shred of evidence to support it. The two men who stood to lose from another Edward on the throne of England were Harald Sigurdsson of Norway and Duke William of Normandy. There is nothing to say that either of these men had set their agents to work on hearing of the ætheling's journey. The strongest case which can be launched against William is that Edward may have travelled through or near to William's patrimony. But as Harold Godwinson watched the ætheling being buried in St Paul's in London, many thoughts must have crossed his mind. Should he now throw the weight of his support behind Edward's son Edgar, who was no more than a child, so that the line of Cerdic continued to preside over the kingdom? Perhaps there was a more obvious and attractive option for England's most powerful man.

Despite the fact that there is a strong likelihood that Ætheling Edward had died of natural causes at a most inopportune moment, there seems to have been a widely acknowledged sentiment that the country was all the poorer for it. Just when the succession issue looked to be solved after the great journey undertaken by Bishop Aldred, the negotiations, the long homecoming of Edward and the journey to London, all the plans had come to nothing. The ghosts of uncertainty had returned to haunt the English succession once again. But the death of the ætheling was not the only death which would have important bearings on the future. Harold must have wondered if his own destiny was being mapped out before his very eyes.

Earl Leofric passed away in the autumn of 1057 and was replaced in Mercia by his son Ælfgar. So too did the hapless Earl Ralph, just before Christmas. Earl Odda[2] had died in the previous year and the upshot of the great reshuffle of 1057, a year of English funerals, was that Earl Harold of Wessex became even more powerful. He received much of Ralph's earldom. Here in the west Harold had proved himself a loyal agent of the king after the battle of Hereford and Odda's earldom vanished into the Wessex patrimony whence it came. The memory of Harold's service in the marcher lands was clearly fresh in the mind of Edward the Confessor.

The scribe who was so agitated at the fate of Edward the ætheling in 1057 must have been suffering from depression when he put quill to parchment for his entry of 1058. He certainly seems to have been keen enough to relate the remarkable visit of Aldred to Jerusalem, a journey which he took by a route that led him through Hungary, but on some spectacularly important domestic matters he is enigmatic to say the least. Here is what he has to say:

> Here Earl Ælfgar was expelled, but he soon came back again, with violence, through the help of Gruffydd. And here came a raiding ship army from Norway; it is tedious to tell how it happened.
>
> *Anglo-Saxon Chronicle.* Worcester manuscript (D) entry for 1058

It almost defies belief that a chronicle which supplies us with such a wealth of information for the years surrounding this entry should have left us in the lurch like this. In fact, out of all the versions of the *Anglo-Saxon Chronicles* which account for this period, the Worcester version is, along with the Abingdon version, the most detailed, but alas not for this time in 1058. It does at least mention the incident. We must be thankful for another man of Worcester, John, who was obviously working from a version of the *Chronicle*. He was a little more energetic in giving us that bit extra that we might at least be able to speculate. The Norwegian force had actually come to England in support of Earl Ælfgar, he says. When we combine this nugget with those gleaned from other sources, including the Welsh *Annales Cambriae* and the Irish *Annals of Tigernach*, a picture emerges. The earl had fled to Gruffydd. Messages had been sent to the king of Norway whose ambitions were widely known. A fleet was sent to England from Norway not to directly challenge Edward for his throne, but to assist Ælfgar in his struggle. This is why it was headed not by Harald Sigurdsson but by his son Magnus. It was clearly a worrying time for the king of England. The great external threat which had occupied the minds of the leaders of England in the internal disputes of 1051-52 had finally materialised in the form of a banished Englishman, a powerful Welsh king and a force of Norwegians. Regrettably, nobody bothered to record what it did. We will never know why it did not achieve what it set out to achieve, or who was behind its failure. In short, it is most likely that Ælfgar had been confounded by the shake-up of the earldoms following the deaths of his father and Earl Ralph. His rebellion had appealed to the natural enemies of the English king, especially to those with a vested interest in gaining some sort of foothold there. Ælfgar had even given his daughter to Gruffydd indicating that his political intentions were most serious. Magnus, for his part, had recruited an army to swell the ranks of his own men and had gone to the Orkneys, the Western Isles and Dublin, these being precisely the same places which Olaf Guthfrithson had visited before his devastating assaults on the northern parts of the English kingdom in 937 and 940.

Although Magnus and Ælfgar's invasion made no lasting difference to the destiny of the English crown, it does not seem to have been easily forgotten by Edward. The campaign had resulted in a second restoration for Ælfgar, but the Mercian earl spent the rest of his life up until 1062 muttering quietly to himself about the house of Godwin. On his death in that year, his young son succeeded to his father's earldom. His name was Edwin.

By 1062 Edward the Confessor clearly realised that he was in the twilight of his life. He had had a remarkable life and there was still a little fire left in the old man yet. He had probably fought alongside his half-brother in 1016 for the survival of the line of Cerdic during the colossal wars of Edmund Ironside; he had spent decades as a prince exiled in the court of the Norman duke and at least twice had attempted an invasion of England himself before finally being restored to the throne in 1042. When in power he had run the gauntlet of civil war and played a political game of brinkmanship with the head of the Wessex earldom and, later still, he had dealt with Scottish and Welsh threats to the security of his kingdom with a degree of determination which makes a mockery of the notion that he was simply an ascetic king with little regard for the hardships of political reality. This notwithstanding, Edward's final years were indeed dominated by an important spiritual matter of great and lasting proportions. Edward's legacy would forever be the great refurbishment of Westminster Abbey. Here, the most important ceremonies of 1066 would take place. It was then and still is now, despite centuries of alterations, one of England's most attractive buildings.

For a while, from 1059 through to 1061, the *Chronicles* record their writers' concerns over ecclesiastical affairs, some of which had an important bearing on what was about to unfold in England. Pope Stephen had died in 1058 and was replaced in Rome by a somewhat unpopular Pope Benedict X. Benedict sent the pallium to Bishop Stigand in England, but shortly after doing so was driven out of Rome by the supporters of Nicholas, the bishop of Florence, who ultimately prevailed in his struggle and took the papacy himself. So Stigand, an archbishop whose credentials were constantly called into question by the Normans, had received his pallium from a pope whose own right to preside in office had been successfully challenged by his enemies in the Church. In fact, as early as 1053, Stigand had been technically unable to ordain the two churchmen Leofwine and Wulfwig, the latter of the two having succeeded to Dorchester on the departure of Bishop Ulf who had left during the purges initiated by the triumphant return of Godwin and his sons. Both these men had found it necessary to travel abroad for their ordination.

Further ecclesiastical developments took place in 1060 when Cynesige, the archbishop of York, passed away just before Christmas. The prominent figure of Aldred took over at York and was succeeded in the devout Athelstan's Herefordshire by Walter, the Lotharingian chaplain of Queen Edith. Aldred, who was clearly no stranger to foreign travel, went to Rome to receive his pallium and with him on this journey were Earl Tostig and his wife Judith. On their way back all three of them were set upon by robbers who took all their possessions, and yet they all lived to tell the tale thanks to the bravery of one of Tostig's retainers, a man named Gospatric. Earl Tostig never forgot his friend's help. Gospatric's subsequent rise to prominence in Northumbria would become just one part of the many motivations for a curious uprising in that earldom which would have a profound influence upon subsequent events along the road to Hastings. Not long after their return Pope Nicholas II died and in his stead came Pope Alexander II whose interest in the state of Church affairs in England would soon be aroused.

As for the unfortunate Earl Tostig, the political picture in his northern earldom would prove to be most colourful. Tostig appears to have had a reasonably close diplomatic relationship with King Malcolm, the recently restored king of Scotland, despite the fact that there is a recorded raid on the coast of Northumbria in 1061. The general picture is that the relationship which Tostig had established with Malcolm was more or less what the king wanted in the north. In fact, Tostig is known to have given Malcolm safe passage through England when the Scottish king visited Edward's court in 1059. And so it must have seemed to the English king that a reasonably sound appointment had been made north of the Humber. But Tostig's family connections were all very much in the south. He had no kinship bond in the land he was set to rule and his wife had come from the court of Baldwin of Flanders. Tostig's predecessor had been a hard-nosed Dane who had married an Englishwoman and had dealt with his political enemies in the ancient tradition of Northumbrian politics. Tostig was a southerner and this was an issue which smouldered until one day it all burst into flames for the son of Godwin.

Before any of these Northumbrian events could turn Tostig's attentions to the north again, he launched himself into a military campaign of co-operation with his brother Harold. Their mutual objective was to crush Gruffydd ap Llewelyn in his seat of power. Mercia had been sufficiently weakened after the death of Ælfgar and the accession of his young son Edwin for the Godwinsons to once again show their love for the king. Edwin could not at this stage, even if he was so inclined, give the type of support to Gruffydd that his father had done. The Welsh king knew that he had lost a very powerful and highly motivated ally. King Edward, however preoccupied his mind may have been on other more spiritual matters, knew precisely what he needed to do. As he sat at the table with Harold and Tostig one winter's night in Gloucester, they pored over a plan which they hoped would remove the thorn from their side. It was an astonishingly successful campaign and it gained for Earl Harold a reputation for speed and surprise which students of the tremendous campaigns of 1066 should not let pass them by.

Memories of Bishop Leofgar's hot-headed and ill-conceived foray across the Wye had left an impression on Harold. Nothing like this should be allowed to happen again. It must have seemed to him that Leofgar's losses in men and horses were due to the fact that he had been bogged down on a gruelling campaign which led only to misery and death. For Harold, speed would be of the essence. The last thing he wanted in Wales was a campaign without decision which would leave him stranded in a hostile landscape. To this end he even ordered his usually heavily armoured housecarles to wear lighter leather armour in preference to the long mailcoat of the more traditional Anglo-Danish heavy infantryman. Before any pitched battle could take place, Gruffydd's capability to resist must be reduced. Harold left Gloucester and struck out across Wales to Rhuddlan with a force consisting entirely of mounted retainers.[3] Here, the master of surprise fell upon the fortification and harbour with everything he had. His arrival was utterly unexpected. His men torched the settlement, destroyed Gruffydd's ships in the harbour and stole much of his military equipment. It had been a campaign of rapid movement focused on the centre of the Welsh king's command and control. Furthermore, his fleet had been caught in harbour, a sure sign that Harold's arrival was a surprise. With no means to resist, Gruffydd melted into the landscape. He was a king on the run.

There followed a lull in the Welsh campaign until the following spring of 1063 when Harold and Tostig put the finishing touches to their campaign plans. From Bristol, Harold took a fleet around Wales and at the same time Tostig brought a huge land force into the country from the east. The devastation of Tostig's force was widely acknowledged at the time. He took much plunder back with him to Northumbria, enough it is thought to impress his thegns there. But to the west, there was no seaborne escape route for the fugitive Welsh king. To the east there could only be certain death. Gruffydd was done for and he was not the only one to realise it. By August, his own men had had enough of the war that he had brought into the heart of his own kingdom. He was brutally murdered by them and they even took the trouble to preserve his head. Harold, the grateful recipient of the head of Gruffydd ap Llewelyn, added this prize to the trophy of the figurehead of the Welsh king's flagship and presented the whole macabre package to his king who was growing used to this sort of conclusion to wars in the west.

Edward, whose power to resolve such matters had been more or less resolved by his earls' campaigns in Wales, decided that the land there should be ruled by the half-brothers of the late Welsh king. Bleddyn and Rhiwallon, having sworn allegiance to Edward and promised him good behaviour and support by land and sea, would rule Gwynedd and Powys for a few years until Rhiwallon died in 1069. From then Welsh power was in the hands of Bleddyn until 1075. Thus it seemed that a job had been well done in the west on behalf of the English king. Perhaps there would be no problems there for a while for whoever came next. But by August of 1065 a clear signal had been sent by the Welsh that this could never be the case. During the late summer Earl Harold had built a fortification at Portskewett to which he wished to invite King Edward for the purposes of hunting. The place was crammed with goods, materials and people. But when Caradog, the son of Gruffydd ap Rhydderch[4] came to the place with a huge band gathered from the Welsh countryside, the buildings were torched and the inhabitants killed. If this had been an unwelcome reminder for Harold that his Welsh problems were far from over, then it pales into insignificance when compared to what his brother Tostig was about suffer in the north.

II

UNEXPECTED JOURNEYS

Shortly before trouble blew up again in Northumbria, Harold had made a journey for which he is famous. The Bayeux Tapestry records the visit of Earl Harold, sent to Normandy on behalf of King Edward to inform Duke William once again that the kingdom of England was to be his. After a difficult crossing which saw his ship fetch up on the shores of Ponthieu, the English earl was taken to William where he swore an oath to support the duke's claim, became his man, then travelled on a campaign to Brittany with the duke where he acquitted himself admirably. After this, Harold was allowed to return home and William was left safe in the knowledge that, when the aging king of England died, the crown would be his. This, at least, is the version of the story which is to be found in most modern accounts. Reality was somewhat different.[1]

Count Guy of Ponthieu could scarcely believe what the waves had brought him. He had his men arrest Earl Harold and then he imprisoned him at Beaurain. Guy had reckoned on a payment of a ransom from Duke William, so that Harold would be allowed to continue his journey. Guy may have expected this as his right since the lee shores of Ponthieu were treacherous for sailors and the men of the ports there had wrecking rights, or claims to the contents of ships wrecked on their coasts, contents which included people. In contrast the duke was far from pleased to be bargained with by the man he had defeated and subjugated at Mortemer. Guy was forced to go to Eu with his charge and hand him over. If William of Poitiers is to be believed, then Guy did indeed get something for his troubles from William, which manifested themselves in terms of land and money. The main point, however, is that Harold was handed over to William. For Guy, the whole thing had been a surprise. For William, he simply wanted the earl to complete the journey upon which his kinsman the king of England had sent him (if indeed we accept this version of the tale). At Rouen the duke gave the earl the sort of respect and hospitality denied him by Count Guy. It was decided that Harold should go with William into Brittany on an expedition against Duke Conan. Harold showed no signs of reluctance in this matter. Perhaps we should remember that his own kin were still in Normandy as hostages and that at least part of his intention would be to negotiate for their release. The campaign, which is beautifully illustrated in the Bayeux Tapestry, shows the earl bravely rescuing some Norman soldiers from the quicksands by the river Couesnon and perhaps significantly shows that Harold had joined an entirely mounted force, something which he himself had done in Wales and would do again. Conan had been facing a rebellion in his own country from Rhiwallon of Dol. William's support of Rhiwallon would effectively weaken Conan and make him more likely to come to terms with William. Ultimately, the campaign ended with the surrender of Conan's castle at Dinan, but there would still be a little more trouble as Conan went to Count Geoffrey of Anjou to solicit his aid. The result was a threat to the very borders of Normandy. William and Conan continued with a game of cat-and-mouse in the border countryside, before both returned home without any major battle having taken place.

But the most important thing about Harold's time with William was that he certainly seems to have sworn an oath. The strongest likelihood is that the oath, which was made at a gathering in Bonneville, was a renewal of the one which Godwin had sworn in 1051 (see pages 102-103). The oath of 1064 has often been taken as evidence of William's opportunism, but it is more reasonable to see it as an expected formality. Harold may have bitten his lip when he gave it, just like his father had done, but he had been sent to Normandy by his own king and he had been told what to do. In fact, there is reason to believe that Harold himself, before swearing the oath, made some of his own demands. William of Poiteirs says that Harold had asked William to recognise the legitimacy of all of Harold's land holdings held with full honours at the event of Edward's death. This sounds more like a negotiation than a one-sided imposition, but there are troubling contradictions in the medieval historians' recollections of the story. According to the *Carmen de Hastingæ Proelio*, Harold came with a ring and sword for the duke, symbols of office for his forthcoming elevation to the throne. Eadmer[2] on the other hand, thought that Harold had gone to Normandy against the wishes of the king, to get his relatives back from the Norman court. He also suggests that Harold's sister was to marry a Norman nobleman and that Harold would take Agatha, William's daughter, for a bride. William would allow Harold to return to England with Hakon and would release Wulfnoth on his smooth accession to the throne which Harold, of course, would mastermind for him. Although Eadmer paints a picture of the entrapment of Harold by William in Normandy, these negotiations sound like those of two high-ranking politicians in conference, more than anything else. But the reason why Harold's trip has remained controversial for so long is that by the time of Wace, who wrote in the 1160-70s, the truth about the matter had been lost to everyone.[3]

The fact that Harold had to swear an oath could not have come as a surprise to him. The subsequent offer to Harold of William's daughter Agatha's hand in marriage may well have come as a surprise, both to the Englishman himself and to the mother of his children, Edith Swansneck.[4] It has been argued that such a move shows that William was attempting to bind Harold to his oath. This was usually done with hostages, not marriages and Wulfnoth, Harold's brother, was already in Norman custody Instead, the move may show that William was making a genuine attempt to link himself with a man who would be very powerful beneath him when he was king. Certainly the oath was exacted under duress, of course Harold had no choice but to acquiesce in the matter and of course it was going to be used against him should he dare to turn his back on William, but there remains the possibility that William intended to work with Harold in the future. The conferment of arms from William to Harold as illustrated in the Bayeux Tapestry presents an interesting concept which has been variously interpreted. It is clearly a symbolic act, but it had an explicit meaning. Harold was William's man. He would act in England as William's sub-regulus. This is what it meant. But it would be Harold who would hear the last words of King Edward before he died, a privilege not experienced by Duke William.

Although Wulfnoth stayed as hostage at the Norman court, William was sufficiently pleased with the arrangements he had made with Harold to allow him to take Hakon, his nephew, back to England with him. So to those who see the trip as a conspicuous failure on the part of Harold must be served this one fact. Harold came to King Edward and told him of his Norman adventure. We do not know what was said. Ordericus Vitalis suggests that the earl made up a downright lie and told the king that the duke had given Harold his own daughter and resigned his claim to the throne in favour of Harold himself, his new son-in-law. A surprised monarch acquiesced, we are told[5] although this sounds rather far-fetched.

Perhaps Harold had simply told the king that he had done what was asked of him and that all had gone well. Perhaps he had told him that he had not enjoyed it a single bit. Whatever was said, the two men would soon have something else to talk about. The writing on the walls of York was about to spell disaster for Tostig in the one earldom above all others where the crown could not afford instability. The Northumbrian revolt of 1065 marks the beginning of the final journey on the road to Hastings. Its consequences led to the last wide-scale political shake-up before the Norman Conquest. Concealed within the details of how it all happened is the one dynamic which characterised the politics of England from the age of Æthelred to the battle of Hastings: factionalism. Let us see how it happened.

Some time after Tostig's triumphant return from his Welsh campaign, a double murder had taken place. Gamal, son of Orm and Ulf, son of Dolfin were killed by Tostig's agents in his own chambers when they were supposedly under his protection. Of course, this act did nothing to recommend the southern Englishman to his northern cousins, but the details reveal a deeper reason for what followed. Later, a certain Gospatric was killed on the orders of Queen Edith, Tostig's sister, who had directly intervened in a dispute between Gospatric and Tostig. This was to be a significant intervention. There are two Gospatrics in this twisted tale of treachery and it is important to distinguish between them. The man who met his death at the Christmas court of the king at the hands of the men of the queen was Gospatric, son of Uhtred, whom we may recall was the earl of Northumbria between 1006-16. The other Gospatric was the man who had taken service with Tostig and who had saved the earl and his family when they had been set upon by robbers on their way home from Rome. This, the second of our Gospatrics, was related to King Edward. Tostig, despite owing him his own life, may well have been encouraged to reward the brave Gospatric by the king himself. Earl Uhtred's third marriage had been to Ælfgifu, the daughter of Æthelred II, who was a sister of the king. Uhtred and Ælfgifu had a daughter, Ealdgyth who married Maldred, the grandson of Malcolm II of Scotland and their son was Gospatric. But there was another side to Earl Uhtred's family from his first union with the daughter of the bishop of Durham. Our doomed Gospatric came from that line. He had granted a great deal of land to his followers in Allerdale in the time of Earl Siward, and the unfortunate Ulf and Gamal were closely linked to the inheritors of these lands.

So Tostig, by killing these two men and through Edith's intervention, was paving the way for the promotion of his favourite: his own man, Gospatric, son of Maldred. But this struggle between the descendants of Uhtred was not enough in itself to cause a wide-scale rebellion in Northumbria, although it clearly gave people with an axe to grind something to use as an excuse. There must have been something else which led the thegns of Northumberland and Yorkshire to cast out their earl. The answer is quite simple: they did not like him. Tostig had a reputation for heavy taxation and harsh government in Northumbria. Even the sources which generally support the earl admit to this fact. The leaders of the revolt were fairly low-level players in national politics. Theirs was a parochial argument, but it had dire national consequences. Gamelbearn, Gluniarn and Dunstan were among the thegns who rebelled against Tostig. The nature of their affinity to the murdered Gospatric is not known in full but their problem was more with the style of government and the nature of the taxation which had been foisted upon their estates by a southern overlord.[6]

Two hundred disaffected thegns descended upon York at a time when Tostig was hunting with the king at Britford in Wiltshire. They wrecked the place. Some of Tostig's chief housecarles who had not gone south with him were murdered in cold blood but, more significantly, the earl's treasury was sacked and the silver and gold regained by those who had suffered such punitive measures in order to pay it. The rebels sat in York and set up an impromptu court and decided, as perhaps only Northumbrians could decide, to choose a new leader. It is an important episode in northern history since it demonstrates that Northumbrians clearly possessed the confidence to make such decisions about who ruled them, despite all the things which had happened in that ancient kingdom's struggle with the lords from the south over the last 150 years. So, the thegns sent for Morcar, son of the troublesome Earl Ælfgar of Mercia. It was a shrewd move. They knew that there was no love lost between the sons of Leofric and Godwin. They perhaps also knew that Tostig had had much to do with Ælfgar's exile. Factionalism had once again reared its ugly head. The only thing which would appear on the face of it to be surprising, is that the Northumbrians in their anger had not at any stage attempted to nominate their own candidate to the throne of England itself. Edward's power was beyond question, his legitimacy widely acknowledged. The thegns of Yorkshire may not have liked the royal policy of higher taxation which had been put into force by Tostig, but the days of a direct assault on the crown from the north might seem to have faded into memory.

The choice of Morcar was of course a political one. The thegns had other options but did not take them. The aspiring Gospatric, friend of Tostig, was perhaps understandably passed by. So too for now was Oswulf, the son of Eadwulf, who had been murdered in 1041 on the orders of Earl

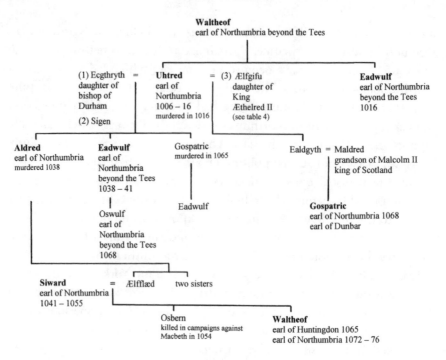

TABLE 10 Descendants of Waltheof, earl of Northumbria beyond the Tees. (Names in bold indicate earls of either Northumbria beyond the Tees or the whole of Northumbria)

Siward, the result of which had been that Siward had acceded to power north of the Tees. Waltheof, Siward's son, whose political career would survive the Norman Conquest, was another curious oversight on the part of the rebels. The answer is obvious. They simply wanted to hit Tostig with a replacement that would hurt him the most, by giving their support to the old enemies from the Mercian house of Leofric. But this was not their role. The king would first of all need to acquiesce. And so to Edward they came, with their new candidate Morcar. And at Northampton they were joined by Edwin of Mercia (Morcar's brother) who, in a move reminiscent of the alliances of his father, had brought some Welsh troops with him. But the sons of Leofric had not come to Northampton in peace. They had ravaged the lands of Earl Tostig on their way to the meeting and caused death and hardship to innocent people. It had taken Earl Harold by surprise. He had come to Northampton not with an army, but with his small retinue in preparations for an expected negotiation. Tostig was of course distraught at the loss of his northern patrimony. He had been one of King Edward's favourite earls and by most accounts had done the king's bidding as he was asked. His sister Queen Edith was also a supporter of the ousted earl. Harold clearly wanted some sort of reconciliation provided that it restored his brother to his seat north of the Humber, but it would not be that simple. Even Harold must have realised that the game was up. When Harold went to see Edward about it, the king readily granted Morcar the earldom. In the end, Harold probably pushed for it as the only obvious option which the Northumbrians would accept. There are hints that Tostig never quite forgave his brother for not intervening strongly enough on his behalf. Henry of Huntingdon is the sole preserver of a tale which describes the jealousy of Tostig over Harold's exalted position in England, and although he describes their lineage incorrectly, Tostig's compulsive and petulant behaviour is perhaps understandable. Tostig was a very proud man, just as his father had been. Nor do the similarities with his father stop there. Tostig chose for his exile his second home, the place where he had gone with his father, and where he had earlier found a bride – the court of Baldwin of Flanders.

An elderly king rode to London that winter. He had been ill for some time and must have had a heavy heart when he realised that he was unfit to attend the consecration of his magnificent Westminster Abbey. The consecration service for the minster was on 28 December 1065 and it came a month after Edward had concluded the formalities of Tostig's banishment with the aid of a somewhat eager Earl Edwin. Still left in power from the house of Godwin were Harold, Earl of Wessex and his two brothers Gyrth and Leofwine. Their combined earldoms stretched from the East Anglian coast to Cornwall. Despite the loss of Tostig's earldom, the family's possessions were still immense. The country was in extreme danger. A childless king lay on his deathbed; his only natural heir who was in any way acceptable to Harold was Edgar, still a youngster at just 14 and inexperienced. Across the sea to the south was a duke who would surely invade the country if Harold did not support his claim as he had promised. In the north the problems were no less profound. Tostig had left Northumbria for Flanders, but Harold knew that he would be back, just like his father, and that he would bring with him military aid from Baldwin. To make matters worse there was every chance that King Malcolm of Scotland might intervene on Tostig's behalf to force the issue of his return to power. And then there was Norway. Harald Sigurdsson had never let the agreement between Magnus and Harthacnut escape his memory. It did not matter to him who Edward had promised the throne to either in his youth or on his deathbed. It was his by right. So, these were very unusual circumstances. This is why something unusual happened.

12

SURPRISES IN THE NORTH

Gladly I'd draw my sword
Once more for my King Harald;
But little use his marshals
Would be on board his longship,
If one of England's warriors
Could deal with two Norwegians.
When I was young, my lady,
Things were different then.

The words of Marshal Ulf, from Heimskringla, *King Harald's Saga.* 79

Edward the Confessor's remarkable life came to an end on 5 January 1066 in London. Even a nation prone to factionalism knows when it is under threat from foreign parts. This is why there seems to have been no hint of opposition to the election by the Witan, on the very day of Edward's funeral, of Earl Harold to the position of king. It was a fundamentally important moment for the history of England. The speed at which it all happened need not surprise us. Many leading Englishmen of the day had been around Westminster for a number of weeks in order to attend the consecration ceremony of the abbey. On learning of the king's illness at a time of widely acknowledged crisis, most of them would surely have stayed to see what was to be resolved if the king died. Of course Harold was only too happy to accept the offer that was made to him, but he would have genuinely felt that only he could successfully defend the kingdom in a difficult time. Certainly there were other candidates, but it had been the wishes of a dying king that he should be succeeded by the earl.[1] The decisions made in London that winter were something of an English affair. There is no evidence that any of the duke's representatives were even at the Christmas council when Edward was severely ill. The choice of Harold and the coronation was certainly a departure from the norm, but surely not a surprise to the leading Englishmen of the day. Least surprised would be Aldred, archbishop of York who performed the ceremony in Westminster Abbey, while Stigand, unable to perform it for reasons given above (see page 130), looked on.[2] Other than the Danish kings of England, who are a special case in this regard, no king outside the line of Cerdic had succeeded to the throne. But now, an earl, a son of Godwin was king. Why had it happened?

Some important sources agree that the kingdom was offered to Harold by Edward. The *Anglo-Saxon Chronicle,* while launching once again into alliterative verse at the death of Edward, says quite explicitly:

> However, the wise man committed the kingdom
> To a distinguished man, Harold himself.

The author of Edward's *Vita* goes further by placing some words into the mouth of the dying king. Edward may or may not have spoken these words. It is well known that the *Vita* has oceans of propaganda in it which can trip up a modern reader. We should bear in mind that the old king had married Harold's sister, too. Nevertheless, the wording hints at something unusual:

> I commend this woman [Edith] and all the kingdom to your protection.
> Serve and honour her as your lady and your sister, which she is, and do not
> despoil her as long as she lives of any due honour got from me. Likewise
> I commend also those men who have left their native land for love of me
> and up till now have served me faithfully. Take from them an oath of fealty,
> if they should so wish, and protect and retain them, or send them with your
> safe-conduct across the Channel.

Where in this statement is the explicit offer of the crown? Look after my wife, take nothing from her, be the protector of this kingdom, use my Normans if you like or send them home. Send them home? Would Edward have offered this option to Harold if he had still been keen on William to succeed? Surely he would have told Harold to keep them in England until William came. The kingdom had clearly been placed

The death of King Edward. *Bayeux Tapestry*

Harold is crowned as King. *Bayeux Tapestry*

under Harold's protection, but there is nothing in these words which suggests that Edward's final wishes had been intended to solve once and for all an age-old succession crisis. Harold knew that in practice it meant that he would have to be sworn in as king, provided that he could win Edwin and Morcar over and this he did. In fact, he took for his wife their sister Ealdgyth, who had formerly been married to Harold's old enemy Gruffydd ap Llewelyn. Moreover, it was Harold's intervention in the crisis of the Northumbrian uprising which led to the royal acceptance of the appointment of Morcar there. By linking himself more closely with the family of the sons of Leofric, Harold had provided some much needed security in Northumbria. The price he must have paid for it at the time was permanently to alienate Tostig. It his hard to see how he could ever have entered into a relationship with the house of Leofric without promising to look after Morcar's interests in the north at Tostig's expense.

Harold knew also that, in the face of the threat of invasion from three different continental powers, he would have to fight to hold his grip on power. But for whom was he securing the kingdom? Events would of course show that, whatever oaths he had sworn to William, these meant very little to him now that he had been given the important job of protecting the kingdom himself. Harold had five sons by his first union with Edith Swansneck and, although they would continue to play a part in the story of the Norman Conquest after Harold's death, there is no real hint that any one of them was acknowledged by King Harold as an heir to the throne of England in his own lifetime.

Did Edward indicate that the kingdom should be held open for a young man of the right blood, Edgar the ætheling? If so, would Harold inevitably disobey the king's wishes in favour of promoting his own line to the throne? Where, when he came of age, would Edgar go to solicit aid to prosecute his own claim? Were Edgar and Harold natural enemies or was one the long-term protector of the other? There are, unfortunately, more questions than answers generated by the short reign of Harold II, king of England. It is a matter of some interest that nobody seems to have loudly championed Edgar's claim during the short reign of Harold. Nor were there any serious signs of internal dissent at Harold's accession. In other words, Harold had used his noted diplomatic skills to make sure that the Earls of Mercia and Northumbria were more or less on board with him and that the small matter of the domestic candidate for the succession would remain in the hands of Harold at least until the foreign threats were overcome. It was absolutely clear to everyone, however, that very soon there would be a bloodbath somewhere in England.

It is likely that very early in the New Year Harold received messengers from Normandy who will have protested their duke's discomfort at the accession of Harold to the throne of England. Baudri of Bourgeuil, writing around 1100, tells the story that Edward, during his terminal illness, sent legates to Normandy confirming his promise to William in writing. An embassy was sent back to England to confirm the acceptance of the offer but, when they returned, they found the king dead. This story is somewhat unlikely since the Normans themselves in numerous writings acknowledged that there had been a deathbed commitment of the kingdom to Harold at this time. So, if they existed at all, whatever Harold said to the Norman embassy, it was as clear to him as it was to William that the duke of Normandy would soon launch an invasion. But first Harold needed to exercise his diplomacy in the one region where there was disquiet about his accession. The thegns of the north needed some reassurance. It is interesting that when Harold went to York in the early part of 1066 he took with him Bishop Wulfstan of Worcester, whose explanation to the people that the country was in very great danger seems to have done enough to stop anything serious coming from the discomfort of the men of the north. In another move which involved a prominent northerner, it has been convincingly argued that it was in fact Harold and not Edward who promoted Waltheof, the son of Earl Siward of Northumbria, to an earldom comprised of estates which had once belonged to the now exiled Tostig.[3] This earldom of Northamptonshire and Huntingdonshire was quite some gift to Waltheof and would surely have demonstrated to the Northumbrians that Tostig's departure, at least as far as Harold was concerned, was a permanent feature.

With a potential crisis smoothed over in the north, Harold made his way to Westminster from York beneath evening skies which would soon be lit up by the famous appearance of Halley's Comet. His concerns will of course have been with the threat to his shores from Normandy but, as it turned out, the first boat to arrive from an overseas land to tread the beaches of southern England belonged to an Englishman. Tostig had returned in force.

Count Baldwin of Flanders had not let Tostig down. During his exile at St Omer, Tostig had solicited the count's aid in terms of ships and men. There is every reason to believe that Tostig's force, with which he sailed to the Isle of Wight in the spring of 1066, posed a very credible threat to the security of his brother's kingdom. Flemish sailors were well known for their skills and their soldiers for their spearmanship. But there is something troubling about what Ordericus Vitalis has to say on the matter of Tostig's travels during his exile. He says that Tostig had gone to see Duke William.[4] After talking to the duke about his plans, Tostig set sail for England from the Cotentin peninsula but failed to reach the shore on account of the unfavourable winds and heavily defended coastline. So Tostig, according to Ordericus, then had to change his plans and eventually teamed up with Harald Sigurdsson in the north. We cannot be sure if the trip to William was ever made, but it is certainly the case that Tostig had been looking for friends during his exile, and the timing of his eventual descent upon his brother's kingdom may indeed have had something more to do with judgment than with luck. Ordericus's unfavourable winds in the Channel certainly have a chime of authenticity about them and, as we shall see, they had a profound effect upon William's plans.

Tostig provisioned himself from the Isle of Wight where he might have expected to easily secure support from some of his former estates and then he headed around the Kent coast. Part of his plan might well have been to solicit aid from the acquaintances of his youth on the Sussex coast, just as his father had done in 1052, but Tostig's recruitment campaign seems to have been executed at sword's edge and will have endeared him to no one there. Indeed, at Sandwich his recruits were less than willing. After hearing that a royal fleet was heading for Sandwich, he sailed north. Harold's grand preparations to guard the southern coast with a land army had already begun and it is likely that Tostig was put off by the probable strength of the resistance he would receive if he made landfall there. Tostig's intentions may be hinted at by a note in Gaimar's writing which tells us that at Thanet he met a force of 17 ships which had come to him from Orkney. What was he up to? On his way north, he raided up the Burnham River in Norfolk and apparently attempted at some stage to seduce his brother Gyrth from allegiance to Harold. Into the Humber estuary he then sailed with a force of 60 ships. Tostig disembarked and raided into Lincolnshire determined to raise hell. Both of Harold's new brothers-in-law were quick to seize the initiative. Edwin and Morcar showed that they were ready to defend the realm, particularly against a man who wanted one of their own earldoms back. They drove him clean out of England. The result for Tostig was that his Flemish soldiers deserted him and the Kentish shipmen who had been press-ganged into service did the same, perhaps then sailing on up the Humber and the Wharfe to Tadcaster. With only 12 remaining ships Tostig sailed to Scotland and cooled his heels with King Malcolm while he pondered his next move. For the petulant and proud earl his next move would go a long way towards permanently tarnishing his memory in the minds of northerner and southerner alike. Nor would it please his brother, the king.

Harold's first emergency then, had been dealt with. The political strength of his union with the family of Edwin and Morcar had brought dividends. It had helped protect the kingdom. But there had been an alarm call or two here. What was the significance of the fleet from Orkney? Had Tostig visited Harald Sigurdsson during his exile and discussed how he might aid the Norwegian king in gaining the English throne for him? Had Harold allowed Tostig to get to the Isle of Wight unmolested? Was it the case that Harold's naval forces had indeed repelled him as Ordericus seems to have suggested? The English king was still putting together a mighty fleet. He soon sailed to Sandwich where his reception would have been much warmer than his brother's. After waiting a while here, he sailed to the Isle of Wight. The Norman invasion was worrying him the most. The maritime defence of southern England seems to have been in the hands of a man named Eadric the Steersman and another, Abbot Ælfwold of St Benet of Holme. It is suggested that, whilst Harold was paying urgent attention to the strategic land defences of southern England, he seized an estate at Steyning which in fact had belonged to the abbey at Fécamp.[5] Thereafter the duke of Normandy promised to restore the estate to the abbey when he became king.[6] What is clear from these references to coastal defences is that Harold had a plan. There is even some evidence that he had spies sent to Normandy who he hoped would bring him news of when the invasion would come.[7] It seems that William must have done the same, as his final arrival at a particular place along the Sussex coast has the hallmarks of military intelligence behind it.

All summer Harold and his giant naval and land force waited in a state of readiness for William to cross to England. Had there not been contrary winds which confounded William and kept his invasion fleet at bay, there would have been a military action somewhere in the south of England even bigger than the one which would come to pass at Senlac Ridge. It is a moot point as to whether the Norman army would not have been swamped by its adversary. In fact, William's military advisors were keen to point this out to him. But William was no fool and knew his preparations would have to leave no stone unturned. He knew also that he could hardly bring with him a piecemeal force. Although it cost him a fortune, he may not have minded too much about the waiting. On 8 September 1066 Harold's land and sea forces were disbanded. They had run out of supplies but, as we shall see, they may have known more about the naval force to the south of them than the contemporary accounts let on. Interestingly and perhaps with hindsight, Ordericus says that Harold abandoned Hastings and Pevensey and other sea ports opposite the Norman coast.[8] This of course would suggest that these two famous ports would be devoid of protection at the arrival of the Norman fleet on the Sussex coast, but also implies something else: the butsecarles of Hastings were somewhere else, perhaps still with the king.

Whatever the reason for the disbanding of the forces of Harold, what happened next must have been the longest expected invasion in European medieval history. And yet to some people it seems to have come as a surprise. Harald Sigurdsson had finally turned his attention to England. His long attritional war with King Swein of Denmark was emptying his coffers and getting him nowhere. In fact, Swein Estrithson and Harald Sigurdsson must have been sick of the sight of each other's mailcoats,[9] perhaps more so than any other two protagonists across the whole of Europe. They had fought each other to a standstill in battle after battle, providing later Icelandic skalds with all they needed for a great yarn. Finally, a treaty was drawn up which is vaguely recalled by the words of a skald in the Heimskringla in *King Harald's Saga*:

> *At long last, fierce King Harald*
> *Turned keen swords into ploughshares;*
> *Weapons had maimed shields at sea;*
> *In the third year* [after a battle at Nissa], *peace was made.*

We are not certain about Tostig's trip to Normandy during his exile, but we have firm assertions about his other diplomatic journeys. If it is the case that Tostig used his months in exile to visit both the Danish and Norwegian courts as Snorri Sturluson suggests, then he is likely in all reality to have got nowhere with Swein Estrithson and perhaps achieved only slightly better with Harald Sigurdsson. Although there was a tenuous claim held by Swein to the English throne through half-remembered promises during the early years of Edward the Confessor's reign,[10] he was unlikely to leave Denmark at the mercy of Harald especially after he had been threatened for nearly 16 years by the Norwegian king. In fact, there is even reason to believe that Swein sent to King Harold of England military reinforcements from his own country later in the year. The injection of Danish warriors into Harold's army would not only give the English king a welcome boost, but it would also be very much in Swein Estrithson's interests to help Harold overcome the Danish king's nemesis.

Harald, on the other hand, seems at last to have been quite receptive to the idea of an English expedition and it is probably from his Scottish base that the final messages were sent from Tostig to Harald in Norway.

In fact, they must surely have corresponded at the very least through an ambassador of some sort because the Anglo-Saxon chronicler, when describing their joining together in the north, says that it had happened 'just as they had earlier spoken about'. Some have said, on the basis of later accounts, that this ambassador may have been Copsi, a Northumbrian compatriot of Tostig's and that he may have been behind the recruitment for Tostig of the fleet from the Orkneys.

It seems to have been Tostig's call to Harald that was the catalyst for the Norwegian king's invasion. However, the notion that Harald had previously had no sort of plan in place is given the lie not only by the failed attempt at a western entry into England by his son Magnus in 1058, but by the paranoia of the English aristocracy throughout the whole of the 1050s and early 1060s. They and their king had been expecting Harald to come. The only surprise – and it was a big one – was the timing. In the event, the Norwegian invasion of England in 1066 bore all the hallmarks of a carefully organised campaign. With something between 300 and 500 ships, the Norwegian king's huge fleet set sail for the British Isles. Sources vary with each other on where he went next and what he did but Snorri Sturluson, who of course is not without his critics in terms of accuracy, says that he first went to Shetland, sending some of his fleet ahead to Orkney. Earls Paul and Erland[11] joined him in Orkney and it was here that Harald left behind his wife and daughters. From here, Harald sailed south down the coast of Scotland, either stopping to pick up Tostig's force or to send messages for him to sail down to the mouth of the Tyne to meet him. Either way, according to Snorri, the first unfortunate Englishmen to feel the brutal force of the invasion fleet were the inhabitants of Scarborough. Here a predictable treatment was meted out to them and their town was razed. Those who remained were left in no doubt as to the Norwegian king's intentions and submitted to him. Interestingly, at about this time, Earl Tostig formally did the same thing. From now on Harald and Tostig's fortunes were bound together in this, the opening campaign of England's greatest year of battles.

The would-be king of England and his man sailed further down the coast into the time-honoured entry point for Viking invasion fleets of yesteryear, the Humber estuary. From here, they took the river Ouse to Riccall where they moored, ready to take York. Edwin and Morcar had got wind of the invasion. After sending messengers south to Harold probably on 16 September, they raced to the defence of the kingdom once again. King Harold, upon hearing the news of the invasion, did what he seemed to have been best at doing. He came north with a huge force, cutting his rest periods and marching, we are told, through the night as well as through the day. It was a march which resembled the great descent upon York of the mighty King Athelstan, the Thunderbolt of the South, who had expelled his Viking foes from the recalcitrant city in 927 and for the first time had taken the place into the custody of a southern English monarch. In 1066, a year full of surprises, perhaps it was the speed of the English king which was the greatest surprise of them all. But even at a rate of well over 20 miles a day, the English king would arrive at Tadcaster no earlier than Sunday 24 September. By then, much would have happened in the north.

Before the dashing king of England could reach his destination, his brothers-in-law had reached theirs. There is a school of thought which suggests that Harald and Tostig had already taken York when Edwin and Morcar arrived to confront him, but the stronger likelihood is that Edwin and Morcar, who had shown their alacrity already this year, had actually succeeded in getting into York themselves via the Roman road which went through Tadcaster and then pushed on south to block the enemy's entrance to York at Gate Fulford. This would explain why there was then a pitched battle. If Harald had taken York first, there would surely have been either a protracted siege or an action which would have taken place on the streets of York itself.[12] But here at Gate Fulford on the Vigil of St Matthew the Apostle, Wednesday 20 September, a battle was hard fought on the northern bank of the river Ouse. It was a good old-fashioned humdinger. Our fullest account of it is our most unreliable as it comes from Snorri once more. And yet there is something which sounds perfectly acceptable about it. The Norwegians had pinned one of their flanks on the river and stretched their line so that their weaker flank could not be rounded by virtue of a dyke at that end. The bulk of the Norwegian force was on the flank nearest the river. For the English earls, their formation was relative. Where Harald had his weakest, they had their strongest, and vice versa. So, when the armies' shield-walls crashed together to sound the first cries of death in a trilogy of famous battles, the results were as they would have been in ancient Sparta. The army with the greatest muscle on one of its flanks won the day, and that army was Harald's. The flank which had achieved the victory by the riverside had succeeded in inflicting heavy losses by pushing their enemy back into the river. Edwin and Morcar had been defeated and it had hurt them. They had both survived the battle, and both would still play a part in the drama of the Norman Conquest, but a defeat is a defeat. York was as open to Harald as it had been to Olaf Guthfrithson on his return to the city in 940. Up to 150 hostages were exchanged on both sides, a great many of whom would have been known to Tostig, but generally speaking the

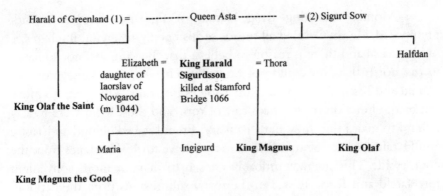

TABLE 11 Norwegian connections of Harald Sigurdsson

(Names in bold indicate kings of Norway)

place was not trashed. This, after all, was the earldom which Tostig wanted back again and York was its capital. Moreover, there are hints that the men of the countryside were responding, perhaps under duress, to the call from the Norwegian king that, if they joined with him and Tostig and came south, they would share ultimately in the rewards.

But the English king was still gathering pace on his journey to York. He must have assumed, like King Athelstan had assumed before him, that his enemies were sat in the Northumbrian capital. Here he would descend upon the city and scatter them. But by the time he reached Tadcaster, it seems that he had learned that Harald and Tostig were not there at all, but were still with their ships. Something else happened at Tadcaster. The *Anglo-Saxon Chronicle* records that here Harold marshalled his shipmen. Quite who these men were we do not know, but there are several possibilities. They may have been the Kentish men press-ganged into Tostig's fleet earlier in the year who had fled from their master when he had gone to Scotland. If this is the case, they will have sailed up the Humber and then the Wharfe to Tadcaster. Harald and Tostig would have known of the whereabouts of these troops when they themselves sailed into the Humber and so the landing at Riccall, which would have denied this fleet any room for manoeuvre, makes a good deal of sense. Alternatively, the English ships may have been part of the royal fleet itself, sent to the north to rendezvous with the land army at Tadcaster. Perhaps the reference to shipmen here refers to the butsecarles of Hastings and Pevensey who had been required to vacate their southern ports. There also remains the intriguing possibility that Swein's Danish reinforcements had in fact arrived in the Humber estuary just in time to join with Harold before the sea was closed behind them.

On Monday morning King Harold of England swept into York unopposed. He then stifled all means of his enemy receiving intelligence of his arrival and there is reason to believe that the king was not so hated in the north that this could not be easily achieved. That same morning Harald and Tostig were dividing their forces into those who were to move out to the junction of the roads east of York, and those who were to stay behind to guard the ships. Earls Paul and Erlend stayed behind and Tostig and Harald went to Stamford Bridge to receive further hostages from the countryside. This site was probably chosen to make it more convenient for Harald and Tostig to call in the many submissions from the earldom which they now expected. The need to receive hostages on such a wide scale reflects the simple fact that the Northumbrians were harder to prize away from their allegiance to the southern English king than perhaps we might expect. But Harald and Tostig were over 11 miles from their ships at Riccall. It would prove for them to be a fatal miscalculation. Worse still, if Snorri is to be believed, it was such a fine morning that the Norwegians had left their armour on shipboard. Snorri, in a stirring passage, says this:

> But as they approached the town they saw a large force riding to meet them. They could see the cloud of dust raised by the horses' hooves, and below it the gleam of handsome shields and white coats of mail. King Harald halted his troops and summoned Earl Tostig, and asked him what army this could be. Earl Tostig said he thought it was likely to be a hostile force, although it was also possible that these were some of his kinsmen seeking mercy and protection from the king in exchange for their faith and fealty. The king said they had better wait there and find out more about this army. They did so; and the closer the army came, the greater it grew, and their glittering weapons sparkled like a field of broken ice.
>
> Snorri Sturluson, Heimskringla, *King Harald's Saga*. 87

Tostig panicked. He wanted to turn back to the ships, but there was no way that this was possible. The army fell back in the face of the English and crossed the Derwent. Harald had sent three messengers on horseback to Riccall. His intention seemed to be to hold his ground until reinforcements could arrive. In fact, up to a third of his force and all of his armour were back there. As the Norwegians fell back across the bridge, later legend has it that there was a famous holding action. The legend, clearly a later insertion in a different hand, appears in the Abingdon version of the *Anglo-Saxon Chronicle*. It may or may not be poetic licence, but something must have happened at this bridge – some sort of attempt to hold the English whilst the Norwegians formed up on the battle flats beyond. Henry of Huntingdon and William of Malmesbury also mention the episode. No account of the battle of Stamford Bridge feels quite complete without it. Here is the Abingdon chronicler's account:

> There was one of the Norwegians who withstood the English people so that they could not cross the bridge nor gain victory. The one Englishman shot with an arrow but it was to no avail, and then another came under the bridge and stabbed him through under the mailcoat. Then Harold, king of the English, came over the bridge, and his army along with him, and there made a great slaughter of both Norwegians and Flemings [Tostig's troops, who appear not have deserted him in this version]; and Harold let the king's son, who was called 'The Elegant' go home to Norway with all the ships.

But there was nothing amusing about the rest of the battle. It was the most complete annihilation of medieval European military history. Ordericus Vitalis, writing in the twelfth century, said that even in his day a huge pile of bones could be seen on the battlefield. Geoffrey Gaimar, a contemporary, said of the battle that 'nobody could count a half of those left on the field'. Were it not for the colossal impact of another battle which took place a few weeks later, Stamford Bridge would have received the attention it fully deserves from historians for centuries.

Once across the bridge, before the action began, Snorri tells us that there was a meeting. An English horseman enquired of the Norwegians whether Earl Tostig was in the army. The earl answered the question himself. The horseman told Tostig that Harold, the king of England would offer the earl his earldom back and a third of his kingdom. The earl was unimpressed and reminded the rider of the harm his brother had done him when he was exiled. Tostig asked of the rider what Harald, his new lord, would get for his troubles. Then came the most famous words of 1066, words which in all probability, were never spoken....

> The rider said, 'King Harold has already declared how much of England he is prepared to grant him: seven feet of ground, or as much more as he is taller than other men.'
>
> Earl Tostig said, 'Go now and tell King Harold to make ready for battle. The Norwegians will never be able to say that Earl Tostig abandoned King Harald Sigurdsson to join his enemies when he came west to fight in England. We are united in our aim: either to die with honour, or else conquer England'.

The horseman now rode back.

Then King Harald Sigurdsson asked: 'Who was that man who spoke so well?'

'That was Harold Godwinsson' [*sic*] replied Tostig.

King Harald Sigurdsson said, 'I should have been told much sooner. These men came so close to our lines that this Harold should not have lived to tell of the deaths of our men.'

'It is quite true, sire,' said Earl Tostig, 'that the king acted unwarily, and what you say could well have happened. But I realised that he wanted to offer me my life and great dominions, and I would have been his murderer if I had revealed his identity. I would rather that he were my killer than I his.'

King Harald Sigurdsson said to his men, 'What a little man that was; but he stood proudly in his stirrups.'[13]

Snorri Sturluson, Heimskringla, *King Harald's Saga.* 91

Battle was about to commence. We should probably not allow ourselves to be seduced by this passage in Snorri's work and yet it speaks to us. Once you have read it or heard it spoken, you cannot remove it from your mind. It is either a powerful fantasy, or something approximating to the real truth. Harold Godwinson had shown himself already to be an extremely clever diplomat. This sort of approach would have been right out of his manual of international negotiations, had he ever written one. He had gleaned all the information from his brother that he needed without being discovered. Harold must have returned to his lines with a clear conscience. The fury of the Anglo-Saxon army would do the rest.

So, a phalanx of well-armed and armoured spearmen and axemen crashed into the brave northerners, deprived of their armour, but resisting with their swords and shields. The defenders fought bravely but had little chance of winning the day. The river ran red. Snorri's account of the battle waxes and wanes between moments of probable truth and those of a clear mistaking of events with those which occurred on the field of Senlac Ridge a few weeks later. Repeated cavalry charges, the defending infantry army's deployment, the pauses in the fighting, all of these things ring far truer of Hastings than they do of Stamford Bridge, right down to the fact that the defending king fell due to a fatal arrow wound. All we know for certain is that Harald Sigurdsson and Tostig failed to survive the battle. After Harald's death, Tostig had found himself beneath the banners at the last. But just then it seems that reinforcements did indeed arrive from Riccall. They were led, according to Snorri, by a man named Eystein Orri. Unlike their compatriots, these new men had arrived with full armour and weaponry. But they were hardly fresh when they got there. In fact, they were exhausted. Their march had been an emergency sprint from the ships of over 11 miles and they were expected to put up a fight at the end of it.

The reinforcements were too beaten by their own fatigue to make much of a difference. Soon Tostig fell in the final onslaught beneath the banners. It was a bloodbath. The Norwegians who remained fled to their ships, being hacked at by the English, who had almost certainly kept a mounted reserve behind for the chase. King Harold allowed Earl Paul of Orkney and Olaf, the son of Harald to take the remainder of the fleet back to Norway on the solemn promise that they would not return. Of the many hundreds of ships which descended on England for that battle, just 24 returned home. King Harold of England was, not for the first time in his career, the successful defender of the kingdom of England.

As the English king dealt with the gruesome business of the post-battle formalities,[14] he could not for a moment have realised what the wind from the south had brought with it. Somewhere on the coast of Sussex, Harold's own family heartland, the duke had landed. If the north of England had been littered with surprises in this extraordinary year, then the south would have the last word in hosting the shock of the century. Somehow, William had defied the odds and got across the English Channel. Now we must turn to look at the extraordinary way in which he did it, for all is not what it seems.

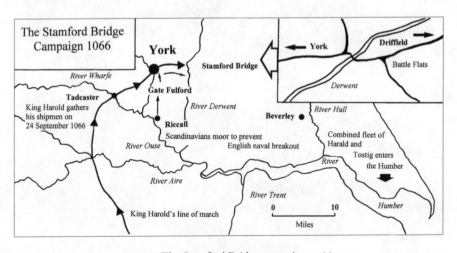

MAP 8 The Stamford Bridge campaign 1066

13

THE WIND OF DESTINY

In Normandy, many ships were already fully equipped, for both clergy and laity devoted their time and money to building them. At the prince's summons, many warriors assembled from all over Normandy.

Ordericus Vitalis

'Sire, we fear the sea and are not bound to serve beyond it'
The Normans' reply to the exhortations of William Fitz Osbern.

Wace

For those men who walked along the quay side at Rouen towards their ships in the summer of 1066, grave doubts must have crept across their minds. They saw the rotting hulks of their father's ships in the water and remembered what had happened on a fateful day in 1033 (see pages 68–69). And here they were, being asked to join an invasion fleet in order to cross to an extraordinarily resilient country whose forces were likely to dwarf their own. These men were to fight for a duke whose right to claim the throne of England was based on a promise made to him 15 years earlier, regardless of when it had been renewed. Even for the hardened mercenaries amongst this spectacular force, these were very nervous times.

But these fears notwithstanding, the preparations made by the duke were nothing short of impressive. The political climate in northern France had recently turned very much to William's favour. For years he had fought to protect Normandy from incursions and rebellions. Brittany, as Harold had seen for himself, was clearly a long-term problem for the Normans, but

The invasion fleet is ready. *Bayeux Tapestry*

by now this troublesome region had been brought under the wing of the duke of Normandy. The count of Anjou, the powerful Geoffrey Martel, who had caused so much trouble for William, had died by 1060 as too had the king of France himself. Anjou had descended into an internecine war thereafter and the throne of France was now occupied by Philip I who was no more than a boy. Philip had been placed under the regency of none other than Baldwin of Flanders, the father of William's diminutive wife, Matilda. Ordericus paints a rather grim picture of Norman domestic politics at this time but with Maine now secure after the death of Geoffrey of Anjou and with all these other factors in place, William's thoughts turned to the biggest prize of all, the throne of England.

First we must address a difficult problem. It is the notion of whether the expedition to England took place with papal backing. It has long been thought, on the basis of the comments of William of Poitiers and the evidence in the Bayeux Tapestry, that William was given a papal banner by Pope Alexander II for his apparent crusade against the over-worldly and irregular English Church and that this extraordinary blessing had taken place before he set off. This idea has always sounded faintly absurd. It has been suggested that the whole story was the product of propaganda.[1] Papal banners were normally used in the context of either a religious war against Muslims, pagans or apostates or as an indication of righteousness in a war against a rebel to papal authority. Where were the rumblings of papal discomfort in 1066? There had been no sign of unease for example in 1062 when papal legates sat in council with Archbishop Stigand, the subject of so much Norman propaganda. Stigand, despite the uncanonical appointment which he held, stayed at Canterbury for four years after the Norman Conquest. That year, 1070, saw another development. The papal legate Erminfrid of Sion imposed a penance upon the Normans for their aggressive act against a fellow Christian kingdom. If there was papal unease about anything, then it was about the way in which the new king of England had come to the throne and had far less to do with the way in which the other man had presided over his church affairs. We might remind ourselves of how passionately a different pope had felt about the dispute between two Christian brothers, the duke of Normandy and Æthelred II in the 990s (see pages 23-24). In that particular case, a pope had gone out of his way to pull two antagonists together through a mixture of diplomacy and treaty.

If it was the case that the banner and other blessings were handed over around 1070 as a way of recognising a *fait accompli*, then it would make some sense, provided of course that the penance was done and that the promised church reforms were indeed carried out. William's grip on England was hardly secure in the first four years of his reign, but from 1070 his hold seems to have grown stronger; with a threat to his shores from Swein Estrithson now over and the rise to prominence of Lanfranc, archbishop of Canterbury, Stigand's replacement, things were looking decidedly different for the king. For William of Poitiers, any small amount of guilt that he might have felt about the way in which England was conquered would be absolved. He would now be free to portray the whole episode as a crusade against the apostate. The maker of the Bayeux Tapestry would feel confident enough to picture the Norman troops carrying the papal banner into battle. And so the propaganda developed into the story we have come to accept as true, that William came to England under papal authority. It would seem that in actual fact he did not.[2] The duke of Normandy had known for a long time – perhaps since 1051 – that if he was to be successful in his bid for the throne of England, then it would not be achieved without bloodshed. It is quite clear that between 1066 and 1070 a great deal of explaining had been required by Rome.

So, who were the men who changed the blood lines of English lordship for ever in 1066? We can piece together their names from the surviving roughly contemporary documentation. The ship list of the Conqueror, a document possibly compiled after 1067, names the number of vessels each lord had provided for the expedition and the number of knights they had brought. To the high-ranking nobles in this list can be added further individuals from the surviving copies of the Battle Abbey Roll and assorted other material. The ship list gives the following breakdown: William Fitz

Osbern (whom Henry of Huntingdon says tricked all the other magnates into participating in the expedition) 60 ships; Hugh of Avranches 60 ships; Hugh of Montfort 50 ships and 60 knights; Remigius of Fécamp one ship and 20 knights; Nicholas, abbot of St Ouen 15 ships and 100 knights; Robert, count of Eu 60 ships; Fulk of Anjou 40 ships; Gerald the seneschal 40 ships; William, count of Évreux 80 ships; Roger of Montgomery[3] 60 ships; Roger of Beaumont 60 ships; Odo, bishop of Bayeux and half-brother of William 100 ships; Robert, count of Mortain 120 ships; Walter Giffard 30 ships and 100 knights. Numbers will for ever be in dispute, but the total number of vessels in the list amounts to 776, which is quite an armada.[4] The numbers given in other sources for the size of William's fleet include estimates of between 1,000 and 3,000 ships which, given the logistical necessities of bringing a partly cavalry army with its attendant supplies and equipment plus pre-fabricated fortifications, might not be as ludicrous as it seems, but Wace, whose figures for the combatants are usually taken as ludicrous, says that his own father had told him that he had remembered that the fleet had 696 ships at St Valéry-Sur-Somme, an unusually specific figure.

Many of these men would feature prominently in the politics of England in the post-Conquest Age. To their names can be added Count Eustace of Boulogne; Geoffrey of Mortagne; Geoffrey, bishop of Coutances; Aimeri, Vicomte of Thouars; Ralf of Tosny; Hugh of Grandmesnil; William of Warenne; Robert, son of Roger Beaumont; William Malet; Gulbert of Auffay; Robert of Vitot; Engenulf of Laigle (whose death at the infamous malfosse we shall explore); Gerelmus of Panileuse; Robert FitzErnies; Roger, son of Turold; Turold (who was one of the ducal messengers sent to Count Guy in 1064); Turstin, son of Rollo (who some suggest carried the papal banner, but see above, page 158); Erchembald; Vitalis; Wadard; Taillefer; Guy of Ponthieu (probably); Rodolph, the Chamberlain of Tancerville; Hugh of Ivry, a butler; Richard FitzGilbert and, finally, Pons. The general breakdown of the command structure is thought to have been as follows: the Normans, by far the biggest divison, were to be commanded in the field by the commander-in-chief, the duke himself, then on one flank the Bretons under Alan and Aimeri Vicomte of Thouars with the men of Poitou and Maine, and on the other flank, the Franco-Flemish under Count Eustace and William FitzOsbern, consisting of some of the duke's own men, the men of Boulogne and of Poux in Picardy. Overall numbers in the invasion force have varied with almost every historian who has attempted to work it out. A figure of around 7,500 is often arrived at of which around 2,000 are estimated to have been cavalry, but this seems really to be the result of a consensus.[5]

1 An Anglo-Saxon woman demonstrates a weaving technique. The Bayeux Tapestry would have been made by women like the one photographed here. English women were famous throughout Europe for the quality of their embroidery. *Photograph: Lise Farquhar*

2 An Anglo-Danish thegn, *c*.990-1066. The men of the Danelaw held the balance of power in the north of England. Edmund Ironside, son of King Æthelred, married the widow of Siferth, a thegn of the Five Boroughs of Scandinavian England, and at once found himself able to recruit from a huge stretch of northern countryside in his fight against Cnut of Denmark during the tremendous struggles of 1016. *Photograph: John Eagle*

6 The revival of the community at Mont-St-Michel, here at the base of the Cotentin peninsula, owes much to the reign of Richard I (942-996). Over time, the canons were replaced by monks. It was to this spectacular site that Edward the Confessor came by ship in 1033 after the abortive attempt by Duke Robert I (1027-1035) to invade England and establish Edward on the throne there

3 *Opposite above, left:* St Michael overcoming Satan, 980-1000. *MS. 50 Bibliothèque Municipale, Avranches.* By the time of the re-foundation of the community at Mont-St-Michel in 966, the Norman rise to prominence in northern France had gathered pace. The count of Rouen now wished to style himself as a marquis, one who ruled over counts

4 *Opposite above, right:* The Norman flag flies high above the medieval remains at Fécamp

5 *Opposite below:* The medieval walls of Hereford. The city was strongly fortified against Welsh attack by Earl Harold after the disastrous battle outside Hereford in 1055 where Earl Ralph the Timid fled the field in the face of a combined Welsh and rebel English force. Harold's subsequent campaigns into Wales would be remembered for generations. Little survives above ground of Harold's fortifications, but archaeological excavations have revealed significant ramparts

7 *Above:* The magnificent Hereford Cathedral, home of an important chained library and an extraordinary medieval map of the world. The devastation of 1055 left its mark on the community here. The blind Bishop Athelstan, a committed and holy man, continued as long as he could after the horrors of the autumn, but soon died. Earl Harold's mass-priest Leofgar was given the role and conspicuously failed to impress

8 *Left:* Worcester Cathedral. Worcester had for a long time been an important centre of education, religion and learning. But during the reign of Harthacnut (1040-1042), it was the focus of an extraordinary uprising. Two of the king's soldiers were killed by the townsmen in the minster church when they tried to exact a punitive tax on the people. A widespread campaign of burning and reduction followed, which saw the population seek refuge on an island in the Severn. The incident did not endear the king to historians

9 The shoreline near Fécamp, northern France. From here, in 1033, Edward the Confessor set out with a Norman fleet organised by the duke of Normandy. Their intentions were to invade England, but they ended their journey at the foot of the Cotentin due to contrary winds. The shores of this whole stretch of coastline were treacherous, as Duke William found in September 1066

10 The remains of later medieval buildings at the site of the Norman Palace opposite the abbey at Fécamp

11 Remaining part of the walls of the keep at Richard's Castle, near Ludlow. The activities of the garrison here provided Earl Godwin and his family with a permanent threat to their interests. In 1051, the influence of such garrisons would lead to an extraordinary stand-off between the king and his most powerful magnate

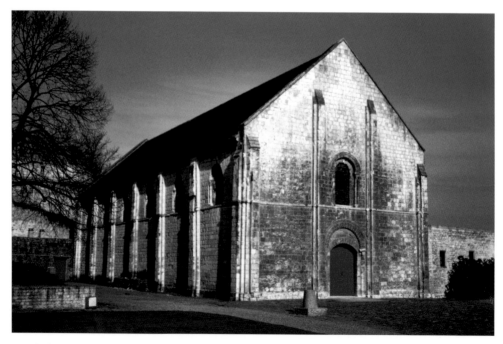

12 The building known as the Treasury at Caen Castle. A perfect example of surviving Norman architecture in Duke William's favourite city

13 Caen, the Abbaye-aux-Hommes. The final resting place of William the Conqueror, this magnificent monument rises above the skyline with spires which seem to represent the very masts of the ships with which the duke achieved his dream

14 The castle at Caen still has some vestiges of the outline plan of the Norman keep. These remains date from the time of Henry I, William's son. William set his castle here in the 1060s

15 Within yards of this outstanding Cathedral church rests the finest historical document of the eleventh century. Bayeux, through its buildings and its 'Tapestry', still exudes a medieval flavour which will stay with it for ever

16 *and* 17 St Valéry-sur-Somme. Looking south along the river towards the modern port (16) and north out to the open sea (17). Wace, writing in the twelfth century, recalled his father telling him that William left St Valery with 696 ships. The original departure point had been the Dives estuary in Normandy, but the ships were blown here by contrary winds

18 *Above left:* An Anglo-Saxon axeman

19 *Above right:* The Bayeux Tapestry shows that mailcoats were put on and taken off over the head. It is quite possible for one man to rid himself of a heavy piece of body armour in a matter of seconds

22 *Above left:* Here, the Anglo-Saxon housecarle carries the famed Dane-axe, which was said to be able to cut through both horse and rider. The shield, being round, is a little old-fashioned for the period, but some are indeed known from the Bayeux Tapestry. *Photograph: Martin Pegler*

23 *Above right:* Re-enactors demonstrate how the shields of the English army would have overlapped to form a shield wall at Hastings. *Photograph: Julie Wileman*

24 *Right:* Caldbec Hill windmill, the traditional point where Harold formed-up his army on the road to Hastings. This was the meeting point of a number of local hundreds and was the site of the hoary apple tree

20 *Opposite below, left:* It is thought that many mailcoats were worn in conjunction with a padded undergarment of some sort. Here, a linen gambeson, lined with fleece, provides adequate protection beneath the mail. *Photograph: Martin Pegler*

21 *Opposite below, right:* An English thegn attends to some repairs. *Photograph: Martin Pegler*

25 The view to the north gives command of the routes through the heavily wooded Weald along which English reinforcements would arrive late in the day of 14 October 1066. Harold expected to march on to Hastings, but was stopped here by William and had to give battle at the end of a narrow ridge at Senlac

26 The lower slopes of the battlefield of Hastings behind most of the Norman lines, looking across towards New Pond and the Horselodge Plantation

27 The field of Hastings from the front of the English lines. The hill in the distance is Telham Hill, where William's army camped before moving out to line the foot of the ridge at Senlac

28 The battlefield of Hastings, looking towards the abbey buildings. Although much truncated by the later buildings, this hill still represents a formidable slope for an attacking army, but King Harold had not intended to go onto the defensive in such a restricted place

29 *Above:* The *malfosse*, or 'evil ditch'. Here, to the north of Caldbec Hill during the chase at the end of the battle, Norman cavalry were deceived by a huge natural feature. Hundreds of them fell to their deaths in an action attributed by some to the arrival of a new English force. The sheer size of Oakwood Gill, the real name of the feature, has meant that many researchers have missed it, preferring to identify the ditch as one of the many smaller ones in the immediate vicinity of the main area of the battlefield

30 *Left:* The monument at the battlefield at Senlac near to where Harold fell is written in French and dedicated to the 'Brave Harold'. It was erected in 1903

31 The Tower of London. Since at least 1016, if not before, the City of London had played a key role in the wars of the age. The traditional duty of Anglo-Saxon Londoners was to accompany and protect the king in his battles. Clearly, after the Conquest, London's role as a centre of power had to be emphasised. So it was here that the mighty White Tower was built

32 The keep was begun in 1077 and the Tower of London became a symbol of Norman power and achievement

The story of the preparations for the most famous amphibious landing in medieval history is fraught with controversy. How did these men get across the Channel? Opinions naturally vary as to exactly how such a feat could possibly have been achieved. This is because all that we know for sure amounts to a mere handful of facts and the rest remains mere interpretation. The facts are as follows: William's invasion fleet initially gathered in the Dives estuary and in some of its neighbouring harbours. This was during the time when Harold's fleet was stationed at the Isle of Wight. At some stage in the late summer the whole fleet moved, for reasons which I shall examine, to St Valéry-sur-Somme undertaking what proved to be a treacherous voyage of some 70 miles. For some considerable time it stayed at St Valéry before finally departing for the crossing of the Channel on the eve of the Feast of St Michael, 28 September. The following morning the fleet arrived at Pevensey in East Sussex. Part of the fleet disembarked and set up a fortification within the walls of the Old Roman Saxon Shore Fort at the abandoned Pevensey which amounted to a fortified reconnaissance-in-force, whilst the rest of the fleet sailed along the coast to Coombe Haven

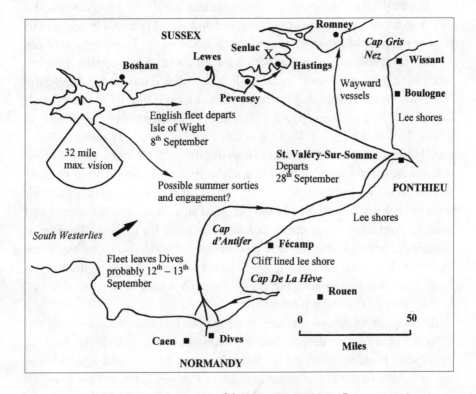

MAP 9 The suggested sequence of the Norman crossing to Pevensey, 1066

in the Bulverhythe estuary near Hastings where the fury of the duke was meted out to the townsfolk, and another fortification, or fortifications, was erected there. What happened next became the most written about battle ever fought on English soil. Before we examine that fateful battle, we must address the untrustworthy business of conjecture whilst making sure that we draw our conclusions from both written evidence and a careful analysis of what was and what was not possible at the time.

As for the treachery of contemporary witnesses, there are two pieces of evidence which might suggest to us a delicious prospect. William's invasion fleet may have been either challenged or in some way blockaded in the English Channel by the forces of Harold's navy, some time prior to its final arrival in desultory fashion at St Valéry-sur-Somme. The Peterborough version of the *Anglo-Saxon Chronicle* states that Harold 'went out against William with a raiding ship army. And meanwhile Earl Tostig came into the Humber with 60 ships'. Of course, it is probable that this passage simply refers to the fact that Harold rode to the Kentish coast not long after hearing that Tostig had press-ganged some of the king's shipmen, but the phrase 'went out against William' is intriguing. Notwithstanding Tostig's intervention, the Norman threat was clearly uppermost in King Harold's mind. To add fuel to the fire of speculation, there is also the mention in the Essex section of the Domesday Book, of a property which once belonged to a certain Æthelric who 'went away to a naval battle with William'. A naval battle? Surely, the compilers of the Domesday Book would not have bothered to record such a claim if it had no basis in fact. Perhaps Æthelric had simply been serving in the fleet at the Isle of Wight and this mention in the Domesday Book merely reflects a popular memory of an important local man's contribution to the war of 1066 without actually indicating that he did anymore fighting than anyone else in the fleet of that year. But it is a troubling reference for those who strive to reconstruct the events of an action-packed summer and autumn. And there is yet more. In a far away place on the river Danube at Neider-Alteich, a scribe wrote in his annal some nine years after the event that there had been a naval engagement between the Aquitainians and the English in the summer after the appearance of a comet in the skies. He said he had learned this from participants.[6]

We may never know for sure if there had been an encounter in the Channel in 1066 but despite his later reputation, one which has suffered many scars from the sharpest blades of Norman propaganda, King Harold was nobody's fool when it came to military matters. Certainly, we know of the limitations of keeping an English fleet in service and of the necessity to disband it at the end of its tour of duty (and indeed when the fleet was disbanded on 8 September, most sources agree that it had run out of supplies). This much is unquestionable. Its departure from the Isle of Wight, however, may just have been accompanied by a sense of confidence in the English high command as it rode back to London, that William would surely not come before the Channel gales of October set in. This might have been a confidence born from the knowledge that something had happened earlier which had demonstrated to William that his crossing would be somewhat against the odds. The notion that William's fleet may well have headed to the south coast of England directly from Dives-sur-Mer only to encounter a retiring English fleet on its way east up the Channel is perhaps pressing the case too far since it is difficult to place William's departure earlier than 12-13 September, a good four or five days after the English abandonment of the Isle of Wight. It is dangerous to suggest that the idea of a naval encounter might explain the confused and desultory manner in which William's fleet arrived at St Valéry-sur-Somme. The port, in fact, held wrecking rights because of its notable position on a windblown coast, where its townsfolk had in the past greatly benefited from foundered vessels. There is also the chronicler's statement that when the remnants of the English fleet arrived in London, they did so mourning the loss of many compatriots. The strongest likelihood is that appalling weather accounted for most of the casualties of both the Norman and the English fleets.

If the *Carmen de Hastingæ Proelio* (a work thought to have been written around 1070 by Guy, bishop of Amiens) is to be believed, then the weather had a profound effect on the whole naval campaign.[7] The rain at Dives was apparently torrential. Even when the fleet had arrived at St Valéry, the skies were said to be hidden by clouds and rain. The physical reason for this was then and still is now the Atlantic lows which frequently bedevil maritime traffic in the English Channel. The south-westerlies which arise from these lows have the effect of producing dangerous shorelines for any fleet trying to cross the Channel from south to north. These dangerous stretches of coastline are known as 'lee shores', due to the fact that the wind could blow a ship aground here. It was upon one of these that Earl Harold had found himself in 1064 after a difficult crossing. The shores are perfectly simple to identify.[8] The first of them which will have been a major concern to the commanders of William's fleet was the stretch of cliff-lined coast between Cap de la Hève and Cap d'Antifer. Anything driven ashore here would be permanently lost. Next, as the shoreline curves away to the north-east and then turns northwards towards a point at Cap Gris Nez, the lee shores of the Somme estuary would have been a great danger, as indeed the Norman fleet discovered. William of Poitiers tells us that the journey between Dives and St Valéry was characterised by westerly winds which brought the fleet to its destination and that there had been drownings along the way as well as desertions. The dead, he said, were secretly buried so as not to affect morale. It hardly sounds as if this part of the operation had been planned.

The fleet apparently left the Dives estuary when it finally received a southern wind sometime in early to mid-September, although nobody seems to be able to agree on the precise day. Somewhere in the middle of the Channel, the wind changed to a strong westerly. Regardless of whether there had been an encounter with the English, the Normans clearly made a decision to turn to the east with the wind behind them and risk the lee shores in search of a safe harbour. But they crashed into the shores of the Somme estuary just a day or so later. The decision to leave Dives may have been inspired by the duke's desire to prevent desertions by putting-out to sea at the first sign of a southerly wind on an evening high tide. His target may have been directly to the north, perhaps even the Southampton area with a view to marching on Winchester, but it would certainly not be here that the duke would ultimately land. At St Valéry, the fleet remained for well over two weeks, waiting once again for a favourable wind to take them to England.

The time at St Valéry was spent partially in prayer and partially in the reparation of the damage to the vessels sustained in the first abortive attempt at a crossing. William of Poitiers says that the duke went so far as to bring out from the cathedral the bones of St Valéry himself to ensure that the contrary wind became a favourable one. It is hard to know if this one act, which William of Poitiers records for us, really took place. If it did, it might have been the duke's masterstroke. During the daytime of 28 September, William must have known that the wind was changing or at least had a strong indication either from local mariners or his own shipmen that it might soon do so. By presenting the bones of St Valéry to his troops shortly before the wind changed, the effect on the morale of the nervous and tired troops would have been extraordinary.

So, a southerly wind at last arrived on 28 of September, the night before the Feast of St Michael. But it is not possible to sail from the Somme estuary when the tide is out as there are miles of flats at this time. William wanted to arrive in England on the morning of the day following his departure in order to maximise the time he would need to disembark and fortify his position. Besides, he wanted to be able to see the shore that he was approaching. As they watched the tide flood into the harbour of St Valéry, the Normans' spirits must have lifted. The fleet stood out to sea, each vessel with a lantern attached to its mast, late in the evening of 28 September; the sky was clear, but the moon had set. The fleet anchored not far out to sea and the ships gathered as close as they could get to William's flagship, the *Mora*. The call to set sail for England would come from the horns and lanterns of the duke's ship as and when he thought that the fleet was in good enough order and the timing was right. The last thing William wanted was to land in the dark.

In the event, despite losing contact with the *Mora* at one stage, the fleet did indeed reach England, arriving in the morning light at Pevensey. However not all of them were present. It had been a tough job keeping order on the voyage and some ships are known to have left the fleet and fetched-up on the shores of England at Romney, perhaps when the wind had changed back to a south-westerly. These crews paid the price for falling foul of the weather and were annihilated by local forces. It was an act that William would not forget after Hastings. We cannot be sure whether Pevensey was the intended arrival point,[9] or whether it was meant to be the heartlands of Harold's Sussex estates to the west or even the Steyning estate seized by Harold from the monks of Fécamp Abbey. But on the morning of 29 September 1066 it was at Pevensey, inside the Roman Saxon Shore Fort, that William set his first temporary fortification, untroubled by the attentions of either a fleet or an army. William of Malmesbury said that the duke stumbled upon disembarking on the beach, but that his retainers had told him not to worry, because he would soon be king.[10] A duke had arrived to claim a kingdom.

14

THE ROAD STOPPED SHORT

The coast upon which William landed bears little resemblance to its modern descendant.[1] Centuries of land reclamation have meant that Pevensey is now some miles from the modern coastline of East Sussex. It is an amusing irony that today the shingle beaches of the shore are lined not only with the usual seaside houses and shops, but with the carefully positioned Martello towers of the late eighteenth and early nineteenth centuries, designed to defend the coast against a seaborne aggressor in the form of the fleet of Napoleon Bonaparte. But in September 1066, what had recently been a defended coastline was now devoid of a significant Anglo-Saxon military presence.

Understanding the eleventh-century landscape in the area between Pevensey, Hastings and Battle is crucial to unlocking the secrets of the battle of Hastings. When William set his fortification at Pevensey, he did so at the head of a bay, an area whose former lagoon had now become an uncrossable salt marsh with tidal inlets. Some of these ancient inlets stretched as far inland as Catsfield and Ninfield, some 5 miles or so from the modern coast.

If the Norman garrison at Pevensey wished to march to Hastings by land, their journey would begin by heading west for a considerable distance before turning round to the north and then to the east along a difficult coastline in order to eventually link up with the road which led to Hastings a mile or two to the north-east of Catsfield. From there they would be able to march down the ridgeway for 7 miles until they reached the famous old settlement of the English shipmen, where their

The Normans land at Hastings. *Bayeux Tapestry*

compatriots had now landed. The fact that there is a place called Standard
Hill in Ninfield has often been taken by the local people there to indicate
that it was here that the Normans landed, right at the extreme north-east
of Pevensey Bay. It is unlikely that the tidal inlet reached quite as far as
Ninfield in the sense that it could accommodate an amphibious landing,
but it is interesting nevertheless. It is quite probable that at some stage
during the Hastings campaign the Pevensey garrison came from their
fortification and passed through Ninfield, on their way to join with their
compatriots who had come from Hastings.

The strongest probability for the sequence of events as hinted at by
the sources, is that William left a sizeable armoured reconnaissance force
at Pevensey, secure in its fortifications and surrounded by supplies and
equipment. Then, as the *Carmen,* the *Anglo-Saxon Chronicle*, the Bayeux
Tapestry and William of Poitiers indicate, he sailed to Hastings. In fact, 'as
soon as they were fit' says the *Anglo-Saxon Chronicle*. The voyage would
have taken place at high tide and took just two hours from Pevensey
to the Bulverhythe estuary where at Coombe Haven the fleet moored.
The estuary here is adjacent to Hastings and provides perfect mooring
conditions with gentle rises and flat beaches flanked by sharper rising
ground. William will also have been told that Hastings was the beginning
of the road to London. If he could secure the town, then he would at least
have the option of following that road to the north before he decided
what to do next. Very soon the defenceless town was overwhelmed by the
Norman soldiers. William then ordered the construction of a fortification
on a mound or motte, which dominated the settlement and was a secure

store for further supplies. Analysis of the relative values of the neighbouring manors in the Hastings area as recorded in the Domesday Book has shown beyond all doubt that William's forces devastated the region. It has been suggested that the reason for this was that William knew Harold's reputation for haste and that William was gambling on Harold's precipitate reaction to the news that Sussex was being wrecked by the Normans. Certainly, it turned out that Harold was indeed quick to head south, but the idea that he did so because his homeland was being destroyed should be set against the fact that the only holding he had in the immediate vicinity of the marauding Normans was the parish of Crowhurst. Harold's lands were further west. Whilst those lands may originally have been the destination for the Dives fleet, William's reduction of the area around Hastings could well have been a necessity as opposed to a cunning plan. Nevertheless, Harold would have been unhappy about what was going on around the town. The shipmen of Hastings, we should not forget, may well have been with him when he heard the news.

There is something else about the countryside around Hastings which is worthy of consideration. In 1066 the town sat at the coastal end of what for a military force must be considered something of a peninsula. It was bounded on the west by the Bulverhythe estuary and on the east by a now disappeared shoreline which turned north from the Fairlight cliffs. It was further bounded to the north by the Brede estuary which stretched inland as far as Sedlescombe, and whose width was of greater consequence and encumbrance then than it is now. All this meant that, while William was protected on three sides by sea and river, he would have to use the ridgeway road to London to get out of the peninsula and into the hinterland. Harold, by the same token, would have to enter the area along the same route if he wished to trap his enemy.

So, where do we suppose that the two commanders really intended to do their fighting? The answer must be that somewhere along the road to Hastings, as dictated by the constraints of the landscape, a battle would take place. This is exactly what happened, although it is not quite as simple as that. The two commanders wanted different things. For William, it was crucial that he have a quick decision now that he was in a hostile landscape. For Harold, fresh from a stunning victory where surprise and speed had been his chief allies, the notion that a second great invader might be driven into the sea in the same way as before, must have been uppermost in his mind. So, to answer the question fully, let us leave the smouldering fires of William's camp at Hastings and join Harold's jubilant crowd of exhausted but happy warriors in the north of England shortly after the protector

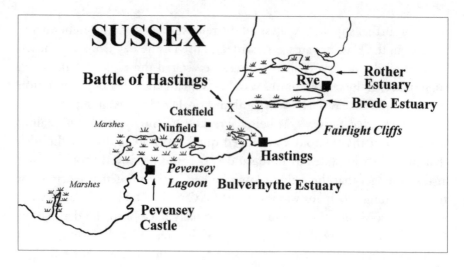

MAP 10 The Sussex coastline in 1066

of the English kingdom had defeated and killed one of the most famous warriors of the northern world. What was Harold thinking?

The news that William had landed 250 miles away from where Harold was camped must surely have come as a shock to the English king. If, as is likely, he was in York when he received it,[2] then it will have reached him on or around 1 October. His reaction to the news is hardly in dispute. He did not hesitate and well within two weeks he was in London, perhaps even by 11 October. He had covered 190 miles at around 20 miles each day. Generally speaking, a march of 20 miles in a day is considered about right for an army of the pre-mechanised era. Here, however, Harold achieved this feat day after day with the same men and horses.[3] He would have to cut his rest periods and start marching early in the morning, finishing late in the evening each day. It was one of the most notable forced marches of history.

The days between Stamford Bridge and Hastings are difficult to account for because the sources are quiet on the subject, but there are possibilities suggested by both William of Malmesbury and Ordericus Vitalis. On Harold's march south, William of Malmesbury alone tells us that there were some desertions on the English side. These had come about due to the king's reluctance to share his booty from Stamford Bridge with his men. He had instead instructed Edwin and Morcar to take it to London.[4] The twelfth-century historian is insistent that other people's ideas of the great size of Harold's army were incorrect. He had with him just his stipendary troops, his housecarles, mercenaries and very few fyrdsmen from the shires. If this was true, there is still no reason to suspect that the force was in any way small. Even with just these troops the army would have been large enough to do the job expected of it.

When he reached London the king took little rest. Tradition relates that Harold stopped at Waltham Abbey, of which he was patron, and gave prayers. He is supposed to have spent several days in London summoning an army and in all probability was heavily engaged in reconstituting his navy. In London, according to Ordericus, there was a conversation between Harold's mother and the king. Gytha had not wanted Harold to fight. His brother Gyrth was also concerned that by fighting against William the king would gain a reputation as an oath breaker,[5] and so offered to lead the army into Sussex himself. The offer was, of course, refused by the king. It may well have been Gyrth's intention to lead the army into the struggle so that the king could have a second chance if things went wrong, but it seems that the idea was not entertained. In a move which has earned him countless critics over the centuries, Harold left London with his army before he had been joined by reinforcements. Much has been written about why Harold should have been so precipitate. Much has been said about why he could not have expected help from Edwin and Morcar, a view based loosely on the argument that these two men were at the head of depleted and demoralised forces which were unable to fight again against a foreign foe. In the past, there had clearly been tension between the houses of Leofric and Godwin, but to argue for its continuance in 1066 is to push the case too far. Edwin and Morcar would continue to play a part in the campaign. There is much that we still do not know about their relationship with their brother-in-law the king, but they had already shown on two separate occasions[6] in 1066 that they were prepared to work with him for the protection of the kingdom.

Harold may well have detailed Edwin and Morcar to follow him, but he clearly had a sense of urgency about him. He had a track record of speeding through the countryside and surprising his enemies. as Gruffydd ap Llewelyn and Harold Siggurdson had both discovered to their cost. He wanted to do it again. If he could trap William at his camp at Hastings, he might drive him into the sea with a hammer blow which would smash him against the anvil of a reconstituted English fleet. In fact, William of Jumièges is insistent that Harold had planned a night surprise on William's camp because he says that the duke had ordered his men to be prepared for it. And what, do we suppose, is the best way to avoid being surprised? By not being where your enemy expects you to be, perhaps. Moreover, there are hints in the sources that Harold had indeed planned to send the ships once again from London to cut off a Norman retreat. William of Poitiers is most clear on the matter:

> ...the king in his fury had hastened his march, particularly because he had learned of the devastation around the Norman camp. He intended

to surprise them and to crush them in a nocturnal or surprise attack. And in case they took to flight he had armed a fleet of seven hundred boats to ambush them on the sea.

The *Carmen* is no less emphatic, recording a conversation between William and a monk which probably took place when the duke had already left Hastings and was camped at Telham Hill:

> The duke said 'Where is the king?' 'Not far off', answered the monk. He said to him in his ear: 'You can see the standards!... He hopes to be able to take you by surprise; by sea and by land he is planning great battles. He is said to have sent five hundred ships to sea to hinder our voyage back.'

Of Harold's urgency John of Worcester has this to say and more besides:

> Thereat the king at once, and in great haste, marched his army towards London; and though he well knew that some of the bravest Englishmen had fallen in his two [former] battles, and that one half of his army had not yet arrived, he did not hesitate to advance with all speed into South Saxony [Sussex] against his enemies; and on Saturday the 11th of the kalends of September [22 October],[7] before a third of his army was in order for fighting, he joined battle with them nine miles from Hastings, where they had fortified a castle. But inasmuch as the English were drawn-up in a narrow place, many retired from the ranks and very few remained true to him.

This little passage is packed with meaning. There are a few things here which we should hold on to for the moment. With half an army Harold marched from London into Sussex. Before a third of that half-army had even deployed, battle commenced. Fighting took place along a restricted front which meant that many of the still great numbers of Englishmen could not bring their weapons to bear on the enemy and retired to the rear. The *Anglo-Saxon Chronicles*, which were closely followed by John, say the same thing, of course. The Worcester manuscript says that

> Then this became known to King Harold [the building of the fortification at Hastings] and he gathered a great raiding army and came against him at the grey apple tree.[8] And William came upon him [Harold] by surprise before his people were marshalled. Nevertheless, the king fought very hard against him with those men who wanted to support him and there was great slaughter on either side.

and the Peterborough version declares that William had surprised Harold 'before all his raiding army had come'.[9] So, at Caldbec Hill, the site of the grey, or 'hoary' apple tree, a known meeting point in the shire, a surprise was sprung upon Harold before he was ready. The road to Hastings had stopped several miles short of its destination for the English king. How had the tables been turned on Harold? Where is the secret to William's success? At what stage did either side discover the precise whereabouts of the other? For the answer to this question, let us examine the curious exchange of messages proposed by the *Carmen* and in particular by William of Poitiers.

The duke himself must have talked at great length to Harold during their time together in Normandy in 1064 about military strategy. He knew his enemy well. In fact, William was visited whilst he was at his camp by a Breton minister of the late King Edward, a man named Robert Fitz Wimarc who told the duke that if he ventured into the countryside he would most likely be swamped by the English numbers which would shortly bear down upon him and that he should stay behind his fortifications. The duke was unimpressed. Had he listened to the advice, he might have lost the campaign.[10] It must have been around about this time that William became convinced that he needed a quick decision. He had to get out of the bottleneck that he was in before Harold could trap him in it. What made him think this way was probably down to the information he had received through intelligence. Scouts are known to have been used on both sides, but there is something else which might have held the key for William and that was the information he gained during the pre-battle embassies. In short, we are told that Harold sent an embassy to William in the form of a trusted monk. The monk gave William the king's message that he should leave the kingdom now that Harold had been given it. He received a predictable reply. An official Norman response was sent to the king the following day. To this Harold replied famously with words to the effect that it would be God who would decide the fate of the armies on the following day. Let us take a closer look at what the sources actually say because it is in the timing of these exchanges that the secret lurks. Beneath the formalities of ambassadorial greetings, two generals were carefully at work, finding out about each other's position and condition before battle.

William of Poitiers says that Harold's monk approached the Norman camp while the duke was inspecting the guards of the ships. On hearing of the monk's arrival it was the duke himself who went up to him, pretending to be his own seneschal. This first conversation is not recorded, because after the monk had been taken into the camp and given hospitality he was then asked on the very next day to repeat the message that he had given William the day before, this time in front of a gathered assembly. This message[11] contained Harold's frank admission that King Edward had indeed offered the kingship some time ago to William. Harold recalled making an oath to the duke too. But it was the strength of the deathbed promise which Harold told William reigned supreme over the issue. William must leave the kingdom or Harold would be forced to act. After hearing the message in public, William asked the monk to go back to Harold with his own embassy Hugh Margot,[12] a monk from Fécamp Abbey who would carry the duke's response. This response was emphatic. William had been made heir to the throne by Edward. The dukes of Normandy had cared for Edward and Alfred during their exile. The leading men of England including Godwin, Leofric, Stigand and Siward had all sworn an oath to receive William as lord after Edward's death. Hostages had been given from the house of Godwin. Harold had been sent himself to Normandy to reaffirm the oath and had even given surety in writing on the matter. After making a plea to have his case heard either in a Norman or an English court, the duke's response ended with the celebrated offer of single combat between the two of them.

Where was Harold when this message was received? We do not know for sure, but it is interesting that William of Poitiers says that at this time the English king 'was approaching' when he heard the response. He was still on the move and had not yet arrived at the place where he intended to fight. 'We will continue our advance', the king is supposed to have said. 'Let the Lord decide today between William and myself according to justice', he added. As the monk was hearing Harold's words, Norman scouts had found their enemy and had reported back to William its position. There is a slight sense of panic in the description of the Norman camp at this time. For William of Poitiers, the duke of Normandy could do no wrong. The author of the *Gesta Wilelmi* was an appalling sycophant. Yet here it seems that William had been genuinely surprised by Harold's speed. Some soldiers were out foraging, others were ordered quickly to don their armour. William himself put his on so quickly that he had worn it inside out. A rallying speech was then delivered to the troops which William of Poitiers records with bellicose writing, but in the speech are these words:

There is no way of escape: on the one hand, an army and an unknown and hostile countryside bar the way, on the other, a navy and the sea.

Harold had surprised William. The road to London was blocked. But William must quickly block the road to Hastings, he must steal the final march. He set out from his camp in an order of march which reflected the way in which he wished to deploy. At the front, the crossbowmen and bowmen, behind them the heavy infantry and in the rear the cavalry. A combined arms force of quality soldiers all, according to William of Poitiers, marching beneath a papal banner.[13] The author then goes on to describe the English army as a huge force, bolstered it seemed by the forces of the Danes. He suggests that the English were frightened of the Normans and had therefore camped on higher ground on a hill close to the forest through which they had marched. They had sent their horses to the rear and went on foot into battle. The duke 'in no way frightened by the difficulty of the place, began slowly to climb the steep slope'. Whereupon the battle commenced. William of Poitiers' story is similar to that in the *Carmen*, but there are important differences. The *Carmen* indicates that the conversation between William and his own monk, in which the duke was told of Harold's intent to catch William by surprise, took place when both armies were in sight of each other. The *Carmen* also has a hill which was seized by the English, who went on to fight the battle on foot.

So, for all his speed, Harold had been caught out at his forming-up point. Somewhere to the north, marching through the thickly wooded Sussex countryside, were reinforcements expecting to rendezvous with the king at the Caldbec Hill forming-up point and also expecting, like Harold himself, to march a further six or so miles in good order to be at Hastings for the surprise attack. Harold had been out-generalled by the only man in Christendom capable of doing so.

15

DECISION AT SENLAC

And so to the battle itself. As William was deploying at the foot of Senlac Ridge[1] he will have felt quietly confident. Harold's army was being sent from Caldbec Hill down a narrow bottleneck to deploy along a ridge incapable of accommodating even half of it. But the upshot of Harold's deployment would be that he had blocked William's route to London. This would not have bothered William too much, for he had blocked Harold's road to Hastings. Whilst the English warriors streamed down what is now Battle High Street and fell in behind a constricted front rank, William's confidence will have been tempered by the notion that he would have to fight a battle quite unlike any which he had ever fought before. What made it so peculiar was the geography of the place. William of Poitiers states that the duke was not necessarily put off 'by the difficulty of the place', but now that he had brought the English onto him on a more even numerical match than he was told to expect, he had only one option left to him due to the steep ravines on either side of the ridge and the absolute impossibility of turning the English flanks. He must fight in the most direct and costly manner known to military men: he must execute a frontal assault.

The numerous sources vary on the nature of William's deployment. Anything between three and five divisions were arrayed at the foot of the slope. William of Poitiers' statement that the duke's force marched with light infantry at its head, followed by heavy infantry and then cavalry is perfectly consistent with what one might expect from an organised combined arms force of the period and this is perhaps the order of march as it was when William left his temporary encampment on Telham Hill.[2] In fact, William of Poitiers was a military man himself and this much should not be forgotten. He may not have been at Hastings and his work is littered with embarrassing sycophancies, but his descriptions of marches, deployment and battle details are to be ignored at the historian's peril. William's account provides the backbone for the following analysis, but where it is necessary to diverge, the words of others are brought into the argument. For example, Wace, in his *Roman de Rou* of the later twelfth century, gives a most explicit account of the duke's deployment. The Bretons were on the left flank accompanied by the men of Poitou (the Aquitainians of some sources) and the men of Maine who had flocked to the duke's standards. In the centre were the units of the duke himself with a few of his own men having spilled over to the division on the right flank under the command of Roger of Montgomery and William FitzOsbern.[3] Here on the right flank too were the men of Boulogne, of Poux in Picardy and probably some Flemings.

It is a matter of some regret that we know next to nothing about the deployment of the English forces. To William of Malmesbury we owe the notion that Harold planted his standards on the highest part of the slope as well he might, but it was not here that he would fall. Gyrth, Leofwine and Harold would have had their direct commands at Hastings but the restriction of the ground and the steep ravines to either side will have prevented them from deploying them anywhere other than along the ridge, consequently leaving them with no flexibility in command and control. Effectively, they were rooted to the spot.[4]

So, there they stood. An English army lined the ridge at Senlac. This immovable object was set to receive an unstoppable force. It would take all day long for a resolution to be found.[5] If we look beyond the words of William of Poitiers, we find more than a handful of references to a most extraordinary opening exchange in the first moments of the battle of Hastings. Whoever Taillefer's parents were, they must have despaired when the young juggler had told them what he would do when he got to England. Henry of Huntingdon has it that this young Norman knight approached the English lines juggling his sword before the enemy, killed one of their standard bearers as the rest stood stupefied, repeated the trick and was then killed himself. Gaimar contends that it was a lance with which Taillefer juggled, catching it by the head and throwing it into the English lines. Then came the sword trick and the maiming of an Englishman before both he and his mount were killed. The *Carmen* simply has him throwing his sword into the air and killing one man, proudly displaying his head. Wace has him too but, whatever he was up to, his bravado seems not to have lasted for long. He was the first casualty of the battle of Hastings, swallowed whole by the English phalanx.

Despite the curious Taillefer episode, it was in fact the sound of trumpets on both sides which heralded the beginning of England's most famous battle. If William of Poitiers is to be believed, the first assault on the English position came from Norman infantrymen, probably the bowmen and crossbowmen. But they got too close. The English infantrymen above them met their enemy with a deluge of missiles, said to include javelins, axes and clubs.[6] Henry of Huntingdon also agrees with the idea that there was preparatory archery from the Normans and he says that, due to the density of the English formation, it was all to no avail. It is a view which chimes perfectly with other accounts of the constricted nature of the place. Interestingly, the *Carmen* suggests the onset of battle came rather quicker than even William had expected: it had been his intention to place his cavalry in the front so that they could affect their well-known shock charge but, in the event, it was the more traditional opening which went ahead. Soon it was clear that the mounted knights were needed not to frontally assault the English line in this instance, but to relieve the pressure on the infantry who had got themselves into trouble close to the English line. Hacking with swords at those who had stepped forward from the English line, the Norman horsemen managed to split their comrades from the enemy who still stood resolute on the ridge. The first significant casualty in the battle of Hastings had been William's plan.

There had been quite a struggle in this opening exchange. The weaponry of the English, largely spears, had been recorded as easily piercing the armour of the Normans and the cavalry had come to the rescue in a manoeuvre which was described by William of Poitiers in terms of an ordered exchange of ranks, bowmen retiring through the advancing horsemen. Even at this early stage of the battle both William of Poitiers and the *Carmen* note the densely packed English formation. So constricted were the warriors that the dead could not even fall to the ground:

> Nor did the dead give place to living soldiers, for each corpse though lifeless stood as if unharmed and held its post; nor would the attackers have been able to penetrate the dense forest of Englishmen had not guile reinforced their strength.[7]

This statement is a natural pointer to one of the most contentious aspects of the battle of Hastings. Did the Normans at any stage attempt to put into effect the feigned flight, a tactic known by horsemen across Christendom, and thereby lure the English in pockets off the ridge?[8] The *Carmen* is not alone in suggesting that there had been a tactical ruse on the part of the Norman horsemen. William of Poitiers has it occurring more than once (in fact, once by accident and twice on purpose); Henry of Huntingdon says it happened, too; Wace has it occurring only after Harold is wounded, and the *Brevis Relatio* is another source which assigns to the event a note of misfortune. We must remember that the duke was restricted to frontal assaults. When they did not work, the natural tendency would have been to retreat and try again. According to William of Poitiers in the first instance it was the Breton cavalry and auxiliary troops on the left wing who fell back relatively early in the battle. This caused almost all the army to yield because William was afraid that his own left flank had become exposed. It was clearly an unplanned and unwelcome episode for the duke. In fact, during this most shaky moment, the duke himself had to personally rally his troops and prevent some of them from fleeing since rumour had it that their leader was dead. It is a scene famously depicted on the Bayeux Tapestry where the duke's helmet is drawn up so that his men can clearly see him. Had King Harold unleashed all his men from the ridge at this one moment, then the history of England would have been quite different. Still they stood there, resolute and undaunted.

The duke must have realised that the repeated frontal assaults were not working. It may well have been the case that he decided to opt for mounted tactics which did not rely upon the shock value of a charge, but instead involved the drawing off of the English infantry with the harassing effect of hurled javelins from horseback. In fact, it seems that William had indeed learned that this could be done by his observation of the Breton near disaster on the left flank. Soon, a whole host of Englishmen were brought down from the ridge and cut off on the famous hillock to the south of the ridge. It is a moot point as to whether this episode is the one depicted on the Bayeux Tapestry, but it does at least come roughly at the right moment in the narrative to suggest that the designer knew what had had happened here. But for William difficulties would continue. He is said to have been unhorsed three times in these struggles as his first wave of troops fell back on his own cavalry. It must have seemed impossible that the English would ever be dislodged. Towards the end of his account, the usually reliable William of Poitiers runs out of steam and leaps to the death of Harold and the aftermath of the battle, so in order to find out what might have happened in the later stages of the battle we have to turn to the words of others.

Norman Cavalry and English Infantry in the thick of the struggle. *Bayeux Tapestry*

The incident on the hillock. *Bayeux Tapestry*

Shortly after the successful feigned flights, the *Carmen* recalls that William and Earl Gyrth faced each other on the field. We can never know if this happened, but we do know that Gyrth failed to survive the battle. One of Gyrth's javelins felled the duke's horse and William was reduced to having to face Gyrth on foot. It seems, according to the author of the *Carmen,* that William thought that he had had a lucky encounter with the king himself:

'Take the crown you have earned from us! If my horse is dead, thus I requite you – as a common soldier.'

The ensuing mêlée cost Gyrth his life and the duke escaped from it only after seizing the nasal guard on the helmet of a passing mounted knight and pulling him off his horse to use the beast himself. The heat of battle is of course a confusing place,[9] but would William really have been unable to identify Harold? They had known each other very well. It may be the case that Gyrth did indeed look like Harold, but Harold may well have been wearing the armour given him by William which William might well have recognised.[10] Poor Gyrth, for it had been he who had advised his brother in London to let him take the field with the king's army. According to Wace, it was Gyrth who had said to Harold at the moment that they received intelligence of William's whereabouts, not to wait any longer because this might be bad for morale. Harold had apparently wanted to wait for the reinforcements he was expecting at the forming-up point. And Gyrth lay dead at the foot of his own standard. It is an interesting point that Wace gives so much credence to the role of Gyrth. He seems to have been responsible for much of the precipitate actions of the English forces. Could it be the case that Harold, quick through the landscape as he was, was not in fact the hothead that some historians have suggested?

The *Carmen* suggests that from this stage in the battle the Normans had the edge in the war of attrition. The casualties were beginning to tell on the English. It is now that Harold seems to have moved his standards to the eastern flank of his army, away from the summit. Here the slope of Senlac Ridge is at its shallowest. Here too there was trouble in the depleting English ranks. And here it is said, according to the *Brevis Relatio*, that the high altar of Battle Abbey was set, for reasons which will shortly become apparent. Harold had at last moved into the front line. The *Carmen* recalls that the duke spotted Harold 'far off on the slopes [indicating that he had indeed come forward] of the hill, fiercely hewing to pieces the Normans who were besetting him.' The very sight of the king made the leading Normans break from what they were doing and head to this section of the line. This was the last stand, the most renowned final stand in all of English history. The fighting was at its thickest and volleys of arrows were ordered to be shot into the English lines at high trajectory. Harold and his housecarles were stoutly resisting the Normans, but four of the enemy would get through to the standards. In fact, an attempt was made by Robert, son of Erneis to do just that. He raced forward to grab the standard, but his action was premature. He was cut down and killed there and later his body was found at the foot of the fallen English standard. But others did get there. A blow to Harold's breast, a decapitation, the earth drenched with a torrent of blood, a lance through the stomach and a leg removed. One of the knights responsible for the mutilation was even deprived of his rewards, so great was the violation of the body of a king. Under the wheeling heavens, which turned a dark day into darker twilight, the king of England was killed. Perhaps, at some stage, Harold had indeed been struck in the eye by an arrow, but this is not how he died. The incident is given a great amount of attention and it certainly seems to have an early root in the sources,[11] but it was this final infantry assault which would mean the most to posterity. The standard of the fighting man, Harold's own personal standard, was taken by the Normans and later sent to the pope.

Harold Godwinson, the protector of the English kingdom, a man who through the necessity of an extraordinary national emergency had been anointed as king, lay shattered in pieces upon Senlac Ridge, his body cruelly dismembered. It does not matter which argument one thinks is the strongest. This was an ignominious end for a proud and successful man. The guilt of the victors at Hastings has never disappeared and nor has the sadness. It is impossible not to feel some extraordinary emotions when we walk the modern-day battlefield at Battle. If we take a view of overt nationality, a view relentlessly pursued by E.A. Freeman, then for English people the emotion is very strong indeed. Something extraordinary happened that day, something shocking. That is why neither side could ever forget it.

But it is to the words of Sir Frank Stenton that we must turn, since he in one sentence seems to have summed up exactly what Hastings was all about: 'he [Harold] lost the battle because his men were unequal to the stress of a purely defensive engagement too long protracted'.[12] No student of the battle of Hastings should let this statement pass them by. This is precisely what happened. This is why the battle was so unusually long. Harold had not intended to fight a defensive action on Senlac Ridge. He had been caught close to his forming-up point. He had not even intended to do any fighting at all there but William had.

The death of Harold and of his brothers marked the end. A medieval army without a leader is a defeated army. Men took flight as quickly as they could, grabbing horses or just running like the wind. The line of the English retreat has been argued over for centuries. It need not have caused such a fuss, because the answer is obvious. They went back they same way they had come. Back along the narrow neck of land which leads up to the Caldbec Hill forming-up place, over that hill and along the road to London they scampered. Yet the battle was not yet over. There was to be one more extraordinary twist in the tale which would send historians into a 900-year spin and it centred on a topographical feature which became known as the *malfosse* or 'bad ditch', so named by the Normans because of the calamity which befell them there.

The incident at the *malfosse* is recorded by at least five of our medieval historians. William of Poitiers says that the Normans, though unacquainted with the countryside, rode after the English until the latter found renewed confidence, having discovered an excellent position on a steep bank with numerous ditches. William of Jumièges explained that the long grass had hidden from the Normans an ancient causeway into which they suddenly fell with horses and armour, one on top of the other. William of Malmesbury is a little more helpful. He says that the English got possession of an eminence and drove down the Normans as they strove to gain the higher ground. The English had got there by a short passage known to them, avoiding a deep ditch and they trod under foot so many Normans as to make the hollow level with the plain. The twelfth-century *Chronicle of Battle Abbey* actually

The rout of the English. *Bayeux Tapestry*

gives the place its name, *malfosse*. 'Between the two armies lay a dreadful chasm', it says. It was a wide open ravine which seemed to the author to have been caused either by a natural cleft or by having been hollowed out by storms. It was overgrown with bushes and brambles and not noticeable to the Normans until it was too late. But to Ordericus Vitalis we owe perhaps the fullest account. Here it is:

> Long grasses concealed an ancient rampart, and as the Normans came galloping up, they fell, one on top of the other, in a struggling mass of horses and arms. At this courage returned to the fleeing English. Seeing that they could be sheltered by the broken rampart and labyrinth of ditches they reformed their ranks and unexpectedly made a stand inflicting heavy slaughter on the Normans. There Engenulf, castellan of Laigle and many others fell; and as survivors relate, about 15,000 [*sic*] Normans met their doom.[13]

Arguments have raged over the location of this famous ditch, which of course should still be visible today. It is still discernible and in fact, it is so huge that it is easy to miss. In the 1850s it was suggested that the ditch lay north-west of the modern town of Battle, and then E.A. Freeman chose a ditch behind Battle church as its location, a place which is not unlikely to have seen some sort of action being so close to the battlefield itself. The ditch here is small however. Francis Baring, writing in 1906, placed the ditch on the western side of the battlefield and, for some time, here at Manser's Shaw was the famous *malfosse*. Something still did not sit quite right. Why would an army positioned on a narrow isthmus choose to flee sideways into difficult countryside when they were defeated? Surely an army retreats the way it came? So, the logical place for the *malfosse* would be to the north of the battlefield in the direction of the routeways which had led the English army to Caldbec Hill and then on to Senlac Ridge.[14] We must remember that William, despite the death of Harold and his brothers, will have known that it was essential to hold the enemy camp and baggage after the battle. It seems that after the fall of the king Eustace of Boulogne, who was closely involved in that struggle, rode up what is now Battle High Street, following the contours along modern Mount Street, climbed the hill at Caldbec and then pushed further north, giving chase in what was proving to be difficult countryside. As the Norman cavalry galloped across what is now Virgin's Lane, the slope down which they were travelling suddenly opened into a chasm of massive proportions. This place is known as Oakwood Gill and its dimensions are extraordinary; so big that it is easily missable, being partially removed from everyday

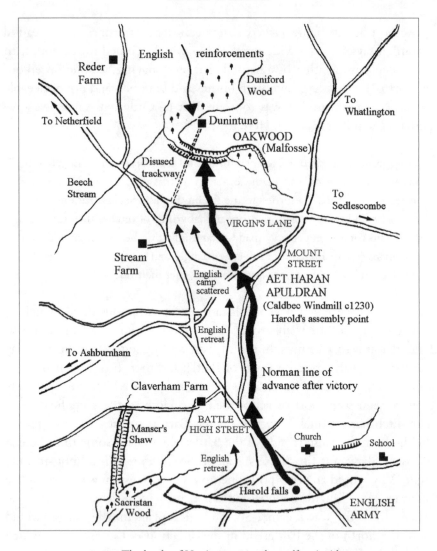

MAP II The battle of Hastings 1066 – the *malfosse* incident

view by the modern road to Hastings which is built over the ditch at an impressive height. The ditch runs right across the northernmost sector of the battlefield of Hastings. It is precisely the place where one might expect a disaster in the chase.

Some problems remain in the interpretation of the whole incident. It is a military fact that, in medieval armies, leaderless troops in rout are utterly incapable of rallying unless they are brought into direct contact with a friendly command who is himself unbroken. And yet several of our medieval historians suggest that the English (some of whom seem to have known about the ditch) were revived in their morale enough to make a stand. This is extremely unusual. It could only have happened if the men who lined the ditch were under new command. In fact, William of Poitiers goes as far as suggesting the duke himself believed this to be the case. It is more probable than possible that the *malfosse* action was masterminded on the English side by a commander who had arrived at the battle late in the day with fresh troops. This is why the *malfosse* is described as lying 'between the two armies' and not between the pursuers and the vanquished. But who was he?

Snorri Sturluson is insistent that Earl Waltheof was at the battle of Hastings. Nobody else, however, makes such a bold claim. There are hints in what Snorri has to say about Earl Waltheof at Hastings, that he might well be referring to the great struggle in the north of 1069-70 in which Waltheof and Swein Estrithson of Denmark joined forces with the result that Norman-occupied York was set ablaze. Waltheof would continue to have a colourful career in the years after Hastings. However, what Snorri has to say about Waltheof at Hastings does have a certain ring to it:

…Earl Waltheof managed to escape, and late in the evening he met a troop of William's men. When they saw the earl's men, they fled into an oak wood; there were about a hundred of them. Earl Waltheof had the wood set on fire, and they were all burned to death. This is what the poet Thorkel Skallason says in his Waltheof poem:

> Waltheof burned a hundred
> Of William's Norman warriors
> As the fiery flames raged;
> What a burning there was that night!
> William's sturdy warriors
> Lay under the paws of Wolves;
> The grey beasts of carrion
> Feasted on Norman flesh.[15]

So Waltheof fought the rearguard action at the *malfosse*? Unfortunately the evidence is not strong enough to suggest that he was even present at Hastings and thus the mystery deepens. Why was Harold so reluctant to take his brother's advice when they had spotted the Normans? Why did he want to wait at Caldbec Hill for reinforcements? Whom was he expecting? Somebody must have turned up with a fresh command at the *malfosse* and it is not beyond the realms of possibility that it was Edwin and Morcar. John of Worcester says that the brothers had withdrawn their men from the conflict on hearing of the king's death and went to London. Their withdrawal from the conflict indicates that they had been in one. Had it been the men of Edwin and Morcar who had lined the ditch at *malfosse* before turning back to London? We shall never know.

Whatever the result at the ditch, William knew he had won the day. He caught up with Eustace there and the count had told him that they should not venture further north into this dangerous countryside. Whilst they were talking, a lone housecarle sprang from the woods and delivered such a blow between the shoulder blades to Eustace that he spat blood in front of his duke. But to no avail for the English: Eustace was quickly spirited away and the duke and his men returned to the scene of carnage on Senlac Ridge. It is probable that a victory cairn was set up at the site of Harold's devastated camp at Caldbec Hill and that this was named *Mountjoy*. A part of that hill still bears the name today. But soon William was back at the spot where he had won a kingdom at the sword's edge.

> That was a day of destiny for England, a fatal disaster for our dear country as she exchanged old masters for new.
>
> William of Malmesbury, *Gesta Regum Anglorum*. vol I. Book iii. Para. 245

The duke is supposed to have spent the night at the battlefield, tending to the business of post-battle formalities. Wace has it that he slept on the spot where Harold and his standards had fallen. Perhaps it was here that he decided that there should be a great abbey built over the spot where Harold had died, a tradition which later was promoted by the monks of Battle Abbey. But first they had to identify Harold. He had looked similar to his brothers, but as they lay bloody and mutilated the sad task of identification was given to Edith Swansneck who, according to tradition, had been at Caldbec Hill with the camp. She was called to the scene of carnage to identify the body as only she could do, on account of certain marks. Harold's mother, Gytha had lost three sons at Senlac and made an offer for the fragments of Harold's body in return for their weight in gold, but this was refused by the duke. Instead, the shattered body was taken by a man, half-Norman, half-English, named William Malet. He wrapped it in purple linen and took it on the duke's orders high upon a cliff where a cairn was erected around it. The *Carmen* speaks of an epitaph being written here for Harold:

By the duke's commands, O Harold, you rest here a king,
That you may still be the guardian of the shore and sea.

It is tempting to think that in these few words the author of the *Carmen* has managed to sum up Harold's role on the stage of England's greatest drama. There is a hint of sarcasm about the passage, but it is interesting that what may have been widely acknowledged as the main reason why Harold had taken the throne is mentioned here in jest, perhaps as a form of irony. He had aspired to the kingdom for its protection at a time of great crisis and despite some spectacular successes, he had ultimately failed. The tradition soon arose however, that Harold's body was taken ultimately to his own Waltham Abbey in Essex, perhaps on the request of his mother, where a plaque commemorates the position of the tomb to this day.

For five days William waited back at his camp in Hastings, expecting a submission from the remaining English leaders, but it did not come. He knew now that he had to go to them and he was not happy about it. He appointed Humphrey de Tilleul over the garrison there and with a depleted but confident force he set out on a famous and punitive march through the south-east of England, arriving first at Romney where he had heard that some of his wayward crews had been eliminated by the people there. He dealt with them in a manner for which he would long be remembered. Then to Dover where, interestingly, William did his best to prevent a repeat of the scenes of carnage of 1051. We might recall that Dover had long ago been promised to William. One of England's greatest Norman castles can still be seen in that town. After a stay of over a week, a period spent in the construction of fortifications and in the overcoming of a bout of dysentery in the ranks suffered as much by the duke as by his own men, the bulk of the army moved out from Dover, leaving behind a garrison. And then they went to Canterbury, where surrender was swift.

William's illness had kept him in Canterbury for some time. Meanwhile, reinforcements had sailed from Normandy and had seized important ports along the south coast of England with some forces moving out to join with the duke. While towns in the south were falling under the Norman yoke, London still stood firm. Here, in the city which so often had much to do with the election and protection of England's Anglo-Saxon kings, sat Aldred, Edgar the ætheling, and the brothers Edwin and Morcar. The London garrison chose Edgar as their king and it is quite probable that at this stage Archbishop Stigand, who was also present, acquiesced. The choice of Edgar should not come as a surprise. He was the only remaining male descendant from the line of Cerdic and his right to assume the throne was even acknowledged by the most pro-Norman of the medieval historians. Nor should we forget the role played by Aldred in the soliciting of the return of Ætheling Edward, Edgar's father in 1057. We are told by the Anglo-Saxon chronicler that Edwin and Morcar promised the young prince that they would continue to fight for him, a statement which indicates that it had been Edgar for whom they had been fighting in the first place and that they had both considered that the campaign was still far from over. It was an extraordinary few weeks in London. Had it not been for certain events which put paid to the things which seemed to be developing, we might have had some very revealing truths about the way in which the remaining English leaders viewed the succession issue.

The decision made in London explains why William received no embassy at Hastings. England had its natural heir in London. For as long as the political will survived to promote the ætheling, William would have to continue to campaign for his throne. There followed a brief moment in English history where Edgar got to experience what it was like to be a king. There he sat in London surrounded by archbishops and earls. There is more than a hint that the people of the countryside, as well as the remaining magnates of Anglo-Saxon England, had expected Edgar to be king. The monks of Peterborough had recently chosen a man named Brand as the replacement for Abbot Leofric and so they sent him to Edgar because it was said that the local people had thought that Edgar should be king. The prince, it was said, gladly gave consent. Later, William would vent his fury upon the community at Peterborough for their insult towards him.

Just as Cnut had discovered in 1016, London held the key to the kingdom. It contained soldiers loyal to the English monarch, a fleet and the leading men of the country. But by now even Winchester had gone over to William. Queen Edith had been forced to hand over the royal treasure there in a move which must have dealt a huge blow to English morale. And yet London still had to be taken by the aspiring duke if he were to claim his kingdom. When he was somewhere beneath London travelling across the north of Surrey, he sent a detachment of 500 knights to Southwark. The rest of his army headed west, continuing its circuitous route towards Wallingford where it would cross the Thames as so many Danish armies had done before it. The southern end of London Bridge was denied to the detachment and they proceeded to torch Southwark. The encounter may seem to have been an English victory, but it is likely that the action was intended by William to occupy the London garrison whilst the bulk of the army passed by to the south thereby preventing any sortie which might fall on the flank of the westerly marching Norman columns. The encounter at the bridge had in fact been rather costly in lives to the men of London. Word may well have begun to spread that their adversary was something out of the ordinary. London began to wobble.

Whilst Stigand was preparing his horse in order to ride out to Wallingford and submit to the duke, Edwin and Morcar had packed their sister (Harold's wife) off to the safety of Chester. She was pregnant with Harold's child. There is the possibility that despite their promise of support to Edgar, the Mercian brothers, through Ealdgyth, were in fact pinning their hopes on this unborn child as a way of promoting their own interests at the expense of others. Events would prove the hopes to be false, but this might at least explain the subsequent abandonment of Edgar by the brothers.

William's force had left a remarkable trail of fortifications and storage dumps on its road to ultimate victory. Many of these places, because of their strategic location, developed into full motte-and-bailey-style Norman castles in the next generation and are among the earliest in England. It was the kind of campaign which few Englishmen had seen. By December, the Normans had executed a huge sweeping arc around the north of London and had arrived at Berkhamsted, where it seems that out of necessity Aldred, Edgar, Edwin and Morcar,[16] Bishop Wulfstan of Worcester and Bishop Walter of Hereford submitted to William. It was deep into the winter. William's road to London had covered over 350 miles. For the English, the beacon which had once shone brightly for the house of Cerdic was little more than a fragile candle. Edgar's submission would not be the end of his contribution to English history by a long way, but this was undoubtedly the beginning of a new age. At last the road to London was unopposed for William. We might recall that it had been denied him just a matter of weeks after he had first landed in England. The duke of Normandy entered London more or less unchallenged and on Christmas Day 1066 he was crowned by Archbishop Aldred in Edward's magnificent Westminster Abbey. For the first time in his adult life William was nervous. There is nothing quite like a formal ceremony to bring home the full impact of the great events of 1066. William would slowly come to understand the strange land and its customs, but it seemed that some of his followers would take longer to learn. According to Ordericus Vitalis, upon hearing the traditional shouts of acclamation which accompanied the coronation of an English king, the Norman armed guard standing outside the great abbey mistook the noises for a riot and proceeded to burn nearby houses as a knee-jerk reaction. It was the first of a thousand misunderstandings. Men ran from the abbey to see what had caused the commotion and, despite the fact that the new king would recover from the incident, it is said that he was left ashen-faced. As soon as he realised that the fracas had not amounted to much, it must have been painfully obvious that William would have much work to do in the years which followed. Two cultures had clashed at Senlac Ridge on 14 October 1066. The nation which was born from this curious union would shed many tears before it grew up.

16

THE REALM OF TRADITION

It was then too that a portent appeared on the borders of Brittany and Normandy: a woman, or rather a pair of women, with two heads and four arms, and everything else double down to the navel; below that two legs, two feet, and everything else single. One of them laughed, ate and talked; the other cried, fasted, and said nothing. There were two mouths to eat with, but only one channel for digestion. In the end one died, and the other lived; the survivor carried round her dead partner for nearly three years, until the heavy weight and the smell of the corpse were too much for her also. Some people thought, and the idea was even published, that these women signified England and Normandy which, although geographically divided, are yet united under one rule. Whatever money these two engulf in their greedy jaws descends into a single maw, which may be either the greed of princes or the ferocity of neighbouring nations. Normandy, dead and nearly sucked dry, is supported by the financial strength of England, until maybe she herself is overwhelmed by the violence of her oppressors. O happy England, if the moment ever comes when she can breathe the air of that freedom whose empty shadow she has pursued so long! As it is, she bewails her lot, worn by calamity and wasted by taxation, with all the nobility of ancient days extinct.

William of Malmesbury, *Gesta Regum Anglorum*. vol. I. Book iii. Para. 207

It is a long passage written by William of Malmesbury. He has plenty more to say on the subject, but this part more than any other demonstrates one important thing: history is a treacherous business. Very little time needs to pass after an event as momentous as the battle of Hastings before accounts of it begin to vary wildly in their interpretation. So too with the varying interpretations of its lasting effects. The tales which grew up around the legend of King Harold, the fate of his family and the career of one remarkably long-lived Englishman are examined in this final chapter. Like William of Malmesbury, we must also return to the famous struggle between Godwin and the king, which William said so occupied the minds of twelfth-century Englishmen. So much of this lies in the realm of tradition.

First, to Battle Abbey where historical evidence for the high altar of the Norman abbey church being placed over the spot where Harold fell is quite strong. The building was not consecrated until 1094, but there is good reason to suggest that its location on a difficult slope was quite deliberate. In fact, King William is supposed to have dismissed attempts by his architect to place the building further west. Perhaps he was under papal duress. The *Brevis Relatio* says that it was built in memory of his victory and for the absolutions of the sins of all those killed there. The *Battle Abbey Chronicle* said that the high altar was placed over the spot where Harold's standard was seen to fall and William of Malmesbury says that this was where Harold's body was found. Any visitor to the modern abbey remains will be struck by the steepness of the slope and the obvious architectural difficulty encountered by the builders of some of the extant thirteenth-century buildings which require immense buttressing at their southern end, further down the slope. It is not the ideal place to build a community and the physical appearance of the place speaks volumes for the notion that, in this instance at least, tradition and truth are one and the same.

Battle Abbey was, according to the *Battle Abbey Chronicle*, the recipient of some gifts on the death of King William in 1087. The gifts were apparently the relics he had worn around his neck during the battle, the same ones according to tradition that Harold had sworn an oath on in 1064. But the gift did not stay long at Battle. In order to rid himself of the persistent attentions of the monks of St Germer in Fly who were beseeching him for funds for a chasuble, King William II Rufus, the Conqueror's son, ordered that they go to Battle Abbey where Abbot Henry would pay them. But Henry was not as rich as William thought he was and had to sell the amulets to find the money. Soon, the garment obtained by the monks was destroyed by lightning in an apparent freak incident and this was seen as a sign from God. The leading men of Fly later came to offer a direct apology for what they had done. Battle Abbey had entered the realm of tradition.

Waltham Abbey is also the source of a number of traditions, some of them quite peculiar. The generally accepted version is that Harold was taken to Waltham perhaps some time after his internment in a temporary cairn on the south coast. Here at Waltham Abbey the sacristan Turketil had seen Harold on his way back from Stamford Bridge to London. The story went that two canons from Waltham had managed to secure the king's remains and bring them back to Waltham. But there is confusion in these stories. From the same place comes the tradition that Harold had not been killed at all at Hastings, but was stunned or knocked unconscious and then found by certain women who bound his wounds and carried him off to a nearby cottage. He was taken to Winchester where he lived in a cellar for two years before being taken to Germany.[1]

Of the fate of Harold's family we are only partially informed. Edith Swansneck is not heard of after her miserable appearance on the field of carnage at Hastings, though she may have joined Harold's daughter Gunhild as a nun at Wilton. She may also have found a home at the community of St Omer in Flanders, where Harold's mother Gytha had fled after holding out at Exeter and then the island of Flatholme in 1067–68. The Norman siege of Exeter had been a costly affair for the besiegers, but they eventually took the city. Gytha had managed to escape with her granddaughter of the same name and it seems that there had also been Harold's sons Magnus, Godwin and Edmund, who had managed to flee to Ireland along with their retinues.

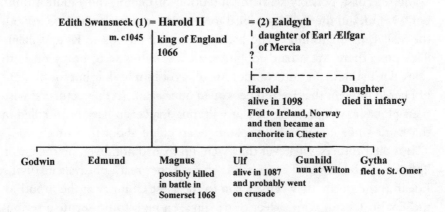

TABLE 12 Descendants of King Harold II of England

As for Ealdgyth, who had fled to Chester on the orders of her brothers Edwin and Morcar, not much is known. But the boy she gave birth to in 1067 was named after his father. A very young Harold Haroldson had accompanied his mother to Dublin during the flight of the rebels from William's impressive punitive northern campaigns of 1069-70. Chester was taken by the Normans and, when he grew up, the Dublin-based Harold Haroldson is supposed to have gone to Norway where he was accepted by King Magnus on account of his father's magnanimity after the battle of Stamford Bridge, which had allowed the remnant of the Norwegian fleet to sail home to safety. After a relatively long life, Harold returned to Chester where he became an anchorite. Some traditions get Harold Haroldson mixed up with the memory of his father and claim that the hermit to whom King Henry I (1100-1135) spoke while he was in Chester was in fact an elderly Harold Godwinson, but for this to be the case Harold Godwinson would have to have been around 100 years old. The hermit who exchanged words with the Norman king was in fact Harold Haroldson. It would certainly have been a conversation worth hearing.

Harold's elder sons certainly seem to have made an attempt to restore their family's fortunes in England, but it is not certain whether the descent upon the English coast with a fleet of Norse-Irish mercenaries in 1068 was a direct attempt to promote one of Harold's sons to the English throne itself. They came by surprise to Bristol and attempted to take the town there, but the local people held out against them. The brothers, realising that resistance was strong, took what booty they could and sailed to the Somerset coast, possibly with the intention of raiding the Taunton mint, but were met in the field by a local force under the leadership of Eadnoth the Staller, an Englishman who had given his submission to King William. This time, there was a hard-fought battle and losses were heavy on both sides. For Eadnoth, his intervention would cost him his life, but for the sons of Harold it seems that Ireland beckoned once again, so they returned with their plunder. Magnus, one of Harold's sons, may even have been killed in this battle since it seems that the sources are silent about him afterwards.[2]

But the brothers, whatever they were up to, had not given up the ghost. Towards midsummer of 1069, while there were great upheavals involving Edgar in the north, they came again to the West Country at the mouth of the Taw in Devon with a fleet of 64 ships, enough to prosecute a serious military campaign. But we are told that the brothers were incautious and allowed themselves to be caught completely flat-footed by the Norman forces of an Earl Brian. The result was a huge defeat for the sons of Harold, who once again turned to Ireland. Eventually, Edmund and Godwin would come to Swein Estrithson of Denmark in their bid to regain a power base in England and Swein himself would attempt an assault on William's England in a move which would involve Earl Waltheof.

One more son, Ulf, deserves mention. He spent the whole of King William's reign in prison. This was not unusual, we might recall that Wulfnoth Godwinson had been a long-term Norman hostage and he would die in captivity in 1094. But Ulf, it seems, gained his freedom in the general amnesty which followed the death of King William and the accession of his son William II Rufus. He became a knight of Robert Curthose, King William I's son and it is likely that he went off to fight in the first Crusade as one of the few surviving Englishmen of former rank who did so.

The politics surrounding the English resistance after the Norman Conquest is necessarily complex and legends are hard to divorce from the truth.[3] The activities of Hereward the Wake at Ely, the assault on the castellans of Hereford by Eadric the Wild and the continued involvement of Swein Estrithson of Denmark and also of the king of Norway, are all factors which gave the sons of Harold some cause for optimism, but these struggles are not the focus of the present volume. It is to the involvement of one man in the politics of post-Conquest England that we should now look, for the story of the ætheling Edgar is the one which holds the key to understanding much that has unfolded in the pages hitherto.

Edgar lived an extraordinarily long life. Only a teenager in 1066, it is perhaps surprising that he was not eliminated by William in the same way that Cnut had dealt with blood threats to his throne in 1016-17. But William viewed his right to rule in a slightly different way to Cnut. He was far cleverer about it, too. Cnut had made a direct appeal to a sense of continuity from the reign of Edmund Ironside, whom he referred to as his 'brother', but quickly engaged in a campaign of murder and enforced exile against any member of the line of Cerdic who might put in a claim for the throne. William treated Edgar in a very different way. According to Ordericus Vitalis, Edgar was like a son to William. This is no surprise. William's claim to the throne was based not only on a promise from Edward the Confessor, but on a relatively distant kinship link to that king. Now, after a time, Edgar would join the rebellions against the new Norman monarch, but for the first few years the accommodation and financial support provided by William for the young prince suggests that there may have been a genuine note of affection, if not actual recognition for Edgar. Although Edgar would fall in and out of favour with William, there seems to have been good reasons for both the rebellions and the reconciliations. John of Worcester and William of Malmesbury, along with Ordericus, follow the fate of the young prince with keen interest. It is obvious why they did so. Edgar was the last surviving male descendent of the line of Cerdic. The Normans themselves had bought into this line of argument with the promotion and protection of the æthelings Edward and Alfred during their exile and therefore had to tread a very careful path when the duke finally won his kingdom. If William had done to Edgar what Cnut had done to his potential enemies, then the real justification for the Norman Conquest would have been lost in an instant. This is why Edgar was treated in the first instance by William like a son of his own.

There were, however, problems for Edgar. These had clearly displayed themselves at the death of Edward and the rise to power of Harold. For the first time in living memory, perhaps for the first time ever, there was little or no kin-group support for an aspiring ætheling of the ancient royal line. In the past, the Witan had organised something approaching a regency for young princes not yet old enough to succeed with full power to the throne. The engine of the regency was usually powered by the kin group of the ætheling as expressed through the connections of the mother. But Edgar's mother was a foreigner with little or no clout in the dynastic politics of England. This one factor goes a long way towards explaining the problems which Edgar faced. In fact, without this traditional support network Edgar's actual achievements in his life seem all the more remarkable. Because this aspect of Edgar's political disposition was missing, some have sought to imply that Harold's rise to the throne in 1066 was an act of usurpation. But what we have discussed in earlier chapters should demonstrate that the call for the return of Edward the exile, Edgar's father, which materialised in 1057, was in fact the result of the wishes of the house of Godwin, with Harold its chief figure. The line of Cerdic had become their preferred option. Harold had not murdered Edward the ætheling before that noble prince had had the chance to gaze upon the face of his kinsman as some have suggested, although he may have secretly harboured something approaching a vaulting ambition at the time. Harold's rise to the throne of England in 1066 occurred because the wishes of the presiding monarch on his deathbed dictated it. The one person who provided the canvas upon which the colourful events of 1066 were painted was the boy. Dare we suggest that the paternalism which William initially showed towards Edgar was merely a repeat performance of that which Edward and then Harold after him had shown? Even Ordericus Vitalis tells us that Edgar's claim was greater than William's by the very blood which coursed through his veins.

So William, a consummate politician, kept his enemy close, showering him with gifts and money, but it seems that Edgar was given very little land with which to create a dangerous power base. Even the relatively wealthy Edmund Ironside had been forced to create a landed power base through marriage to Siferth's widow in order to launch a credible bid to rule at a time of upheaval in 1015-16. But what Edgar did have was moral support. His flight to Scotland in 1068 was an act which would have deprived him of the generosity of the king from which he had benefited greatly. But this and his subsequent actions show how far he was prepared to go. He took with him to Scotland his mother Agatha and his two sisters Christina and Margaret as well as Mærleswein and 'many other good men with them'. There they stayed under the protection of King Malcolm of Scotland. Malcolm soon took a shine to Margaret and the proposed marriage arrangement met with the approval of neither Margaret nor her brother Edgar but took place, nevertheless. The *Anglo-Saxon Chronicle* devotes a huge passage to the importance of this union, it being clear to the chronicler that the line of Margaret's descent was of paramount significance, as it would eventually prove to be with the marriage of Maud, Malcolm's daughter by Margaret, to Henry I of England (1100-1135). That union would bring many children of whom Maud Æthelic would go on to raise the future King Henry II of England (1154-1189). In this way the line of Cerdic would just about survive enough to pump some of its blood back into the veins of the English monarchy.

In 1068, a popular uprising had deprived Robert de Commines of his Northumbrian earldom, accounting for a full 900 of his men. Into the vacuum came Edgar once again from Scotland, supported, it is said, by a number of Northumbrians, and at York peace was made. Edgar was looking for a power base. William came quickly to York and drove out Edgar's forces in a most punitive campaign which saw Edgar return once again to Scotland.

So, Edgar the indolent ætheling had gone over to the rebellion, but had failed in his bid. William of Malmesbury tells us that he was too fond of spending his stipend on his horse than anything else during his time at court, but this episode was not the end of his story. Edgar was finally forced to flee Scotland when William came to the country in a campaign of some magnitude in 1074. He went to Flanders but returned when he knew that William had gone to Normandy. It was a life on the run for Edgar, but it was not without some curious offers of help. The King of France even offered him a castle at Montreuil so that he could 'daily do ill turns against those not his friends'. The trip back to Scotland nearly cost Edgar his life at sea and, when he finally arrived to speak with Malcolm, the Scottish king urged that it would be wise for Edgar to settle his differences with William for all their sakes. William accepted Edgar once again, preferring, it seems, to repeat the policy of keeping his natural enemy closer than his friends. During the next few years Edgar enhanced his friendship with Robert Curthose, the king's son. Their relationship would seem to have been close. Edgar is known to have witnessed some of Robert's charters when the son of the king was duke of Normandy.

By 1086 the Norman grip on England was so firm that Edgar could not seriously have entertained a notion of seizing the throne. He took with him a group of knights to Apulia, only to return in 1091. But William II Rufus invaded Normandy in 1091 and Edgar was deprived of much of his English property. Still the ætheling would get involved in Scottish politics where there is evidence that he did indeed live to a very old age. Also, there is the interesting friendship which Edgar seems to have formed with Robert, the son of a certain Godwin, who was his dependent. They went together on crusade and had many adventures. There are many questions and few answers to the life of the last male descendant of the ancient house of Wessex. But to William of Malmesbury, who might have known much about Edgar, we owe the final words:

> After the loss of the knight [this being Robert, who was martyred by the Saracens], Edgar made his way back and, after receiving many acts of kindness from the Greek and German Emperors – for they had even tried to retain him in view of his distinguished lineage – he spurned all their offers in his longing for his native land; for some people are simply misled by the love of their country, so that they can enjoy nothing unless they can breathe familiar air. Thus it was that Edgar, deceived by this foolish longing, returned to England where…he suffered a turn of Fortune's wheel, and now, in solitude and silence, wears out his gray hairs in the depths of the country.
>
> William of Malmesbury, *Gesta Regum Anglorum*. vol. I. Book iii. Para. 252.1

We may never know why Edgar did not marry and have children. We may never know a great deal about this curious figure, but some things seem obvious. From 1057, when he came to England with his family, he was the subject of a thousand debates at court and in the countryside. Noblemen lost their lives over the future of the young prince, kings were compelled to treat him with some respect, perhaps in some instances even to the detriment of their own sons, and yet there he sat in the English countryside, during the reign of a third successive Norman king, silent and unmoved to political aspiration. Perhaps the marriage of Henry I to the blood line of Cerdic had put the final nail in the coffin, perhaps the world had simply changed too much, but of all the stories worth gathering around the medieval fireside to hear Edgar's must have been the most compelling.

Now to the small matter of whether England had really formed anything like a national cultural identity on the eve of its conquest. It is an issue which has divided historians for years. It need not have generated quite such controversy. For those who insist that England's identity really grew out of the achievements of Norman monarchs in the centuries following the Norman Conquest, there is much which they must contend with. The evidence for the increasing idea of the notion of Englishness stretches from the contemporary tenth-century accounts of a blood-soaked battlefield somewhere in the north of England called Brunanburh to the greatest political comeback in medieval European history when Earl Godwin appealed to a sense of nationality to oust every Frenchman of consequence that he thought he could get away with. Or so it would seem.

The reasons why such matters have caused controversy are that there were a number of dynamics at work in later Anglo-Saxon England, some of which might seem to lead us in opposite directions of interpretation. Indeed the English people did possess a strong sense of cultural identity which stretched from Bamburgh in the north to Hastings in the south. But few of the political leaders whose careers we have traced in this book would have allowed this affinity to stand in the way of their political interests, for the second dynamic at work in later Anglo-Saxon England is the one which this volume has shown to have been the main force in decision making at the highest levels, and that is the strength of the kin-group as expressed in the dynastic power politics whose fabric was sewn together by familial ties and through the bonds of lordship. We should never forget that the word 'king' comes from the early medieval idea that a man could be chief amongst his kin and rule them accordingly. That is why in the early days there were so many of them. Early medieval Ireland, for example, was awash with 'kings'. So, in a way both dynamics, that of an embryonic national identity and that of the brutal prosecution of territorial dominance through familiar power politics, had their roots in the medieval idea of the kin-group. The chief kin-group, for the duration of this volume, was the house of Cerdic, a group which might seem to have behaved in the same way that a modern Mafia family would do in order to protect its interests. Their main concerns were to keep the line going.

This really is as far as we should allow ourselves to go. The danger, as we have set out at the start of this volume, is that we allow our ideas of

English national identity to become discoloured by our modern notions of what that really means. In 1052, Earl Godwin's main motive was to restore himself and his family to power, before he could then set his mind on the idea of promoting his own choice to the position of chief kinsman in the kingdom and, of course, the continued development of his own family's interests. The fact that there does indeed seem to have been a general popular feeling for him, set against the background of foreign influences at court and in the countryside, was simply something which worked in his favour. And yet in the same year the senior earls of England were reluctant to fight their own countrymen because they knew that it would leave the kingdom open to foreign predators – a very statesmanlike view for each of them to have taken.

It is because there was this growing sense of national identity on the eve of conquest, that the date of 1066 has seemed like such a watershed involving the huge-scale importation of French men who replaced thegns and native earls, had foreign-sounding names and administered harsh justice to the long-suffering peasant. All this may be true, but it is a point of the most profound significance that many of the historical sources which have been drawn from in this book are in fact the works of twelfth-century Anglo-Norman historians who seemed only too happy to keep alive the Anglo-Saxon tradition in its new form. But the cry of foul play was based mainly on the sweeping changes in the nature of lordship within the country as opposed to the supposed foreign nature of the king himself. This latter argument would be the basis for complaints a very long way into the future.

One final observation on Anglo-Saxon politics remains. In this volume there have been recorded countless political murders; numerous acts of treachery involving the changing of sides; several blindings, designed to make inheritance an impossibility; countless acts of outlawry and returns from exile; brutal abductions; romantic abductions; battles and unexpected deaths. There have been claims to the throne of England from at least three foreign sources and numerous internal ones. Prayers and promises have helped to oil the machinery of the politics of this age, but the public face of it all would have been as misleading then as it is today. Enemies would have greeted each other at court with smiles and embraces. Prodigal sons will have been welcomed into the king's bosom in a widely witnessed public event. Godwin and his sons dined with the king after their return from England's most dangerous period of pre-Conquest politics. Edgar was received back into King William's house with similar outward displays. And yet under the surface something else was going on. You never saw your enemies coming in Anglo-Saxon England. All too often they were standing next to you when you thought that you were facing your enemy. This much remained for centuries.

To rule in England in the eleventh century, you simply had to be better than anyone else at it, regardless of the claim. The motor which drove the machine of succession had spluttered. One man, above all others, showed an extraordinary ability to master the politics of his age, an ability to persuade by both diplomacy and force way beyond his peers, but the price he paid for it was to leave England's rightful heir living in obscurity and to create generations of historians who would condemn him for his ruthlessness. What William did to England played even upon his own conscience. He had left the country's protector shattered on the field of Hastings, and after a time presided over the wholesale removal of a native nobility from coast to coast. It did not happen immediately, of course. The return of the Anglo-Saxon would be an extraordinary phenomenon which would express itself in a number of different ways, sometimes with sinister overtones, in the centuries which lie between that time and this, but the recovery of England and of the identity of its people is a story worth the telling.

As for the child and his father whose story I told at the very beginning of this volume, I hope that they visit again the field of Senlac Ridge where so much came to pass. The boy who walked alongside his father that day is old enough now to come to terms with the complex story of the road to Hastings, a story worth the telling.

NOTES

INTRODUCTION

1. See Campbell, A. (ed.) 1962 *Chronicon Æthelweardi*. London.
2. The curious and continuing history of Edward the Martyr's bones, rediscovered in the 1930s at Shaftesbury is outlined in Hill, P. 2004 *The Age of Athelstan*. Stroud: Tempus, pp.188-93.
3. King Edward was said to have been short-tempered and intolerant of others.

1 A BLOOD RED CLOUD

1. Thorgils 'Skarthi' and his brother Kormack Fleinn are thought to have given their names to these two places in or around the year 965. See Stenton, Sir F. 1971 *Anglo-Saxon England*. Oxford: Oxford University Press, p.373.
2. The Peterborough manuscript (E) and Canterbury (F) of the *Anglo-Saxon Chronicle* entry for 991 both state clearly that Archbishop Sigeric had decided on payment of the 10,000 pounds tribute.
3. Or Rochester.
4. Forester, T. 1854 (Transl.) *The Chronicle of Florence of Worcester with the Two Continuations*. London, p.154. These texts have traditionally been attributed to Florence of Worcester, whose contribution John of Worcester acknowledges in recording Florence's death in 1118. It seems that John's contribution is beginning to be recognised as being of the greatest significance in the work.
5. Æthelric of Bocking was one such man. See Whitelock, D. 1930 *Anglo-Saxon Wills*. Cambridge: Cambridge University Press, pp.44, 148-9.
6. The events left a mark on the minds of Englishmen of a later generation: Henry of Huntingdon, writing in the twelfth century, recalled that when he was a boy he had heard some very old men speak of the massacre of the Danes on St Brice's Day during King Æthelred's reign. 'Concerning this crime, in my childhood I heard very old men say that the king had sent secret letters to every city, according to which the English either maimed all the unsuspecting Danes on the same day and hour with their swords, or, suddenly, at the

same moment, captured them and destroyed them by fire.' (Greenway, D. 1996 (Transl.) *Henry of Huntingdon. The History of the English People.* 1000-1154. Oxford World Classics. Oxford University Press, II. 1-3, p.7).

7. The translation here is taken from Swanton, M.J. 1997 *The Anglo-Saxon Chronicle.* London: J.M. Dent, p.135. The use of the term 'raiding army' is a generalisation and should not imply that raiding was its main activity.

2 TREACHERY AND AMBITION

1. The proper interpretation of the name Streona is not as fraught with difficulty as many people have suggested. The verb Streonan means to gain, acquire, to beget, to generate or create. The noun is Streon. A Streonand is one who gains or acquires. Eadric's nickname is no mystery at all. See Bosworth, J. (ed. Toller, T.N.) 1954 *An Anglo-Saxon Dictionary.* Oxford: Oxford University Press, p.928. And see also Toller, T.N. 1955 edition *An Anglo-Saxon Dictionary Supplement.* Oxford: Oxford University Press, p.713. The first edition of these volumes was published in 1898. Identifying Eadric is another matter. E.A. Freeman has him as most likely the thegn of Archbishop Oswald to whom a grant was made in 988. See Freeman, E.A. 1867 *The History of the Norman Conquest of England. Its Causes and Results.* Oxford: Clarendon Press. Vol. I, p.354.

2. See Note 4, Chapter 1.

3. According to the Peterborough entry for 1006 of the *Anglo-Saxon Chronicle,* the Danes had been told that if they ventured as far along Ashdown Ridge as the ancient site at Cwichelm's Barrow, then they would never make it back to the sea. See Swanton, M.J. 1997 *The Anglo-Saxon Chronicle.* London: J.M. Dent, p.137.

4. Quite how all these mailcoats have disappeared from the archaeological record remains a mystery, but the presence of huge numbers of mail-clad warriors in later Anglo-Saxon England is given further weight by the statement of Thietmar of Merseburg that when London was under siege in 1016 it held 24,000 coats of mail. *Chronicon,* ed. Holtzmann, pp.446-7; trans. EHD1, p.348.

5. The statement is made in the Peterborough manuscript of the *Anglo-Saxon Chronicle* under the entry for the year 1009. See Swanton, M.J. 1997 *The Anglo-Saxon Chronicle.* London: J.M. Dent, p.139.

6. Ælfheah had earlier saved Ælfmær's life, according to Henry of Huntingdon (Greenway, D. 1996 (Transl.) *Henry of Huntingdon. The History of the English People 1000-1154.* Oxford World Classics. Oxford University Press, II. 6-7, p.10).

7. In fact, this was the line taken by the leading churchman Wulfstan in his sermons, particularly in his 'Sermon of the Wolf'.

3 A FLAME THAT DIED

1. An area which is thought to have included York and Torksey in addition to the traditional Five Boroughs of the Danelaw which were Nottingham, Stamford, Leicester, Derby and Lincoln.

2. Forester, T. 1854 (Transl.) *The Chronicle of Florence of Worcester with the Two Continuations*. London, p.125. But see also note 4, Chapter 1.

3. The reason for Thorkell's departure is not known. Sir Frank Stenton thought that there was some truth in the saga tradition that some of Hemming's men who were in England were killed by the English through treachery along with Hemming after Swein's death, and that this may be an explanation. Eilaf only escaped because he had been warned by his mistress of the plot. See Stenton, Sir F. 1971 *Anglo-Saxon England*. Oxford, p.388.

4. In his *Roman de Rou*, written in the late twelfth century, Wace recalls the tradition that Anglo-Saxon armies had a certain protocol in their order of battle. The men of Kent would always have the honour of going into battle first, and the men of London would always be grouped around the standards of the king. Vol. II, lines 7819-30.

5. An anonymous twelfth-century Durham tradition reports the tale, giving the impression that it was still a famous event in northern history at the time of his writing. The writer's concern was to record the descent of six estates in lower Teesdale which had fallen out of the ownership of the cathedral community. He says that Uhtred's son Ealdred, who became earl of Northumbria, killed Thurbrand. Ealdred was then killed by Thurbrand's son Carl. Carl's sons were later killed by Waltheof, son of Earl Siward, whose mother was Ealdred's daughter. Memories, it would seem, die hard in Northumbria. A recent book examines this tale of treachery in compelling detail. See Fletcher, R. 2002 *Bloodfeud. Murder and Revenge in Anglo-Saxon England*. London: Penguin.

6. This argument, along with the notion that Emma never actually left England in 1016-1017 has been powerfully put forward by Simon Keynes. It is an interpretation most favoured by the present author. See Keynes, S. 1991 'The Æthelings in Normandy', *Anglo-Norman Studies XIII*. Proceedings of the Battle Conference 1990. Woodbridge: Boydell.

7. Forester, T. 1854 (Transl.) *The Chronicle of Florence of Worcester with the Two Continuations*. London, p.128. But see also note 4, Chapter 1. Henry of Huntingdon also assigns this famous treachery to Eadric, but has it at the battle of Ashingdon, not at Sherston.

8. Henry of Huntingdon telescopes events here somewhat. He places Eadric's murder immediately after the murder of Edmund and says that Cnut said to Eadric: 'As a reward for your great service I shall make you higher than all English nobles.' Then he ordered him to be beheaded, and his head to be fixed on a stake

on London's highest tower. Readers will be aware that a rather poor picture of Eadric Streona's character has been painted in the present volume. I see no reasons to apologise for this portrayal of an almost universally despised man, but it is a matter of some interest that recently Eadric has attracted his own apologists. For a good account of the reign of Æthelred and of the interventions of Eadric, see Lavelle, R. 2002 *Æthelred II. King of the English 978-1016*. Stroud: Tempus.

9. A passing mention in the *Inventio et Miracula Sancti Vulfrani*, written in the 1050s.

4 HOUSE OF THE KINGMAKER

1. Brought to light by E.W. Robertson, 1872 *Historical Essays*. Edinburgh: Edmonston and Douglas.
2. It would seem that Cnut himself had to defeat a large fleet of Vikings in English waters in 1017, according to Thietmar of Merseburg.
3. This argument was put forward by Campbell, M.W. 1978 'The Rise of an Anglo-Saxon Kingmaker: Earl Godwin of Wessex', *Canadian Journal of History Volume* 13. For a more comprehensive account of the activities of the whole family of Godwin, see Barlow, F. 2002 *The Godwins. The Rise and Fall of a Noble Dynasty*. London: Pearson/Longman.
4. Gaimar II, 155. Edited by Hardy, D. and Martin, C.T. (Rolls Series, 1888-1889).
5. Olsen, M. 1908 Runestenen ved Oddernes Kirke. In *Afhandlinger Viede Sophus Bugges Minde*. Christiana, p.8.
6. The medieval historian Rodulfus Glaber said that the marriage did indeed take place, but Duke Robert disliked Estrith so much that he divorced her.
7. See Keynes, S. 1991 'The Æthelings in Normandy', *Anglo-Norman Studies* XIII. Proceedings of the Battle Conference 1990. Woodbridge: Boydell.
8. But see page 70 of this volume for doubts cast upon the parentage of Cnut's sons.
9. Alfred died on 5 February 1036. The knife used to blind him had entered his brain.
10. It is likely that Harold Harefoot did not die without issue. A letter survives in Aquitaine recording that an Englishman by the name of Ælfwine, born in London, the son of Harold, king of England and Ælfgifu, came during a pilgrimage to the county of Rouergue and ascended a hill to the castle called Panade where he remained for three days and persuaded the lords to rebuild the church which was re-dedicated in 1060. There have only ever been two Harolds on the throne of England and the father of Ælfwine could not possibly have been Harold Godwinson, neither of whose female partners had the name Ælfgifu, and who certainly was not a king before 1066. See Stevenson, W.H. 1913 'An alleged son of Harold Harefoot', *EHR* 28, pp.112-117.

5 THE RISE OF A PREDATOR

1. *The Ecclesiastical History of Orderic Vitalis.* Vol. II, books III and IV. Edited and translated by Marjorie Chibnall. Oxford: Clarendon Press, p.3.

2. There may have been an earlier version of the text which it is suggested could provide a date for the work at between 996-1015, although this view is not universally accepted.

3. In 1021 Fulbert, bishop of Chartres received a letter written to him by William V of Aquitaine enquiring about the nature of the relationship between lord and vassal. A letter from such a high-ranking person about such a basic issue indicates the extent to which these social relationships were changing.

4. Godwin's son, Earl Swein had died whilst on pilgrimage (see page 111). It is surprising how many men who went on pilgrimage to atone for their sins died before they got home.

5. Some sources describe Herlève's father as an embalmer, whilst others state that he was a tanner.

6. Among the many stories of illicit relationships which brought the disapproval of churchmen upon the guilty party, is that of King Edgar of England who seems to have paid a heavy price for his lustful youth. See Hill, P. 2004 *The Age of Athelstan*. Stroud: Tempus, pp. 182-3.

7. But see the argument presented between pages 109-110 of this volume.

6 A KING'S WISHES

1. The poet here is Odd the Kikina-poet, about whom very little is known and whose work only survives in a few verses here and there.

2. Harald's sobriquet 'Hardrada' was assigned to him in the thirteenth century. He may or may not have had it when he was alive, but I have chosen here to use the name by which all Scandinavians would have recognised him: Harald Sigurdsson.

7 A VERY ENGLISH REVOLUTION

1. The seminal work on the Norman Conquest was and still is that produced by E.A. Freeman. It is a scholarly masterpiece, but it is shot-through with notions of national identity which reflect the time of writing more than they reflect the time about which he is writing. See Freeman, E.A. 1867 *The History of the Norman Conquest of England. Its Causes and Results*. Oxford: Clarendon Press. Vol. I. Especially p.449 and pp.125-62. For a modern view of the great diversity of French and not just Norman influence in England prior to the Norman Conquest, see Lewis, C.P. 1994 'The French in England Before the Norman Conquest', *Anglo-Norman Studies* XVII, pp.123-44.

2. The practice of fetching this ecclesiastical vestment from Rome was revived in the tenth century for the archbishops of Canterbury. By Cnut's reign, it was extended to the archbishops of York as well.

3. The paper which addresses the issue of a Norman occupation of strategic sites in England is Campbell, M.W. 1971 'A Pre-Conquest Norman Occupation of England?', *Speculum* 46, pp. 21–30. The strength of the argument in favour of the imposition of a Dover garrison by Eustace is given further weight by the observations of R. Allen Brown in Brown, R.A. 1985 *The Normans and the Norman Conquest.* Woodridge: Boydell, p.106.

4. The marriage of Edward's sister to the count of the Vexin, an important border area of Normandy, may be seen as an attempt by the English king to place his own family firmly in the struggle for Norman security in northern France.

5. Known as 'aux grenons' – he with the moustaches.

6. This reference to the 'king's men' need not necessarily confuse us. Godwin had become upset at the total lawlessness of these foreign garrisons who had no real reason to answer to anyone other than themselves for their actions and he would have been quite happy to point out to the king that these men were interrupting the king's peace.

7. It is extremely surprising that so many historians have agonised over the identity of the castle in which these Frenchmen had been placed. There had been an explicit request from Godwin that the king should hand over Eustace and his men. The men Eustace had left at Dover were to be given up too. As if this was not a strong enough argument, John of Worcester tells us that the castle was on Dover cliff and that it was held by Normans and the men of Boulogne. See Forester, T. 1854 (Transl.) *The Chronicle of Florence of Worcester with the Two Continuations.* London, p.151 (see note 4 in Chapter 1 for 'Florence').

8. It is a source of great irritation to the present author that William's visit to England has been called into question. See pages 109-110 of this volume for the arguments and counter-arguments regarding this matter. For an argument against the visit, see Douglas, D.C. 1964 *William the Conqueror.* Newhaven and London: Yale University Press, p.58-9 and p.169.

8 AN EARL'S VENGEANCE

1. For a full and frank account of Emma's impact on English and continental political life, see Searle, E. 1989 'Emma the Conqueror'. In *Studies in Medieval History. Presented to R. Allen Brown.* Edited by Harper-Bill, C. *et al.* Woodbridge: Boydell, pp.281-8.

2. Forester, T. 1854 (Transl.) *The Chronicle of Florence of Worcester with the Two Continuations.* London, p.155. See also note 4 in Chapter 1.

3. Robert died in Jumièges in 1055 where William was already working on his *Gesta Normannorum Ducum*.

4. Much later as it might seem. See page 158 of this volume.

5. I am aware that the idea that there had been a significant Norman garrison in England before the Conquest is a controversial one. It is, however, a phenomenon which has a good deal of evidence to support it. See also note 3 in Chapter 7.

9 RESTLESS KINGDOMS

1. Most modern authorities who have offered an opinion on the subject seem to agree that the earl suffered a massive stroke before he died. It is therefore extremely likely that he had a minor one late in 1052. Henry of Huntingdon, however, suggests that the earl choked on a piece of bread and that this was a judgement from God for his treachery.

2. Let us not forget the epithet 'Ralph the Timid'.

3. For a detailed discussion of the role of the horse in later Anglo-Saxon warfare see Hill, P. 2004 *The Age of Athelstan*. Stroud: Tempus, pp. 117-18. For comprehensive coverage of Harold's activities in Wales, see De Vries, K. 2001 'Harold Godwinson in Wales: Military Legitimacy in Late Anglo-Saxon England'. In *The Normans and their Adversaries at War. Essays in Memory of C. Warren Hollister*. Edited by Abels, R.P. and Bachrach, B.S. Woodbridge, pp.65-85.

10 ECCLESIASTICAL AFFAIRS

1. King Stephen of Hungary had married Gisela, a niece of the Holy Roman Emperor. Edward married their daughter.

2. Whose real name was in fact Æthelwine, according to John of Worcester.

3. A fact which the flag-bearers for the school of thought that the English had no cavalry should ignore at their peril.

4. Gruffydd ap Rhydderch, Caradog's father, had been murdered by Gruffydd ap Llewelyn.

11 UNEXPECTED JOURNEYS

1. Quite what we are to make of William of Malmesbury's suggestion that Harold had been out fishing in his ship and was then blown to Ponthieu, is anyone's guess. Henry of Huntingdon suggests that Harold was not even destined for France at all before his ship was driven ashore; instead he was heading for Flanders, he says. The stronger likelihood is that he was a man on a mission and not a man out fishing.

2. Eadmer of Canterbury. *Eadmeri Historia Novorum in Anglia*. Edited by Rule, M. (Rolls Series, 1884); trans. G. Bosanquet.

3. Wace *Roman de Rou*. Lines 5543-5604.

4. Harold had married Edith 'Swanneshals' (Swansneck) and had many of his children by her (see Table 12). The marriage was said to be in the 'Danish fashion' in that it seemed not to prohibit further marriage arrangements. An analogy can be drawn with the union between Ælfgifu of Northampton and Cnut, whose partnership was superseded by the marriage of Emma of Normandy to Cnut. By all accounts, Edith's beauty matched her noted wealth.

5. *The Ecclesiastical History of Orderic Vitalis*. Vol. II, books III and IV. Edited and translated by Marjorie Chibnall. Oxford: Clarendon Press, p.137.

6. The effects of Tostig's taxations are expertly brought to light by Ian Walker in Walker, I. 1997 *Harold, the Last Anglo-Saxon King*. Stroud: Sutton, pp. 106-110. Walker points out that the general taxation system in Northumbria was not as onerous as it was in other parts of Edward's kingdom, but that it was the nature of the increase which caused the problems. The rises were equivalent to a fifty percent overnight increase. Nobody had ever liked paying taxes, and we can perhaps understand why feelings ran so high. There is also the enigmatic statement made in the *Vita Eadwardi* that the Northumbrian rebellion was in fact incited by Harold, though it may be biased in this regard.

12 SURPRISES IN THE NORTH

1. Ordericus Vitalis saw Harold's takeover of the English crown as nothing short of usurpation by a cruel perjurer, a view reflected by many pro-Norman writers. *The Ecclesiastical History of Orderic Vitalis*. Vol. II, books III and IV. Edited and translated by Marjorie Chibnall. Oxford: Clarendon Press.

2. Ordericus Vitalis suggests that Stigand did indeed perform the ceremony, but John of Worcester and northern sources, both of whose churches were closely associated with Aldred are in disagreement with this view and they were in a better position to know.

3. See Walker, I. 1997 *Harold, the Last Anglo-Saxon King*. Stroud: Sutton, p. 141.

4. *The Ecclesiastical History of Orderic Vitalis*. Vol. II, books III and IV. Edited and translated by Marjorie Chibnall. Oxford: Clarendon Press, p.143.

5. See Walker, I. 1997 *Harold, the Last Anglo-Saxon King*. Stroud: Sutton, p. 145.

6. There had in fact been quite a long history between the kings of England and the community at Fécamp, as we have seen from Edward's associations with the abbey during his period in Normandy. The relationship probably has its roots in the visit paid to the community by King Æthelred during his own period of exile in Normandy when he had promised to Fécamp some lands in Sussex.

7. One of these spies seems to have been captured by William in Normandy, according to William of Poitiers. *Gesta Willelmi ducis Normannorum et Regis Anglorum.* Reprinted in Morillo, S. (ed.) 1996 *The Battle of Hastings. Sources and Interpretations.* Woodbridge: Boydell, p.7.

8. *The Ecclesiastical History of Orderic Vitalis.* Vol. II, books III and IV. Edited and translated by Marjorie Chibnall. Oxford: Clarendon Press, p.169.

9. Not as flippant a statement as one might think. King Harald Sigurdsson was a huge man. His mailcoat was known to have come well beyond his knees. He even had a name for the garment. It was called, amusingly enough, Emma.

10. Adam of Bremen mentions these offers as having taken place twice in the 1040s. Eventually, after the Norman Conquest of England in 1069-70 Swein would indeed try his luck in England.

11. The sons of Earl Thorfinn the Mighty who had died in around 1065 and who had reigned sometimes independently from Norway and sometimes as an agent of the Norwegian king in the Shetlands, Orkneys, coastal areas and other islands off the Scottish coast.

12. Much like the appalling bloodbath at York in March 867 when Ælla the usurper and Osberht, the natural king of Northumbria set their differences aside and launched a combined assault on the city to oust the Viking Great Army. Their attempt was a costly failure. Both of them were killed in the streets of York along with eight of their ealdormen.

13. Perhaps it is worth noting that *everybody* was 'little' to Harald Sigurdsson.

14. Tostig was apparently recognised on the battlefield by virtue of a wart between his shoulder blades. Mynors, R.A.B., Thomson, R.M. and Winterbottom, M. 1998 William of Malmesbury. *Gesta Regum Anglorum. The History of the English Kings.* Oxford: Clarendon Press. Vol. I, book iii, paragraph 252.1.

13 THE WIND OF DESTINY

1. See Morton, C. 1975 'Pope Alexander II and the Norman Conquest', *Latoumus* 34, pp. 362-82. In particular pp.378-80.

2. It should be borne in mind that the view expressed here that William did not have a papal banner until around 1070 is not yet universally accepted and is likely to remain a controversial issue. Against the argument must be set the facts that the banner is described by Ordericus Vitalis as the banner of St Peter the Apostle and that he says that Gilbert, the archdeacon of Lisieux, was the envoy who went to Rome. Most of the Norman sources, including the Bayeux Tapestry, have the banner being carried into battle as well. Most modern accounts still suggest that the banner came before the battle and not after it. See Lawson, M.K. 2002 *The Battle of Hastings 1066.* Stroud: Tempus, p.41

3. Professor Douglas thought that William actually left Roger behind in Normandy as regent. See Douglas 1943 'Companions of the Conqueror', *History XXVIII*, p.132.

4. For a thorough analysis of the ship list and an argument that it is indeed a roughly contemporary compilation, see Van Houts, E. 1987 'The Ship List of William the Conqueror', *Anglo-Norman Studies X*, pp.159-83.

5. For the estimate of numbers in the invasion force and for that matter on both sides, Lawson is the best modern summary of the history of the research. See Lawson, M.K. 2002 *The Battle of Hastings* 1066. Stroud: Tempus, p.134. Estimates have varied from below 7,000 men to above 14,000 over the years and it is unlikely that the issue will ever be laid completely to rest.

6. The reference to Aquitainians here may seem puzzling, but it is clear from some sources that Aquitainians were indeed participants in the Conquest. It is thought that Aimeri of Thouars was in fact an Aquitainian and that many of his Poitevins may also have been. Even more interesting are the people whom the annalist must have spoken to in 1075. English exiles, some of whom had joined with the Byzantine Varangian Guard who participated at the disastrous battle of Manzikert of 1071, may be candidates. See also Beech, G. 1986 'The Participation of Aquitainians in the Conquest of England 1066-1100', *Anglo-Norman Studies IX*, pp.1-24.

7. See Grainge, C. and Grainge, G. 1996 'The Pevensey Expedition: Brilliantly Executed Plan or Near Disaster?' In Morillo, S. (ed.) 1996 *The Battle of Hastings. Sources and Interpretations*. Woodbridge: Boydell, pp.129-42. Their observations on weather conditions and the dangers of the lee shore have gone some way towards restoring the *Carmen* as a credible source.

8. Ibid., pp.132-3.

9. William of Malmesbury intriguingly says that Duke William had informed Harold that 'he would claim what was his due by force of arms, and come to a place where Harold supposed his footing secure'. Mynors, R.A.B., Thomson, R.M. and Winterbottom, M. 1998 William of Malmesbury. *Gesta Regum Anglorum. The History of the English Kings*. Oxford: Clarendon Press. Vol. I, book iii, paragraph 238.1.

10. Mynors, R.A.B., Thomson, R.M. and Winterbottom, M. 1998 William of Malmesbury. *Gesta Regum Anglorum. The History of the English Kings*. Oxford: Clarendon Press. Vol I, book iii, paragraph 239.3

14 THE ROAD STOPPED SHORT

1. Recently, a British Channel 5 documentary, produced by Granada TV showed through modern GIS technology and soil sampling in the Coombe Haven area exactly how the coastline would have looked in 1066. The results, upon which the current summary is based, are further outlined in Wason, D. 2003 *Battlefield Detectives. What Really Happened on the World's Most Famous Battlefields*. London: Granada Media, pp.40-3.

2. Both Freeman and Stenton plump for this date, although Ordericus Vitalis says that Harold was actually in London when he heard that William had landed, but this version of events is not one that has gained popular acceptance.

3. There is a strong likelihood that the king's forces would have been provided with remounts along the way.

4. Geoffrey Gaimar says that it was Aldred who had been entrusted with the booty.

5. The *Vita Eadwardi* also notes that Harold was 'rather too generous with his oaths'.

6. The expulsion of Tostig from Lindsey and the battle of Fulford Gate respectively.

7. John is in error here. The battle was fought on Pope Calixtus's Day, 14 October 1066.

8. The site is marked today by the Caldbec Hill windmill. It was a known meeting point of the boundaries of three separate hundreds and is often referred to as the Hoary Apple Tree.

9. Both the Worcester and Peterborough texts are taken here from the translation by Swanton, M. 1997 *The Anglo-Saxon Chronicle*. London: J.M. Dent, pp.198-9.

10. This view was suggested by Sir Frank Stenton, one of England's finest Anglo-Saxon scholars. It is very evident that Stenton had a keen understanding of what both commanders were thinking at this stage in the campaign and his brief summary of the battle of Hastings is worth anybody's time since it is perfectly straightforward and to the point. See Stenton, Sir F. 1971 *Anglo-Saxon England*. Oxford: Oxford University Press, pp.593-7.

11. See page 89 of this volume.

12. Wace said that he had found out that this monk had been Hugh when he visited Fécamp and was told in person.

13. See page 159 of this volume.

15 DECISION AT SENLAC

1. Ordericus Vitalis is the only source to give the battle this name. It is supposed that the word Senlac means 'Sandlake'.

2. In fact, the *Brevis Relatio de Guillelmo noblissimo comite Normannorum*, written between 1114–20 by an anonymous monk at Battle Abbey, states that William had come to a hill opposite that of the English, this being the place where the duke inadvertently put his armour on inside out. It is also to the *Brevis Relatio*, along with a heavy hint from William of Poitiers, that we owe the crucial observation that in the first instance the famous 'feigned flight' of the Norman cavalry was, in fact, an accident.

3. See Note 3, Chapter 13.

4. There is another option for the English deployment. Lawson has suggested on the basis of the written statements that the English occupied a hill and a valley and on the visual evidence in the Bayeux Tapestry, that not all of Harold's army had lined the ridge at Senlac. Instead, he argues that the English line might have been skewed to face the south-east, thus being more or less at right angles to the Hastings road which is carried by a feature known as 'the saddle'. The lightly armed men at the famous hillock, a scene depicted in great detail on the Bayeux Tapestry, were in fact holding one of the flanks which was pinned upon this topographical feature. It is an intriguing argument, but would not account for the numerous references to the place being so constricted for the English. See Lawson, M.K. 2002 *The Battle of Hastings*. Stroud: Tempus, pp.190–2.

5. The length of the battle gives the lie to the notion that Harold fell in the first wave of attacks. This is something which some modern historians suggest was stated by William of Jumièges and others who followed his work. William's words have been variously interpreted. Here is what he says according to one translation:

> The battle began at the third hour of the day [9 o'clock in the morning], and continued amid a welter of carnage until nightfall. Harold himself, fighting amid the front rank of his army, fell covered in deadly wounds. And the English, seeing their king dead, lost confidence in their own safety, and as night was approaching, they turned and fled.
> Translation from the passage in Morillo S. (ed.) 1996 *The Battle of Hastings. Sources and Interpretations.* Woodbridge: Boydell, p.18.

> The actual Latin words that relate to the fall of the king which are interpreted here as 'amid the front rank of his army' are not faithfully represented. The words were '*in primo militum congressu*', meaning 'in the first military encounter'. Herein lies the problem. Lawson explains that there may have been a scribal slip some-

time in the early life of William's *Gesta* manuscript and that the word '*postremo*', meaning 'final' or 'last' was mistaken for '*primo*' meaning 'first'. Therefore, Harold fell in the last attack and not the first. This is a useful argument.

However, there is one alternative left to explore. For Harold, even though it was late in the day, this action might well have been his first. He had planted his standards at the highest part of the hill and had to move them over to the eastern flank where by the end of the day he had spotted a genuine calamity which he had to shore-up. For much of the battle Harold had a phalanx of soldiers in front of him. Here, however, fighting in the front rank, the king might well have received his first and last direct assault. If so, then there would be nothing at all wrong with William's statement as it currently stands. See also Lawson, M.K. 2002 *The Battle of Hastings 1066*. Stroud: Tempus, p.95. It is worth also noting that Eadmer in his *Historia Novorum* said that Harold fell in the line after heavy fighting and that there had been significant Norman casualties at this stage of the battle, a fact which veterans of the field had told him themselves. The implication is that this was indeed Harold's big struggle.

6. This is an extraordinary statement. The effective range of a javelin hurled by an infantryman is only around twenty yards. The Normans must have thought that by getting close, they could inflict significant missile casualties to weaken the English, but it seems that they were met with a surprising repost.

7. From the *Carmen de Hastingæ Proelio*. In Morillo, S. (ed.) 1996 *The Battle of Hastings. Sources and Interpretations*. Woodbridge: Boydell, p.47.

8. For a good background on the history of the use of the feigned flight in early medieval warfare see Bachrach, B. 1996. The Feigned Retreat at Hastings. In Morillo, S. (ed.) 1996 *The Battle of Hastings. Sources and Interpretations*. Woodbridge: Boydell, pp.189-94.

9. The things which different combatants see on the same battlefield can vary enormously. An account from someone standing just 50 yards away from another witness might make it seem that the two of them were at completely different battles. It is a phenomenon expertly captured by John Keegan, which he calls 'The Personal Angle of Vision', to which he applies the case study of the battle of Waterloo. See Keegan, J. 1976 *The Face of Battle*. Pimlico, pp.128-33. Recollections of the battle of Hastings as reported by veterans and relatives to authors such as Eadmer and Wace, will have been tainted in the same way.

10. The scene in the Bayeux Tapestry where William confers arms to Harold is the only depiction in the entire work of an Englishman wearing a mailcoat with a square patch across the chest. A great many of the Normans, however, are depicted wearing this device. The most compelling argument for its function, as put forward by a number of re-enactors, is that it was a loose flap of mail which was drawn-up over the chin and attached to the underside of

the helmet before the warrior went into action. English mailcoats, although long, did not have this extra facility if we take the Bayeux Tapestry as our sole source. Perhaps the prevalence of beards amongst the English might have had something to do with it.

11. The background of the arrow in the eye issue is discussed in Lawson, M.K. 2002 *The Battle of Hastings 1066*. Stroud: Tempus, p.107, where he assigns the early root of the story to Baudri's *Adelæ Comitissæ*.

12. Stenton, Sir F. 1971. *Anglo-Saxon England*. Oxford: Oxford University Press, p.595.

13. *The Ecclesiastical History of Orderic Vitalis*. Vol. II, books III and IV. Edited and translated by Marjorie Chibnall. Oxford: Clarendon Press, p.177.

14. By far the most convincing research into the location of the ditch was published by C.T. Chevalier who examined every aspect of documentary evidence possible including England's oldest street directory, listing the early tenants and properties of Battle Abbey. The identification of Oakwood Gill, to the north of Virgins Lane, 600 yards north of Caldbec Hill, makes both historical and military sense. It is difficult to see what more evidence short of the discovery of the bones of dead warriors one would need. See Chevalier, C.T. 1963 Where was the Malfosse?, *Sussex Archaeological Collections*. Vol. 101, p.1-13.

15. Quoted in *King Harald's Saga. Harald Hardradi of Norway. From Snorri Sturluson's Heimskringla*. Translated with an introduction by Magnus Magnusson and Herman Pálson. 1966. St Ives: Penguin, p.157-58.

16. Edwin and Morcar may have surrendered later at Barking, but this is not entirely certain.

16 THE REALM OF TRADITION.

1. See Swanton, M. 1984 *The Lives of the Last Englishmen.*, X, series B. New York, p.13.

2. The identity of Harold's sons in this episode is problematic. John of Worcester mentions Godwin, Edmund and Magnus, but Gaimar mentions only Godwin and Edmund with no Magnus, but includes Tostig, the son of Swein Godwinson. There is also a chance that Magnus, perhaps injured in the battle, returned to Sussex, where an inscription was known to have existed recording the presence of a mysterious Magnus, a prince of the royal northern race, but it is not certain to whom this was dedicated.

3. For the latest interpretation of the events surrounding the continuing resistance of Anglo-Saxon England to the Norman Conquest, see Rex, P. 2004 *The English Resistance: The Underground War Against the Normans*. Stroud: Tempus.

LIST OF MAPS AND
GENEALOGICAL TABLES

MAPS

TABLES

INDEX

Numbers in **bold** refer to illustrations

If you are interested in purchasing other books published by Tempus, or in case you have difficulty finding any Tempus books in your local book-shop, you can also place orders directly through our website www.tempus-publishing.com